Down Syndrome Culture

Corporealities: Discourses of Disability
Series editors: David T. Mitchell and Sharon L. Snyder

Recent Titles

Down Syndrome Culture: Life Writing, Documentary, and Fiction Film in Iberian and Latin American Contexts
    by Benjamin Fraser

Cripping Girlhood
    by Anastasia Todd

Blind in Early Modern Japan: Disability, Medicine, and Identity
    by Wei Yu Wayne Tan

Cheap Talk: Disability and the Politics of Communication
    by Joshua St. Pierre

Diaphanous Bodies: Ability, Disability, and Modernist Irish Literature
    by Jeremy Colangelo

Embodied Archive: Disability in Post-Revolutionary Mexican Cultural Production
    by Susan Antebi

Beholding Disability in Renaissance England
    by Allison P. Hobgood

A History of Disability, New Edition
    by Henri-Jacques Stiker

Vitality Politics: Health, Debility, and the Limits of Black Emancipation
    by Stephen Knadler

Blindness Through the Looking Glass: The Performance of Blindness, Gender, and the Sensory Body
    by Gili Hammer

HandiLand: The Crippest Place on Earth
    by Elizabeth A. Wheeler

The Matter of Disability: Materiality, Biopolitics, Crip Affect
    by David T. Mitchell, Susan Antebi, and Sharon L. Snyder, editors

Monstrous Kinds: Body, Space, and Narrative in Renaissance Representations of Disability
    by Elizabeth B. Bearden

Autistic Disturbances: Theorizing Autism Poetics from the DSM *to* Robinson Crusoe
    by Julia Miele Rodas

Foucault and Feminist Philosophy of Disability
    by Shelley L. Tremain

Academic Ableism: Disability and Higher Education
    by Jay Timothy Dolmage

Negotiating Disability: Disclosure and Higher Education
    by Stephanie L. Kerschbaum, Laura T. Eisenman, and James M. Jones, editors

Portraits of Violence: War and the Aesthetics of Disfigurement
    by Suzannah Biernoff

A complete list of titles in the series can be found at www.press.umich.edu

Down Syndrome Culture

*Life Writing, Documentary, and Fiction Film in
Iberian and Latin American Contexts*

Benjamin Fraser

University of Michigan Press
Ann Arbor

Copyright © 2024 by Benjamin Fraser
Some rights reserved

[CC BY-NC]

This work is licensed under a Creative Commons Attribution-NonCommercial 4.0 International License. *Note to users:* A Creative Commons license is only valid when it is applied by the person or entity that holds rights to the licensed work. Works may contain components (e.g., photographs, illustrations, or quotations) to which the rightsholder in the work cannot apply the license. It is ultimately your responsibility to independently evaluate the copyright status of any work or component part of a work you use, in light of your intended use. To view a copy of this license, visit http://creativecommons.org/licenses/by-nc/4.0/

For questions or permissions, please contact um.press.perms@umich.edu

Published in the United States of America by the
University of Michigan Press
Manufactured in the United States of America
Printed on acid-free paper
First published August 2024

A CIP catalog record for this book is available from the British Library.

Library of Congress Cataloging-in-Publication data has been applied for.

ISBN 978-0-472-07691-8 (hardcover : alk. paper)
ISBN 978-0-472-05691-0 (paper : alk. paper)
ISBN 978-0-472-90455-6 (open access ebook)

DOI: https://doi.org/10.3998/mpub.12675824

The University of Michigan Press's open access publishing program is made possible thanks to additional funding from the University of Michigan Office of the Provost and the generous support of contributing libraries.

Contents

Acknowledgments — vii

List of Figures — ix

Foreword: Down Is Everywhere by Michael Bérubé — xi

Introduction — 1

1 Down Syndrome Culture — 15

2 DS Life Writing — 33

3 Disability Ensembles — 57

4 Where Is Down? — 87

5 Interdependence and Individualism — 114

Conclusion: Amplification and Interpretive Power — 139

Notes — 145

Bibliography — 167

Index — 181

Digital materials related to this title can be found on the Fulcrum platform via the following citable URL: https://doi.org/10.3998/mpub.12675824

Acknowledgments

I first became interested in disability studies at a time when there were very few out there working on themes of disability in Spanish-language contexts. Or at least there were very few researchers in the humanities who were in dialogue with disability studies as an interdisciplinary academic discipline. It was absolutely formative for me to read the work of Encarna Juárez Almendros and Susan Antebi, whom I regard as true pioneers, along with a growing list of others whose work I cited in my books *Disability Studies and Spanish Culture* and *Cognitive Disability Aesthetics*. My forays into disability studies have been greatly influenced by their examples and research, and I am fortunate to count them among my colleagues in the field.

I was quite fortunate, also, when I was new to the field, to attend a lecture delivered by Michael Bérubé and his son Jamie at the College of Charleston during my stay there from 2010 to 2014. Also formative was my participation in a film series about disability there. Attendees, copresenters, and colleagues were influential in encouraging me to engage more with disability, and I want to thank in particular Morgan Koerner, Sarah Owens, Cynthia May, Silvia Rodriguez Sabater—and Alison Piepmeier, who passed away in 2016. Thanks to Eduardo Ledesma and the Department of Spanish and Portuguese at the University of Illinois, Urbana-Champaign for inviting me to give a talk there related to themes of disability. David Bolt has been quite encouraging to me in his position as editor of the *Journal of Literary and Cultural Disability Studies*, and I thank him also for generous responses to my email queries. At the University of Arizona, I am extremely grateful to Sue Kroeger, Dev Bose, Amanda Kraus, Sav Schlauderaff, and the extended family of folks from the Disability Studies Initiative, the Disability Resource Center, the Disability Cultural Center, and the Sonoran University Center for Excellence in Developmental Disabilities. I am very grateful to be included in ongoing discussions surrounding academic, interdisciplinary, curricular, historical, and practical issues in disability in global contexts.

An earlier version of part of chapter 2 was originally published in Catalan in as "La trisomia 21, la discapacitat intel·lectual i l'escriptura de la vida a Barcelona" [Trisomy 21, intellectual disability and life writing in Barcelona], *Catalan Review* 37, no. 1 (2023): 1–18, though this English version presents many differences. Part of chapter 3 was originally published as "Down Syndrome Ensembles, Autonomy and Disability Rights in *The Grown-Ups* (2016) by Maite Alberdi," in *Chasqui* 50, no. 2 (2022): 233–52. I thank these journals for their generous permission to republish that material here. Additional thanks go to Aurélie Vialette, Bill Viestenz, and Cynthia Tompkins for their guidance and insights. Mateo Cabeza was extremely generous regarding emails I sent him concerning his wonderful documentary film *Que nadie duerma*, analyzed in chapter 3, and I am grateful for his permission to use three stills from the film. I also want to thank University of Michigan Press, and particularly Sara Cohen, Annie Carter, Marcia LaBrenz, Danielle Coty-Fattal, Sarah Berg, and copyeditor Richard Isomaki, for working with me throughout the process and as the book went to press. My heartfelt thanks go to the anonymous readers of the manuscript whose close readings and suggestions improved the book, and to Michael Bérubé for writing the foreword. I extend my sincere gratitude to Corporealities series editors Sharon L. Snyder and David T. Mitchell for their support of this project. All translations from Catalan, Spanish, and Portuguese are my own unless otherwise noted.

This book is the product of many years of reflection and would not have happened without Abby, without Judd, Margaret, and Daisy, most of all without Ben, my brother in-law and tocayo.

Figures

Figure 2.1: The cover of the forty-first edition of *El teu nom és Olga*, originally published in 1986. Author and father Josep Espinàs poses with his daughter Olga Espinàs. Barcelona: La Campana, 2016.   44

Figure 2.2: The covers of the Catalan and Spanish versions of *Ignorant la SD / Ignorando el SD* by Andy Trias Trueta. Barcelona: Fundació Catalana Síndrome de Down, 2018.   45

Figure 3.1: The group from Coocende's gastronomy program goes door-to-door to sell their baked goods. While Ricardo (not pictured) interacts with residents over their intercoms, Andrés, Anita, and Rita are among those listening in hope of a purchase. From Maite Alberdi's *Los niños* (2016).   74

Figure 3.2: Ensemble thinking during the scene where some twenty actors with Down syndrome are interrogated by the detectives. One interviewee fires pretend bullets from behind the chair. From Marcelo Galvão's *Colegas* (2012).   83

Figure 4.1: Jaime García and José Manuel Muñoz eat breakfast together; Jaime tries to get José Manuel to see things in a positive light. From Mateo Cabeza's documentary *Que nadie duerma* (2017).   103

Figure 4.2: The four performers in the Danza Mobile production *En vano* begin the representation for an audience outdoors. Left to right: Manuel Cañadas, José Manuel Muñoz, Jaime García, and Arturo Parrilla. From Mateo Cabeza's documentary *Que nadie duerma* (2017).   103

Figure 4.3: Wearing his "Where Is Down?" T-shirt and filmed indirectly through the mirrors of the practice space, José Manuel Muñoz weaves through and stands upright in the wooden frame at the center of the *En vano* performance. From Mateo Cabeza's documentary *Que nadie duerma* (2017).   104

Figure 5.1: Anita in the bookstore at the moment that the bomb explodes in the AMIA building, just down the street. Deep focus is used to clearly represent her in the foreground, the shop floor in the midground, and the Buenos Aires city street in the background. From Marcos Carnevale's fiction film *Anita* (2009). 126

Figure 5.2: Pepe is reaching the peak of his success and now has the manager's support for being in the center of the stage. Also pictured: Rita on bass, Agus on drums. Lauro is absent. From Jesús Magaña Vázquez's fiction film *El alien y yo* (2016). 135

Foreword

Down Is Everywhere

MICHAEL BÉRUBÉ

You may wonder why I am writing the foreword to this book. (I certainly wondered, at first, why Ben Fraser would ask me to do so.) For although I am aware that disability studies has become increasingly global over the past decade or so, I have played no part in its globalization. Nor do I have any knowledge—really, any—of the representation of Down syndrome in Iberian and Latin American film. Indeed, my knowledge of Iberian and Latin American film in general is confined to a handful of films by Almodóvar and a few crossover hits in the North American market (Cuarón's *Y tu mama tambien* and *Roma*, del Toro's *Pan's Labyrinth*). Until I read this book, the only non-English-speaking film I had seen involving characters with Down syndrome was Jaco van Dormael's *Le huitième jour* (The eighth day), over twenty-five years ago. So this book came as a revelation—and I realized that I have a great deal of catching up to do.

I have begun: immediately after finishing this book, I watched Marcelo Galvão's *Buddies* (*Colegas*), so I already have Ben Fraser to thank for that. I wasn't sure I could watch through to the end, since (as Fraser notes) its antecedents in the charismatic-criminals-on-the-run genre are *Bonnie and Clyde* and *Thelma and Louise*, and if memory serves, none of those titular characters survives to see the credits roll in the end. I won't offer any spoilers here—but I will say that Fraser's reading of the interrogation scene in chapter 3 seems to me exactly right. And he's right that it's indicative of Galvão's representational strategies in the film more generally.

But of course, I'm not writing this foreword because I have anything interesting or insightful to say about Iberian and Latin American film. I'm writing because, as I learned in the course of my reading, Fraser has found my work in disability studies—my books about my son Jamie and my 2016 book *The Secret Life of Stories*—useful in the course of his own work. This is gratifying in and of itself, but all the more pleasantly surprising because I could not possibly have extended my textual analyses in *Secret Life* to the archive of materials Fraser has assembled here. More important, it is central to Fraser's argument that until recently, this archive of materials could not have been assembled at all: as he writes, "Two decades ago, I would not have been able to imagine putting together a similar corpus of texts. Today, however, researchers and instructors in the humanities disciplines . . . find at our fingertips all the materials necessary to launch a lengthy film series, or a semester-long college course, for that matter. This volume's contents are proof that there is a kind of sea change taking place, in cinema in particular, but perhaps also within a global DS culture."

If you have not heard the phrase "global Down syndrome culture" before (I had not), settle in, make a nice cup of tea, and start reading. Because the title of this book is a provocation: the very idea that we might speak of something called "Down syndrome culture," let alone "*global* Down syndrome culture," was not thinkable until very recently—nor was it possible to write the sentence "Down syndrome culture is an organizing principle for attending to the ways in which the achievements of people with trisomy 21 are having an impact across the globe," as Fraser does in his conclusion. Even if we take the most capacious definition of "culture" in the humanities—Raymond Williams's claim that culture names "a whole way of life"—it is painfully obvious that for most of human history, people with Down syndrome didn't have one. For the most part, either they led isolated lives in their own immediate families, or, for much of the nineteenth and twentieth centuries in the West, they led even more isolated and unimaginably wretched lives in institutions. Even after the 1970s, in the first few decades of (fitful and partial) inclusion, there was no plausible way to claim that people with Down syndrome inhabited or had created a *culture* in the sense that many Deaf communities possessed. Deaf culture has a language and (to cite another of Williams's memorably vague and capacious phrases) a structure of feeling, which is why Deaf community members saw themselves as members of a linguistic minority rather than as people with disabilities; people with Down syndrome, by and large, shared physical features—epicanthal folds around the eyes, flattened faces, creases across the palms of the hands, and short stature—but no linguistic or social commonalities that we would associate with the concept of "culture."

Until now. For as Fraser's work shows, "people with Down syndrome are not merely hypervisible in cultural production, they are also hypervisible as a perceived threat to able-bodied normalcy under the guise of prenatal testing." Though this is a usefully monitory way of framing our current state of affairs, it bears noting that ever since the advent of prenatal testing (especially, but not exclusively, amniocentesis) people with Down syndrome were hypervisible in the discourse of screening *without* being hypervisible in cultural production. When I was writing *Life as We Know It* in the mid-1990s, the only actor with Down syndrome I could think of was Chris Burke. Now, as Fraser shows, there has been a sea change across all the seas on the globe, with substantial consequences for how we should think about the representation—and the lives—of people with Down syndrome. Particularly when there are sixty of them in one film.

For scholars in literature and film, this means revisiting some of the most groundbreaking and influential monographs in our fields: as Fraser remarks, "One looks back at Martin Norden's classic study *The Cinema of Isolation: A History of Physical Disability in the Movies* (1994) and finds the current state of affairs hard to believe." The same is true of David Mitchell's and Sharon Snyder's 2000 book *Narrative Prosthesis: Disability and the Dependencies of Discourse*. Fraser demonstrates that most of the texts under discussion here do not exhibit the dynamic described by Mitchell and Snyder, in which (*a*) disability is used as a mere narrative device to get a story going and/or (*b*) characters with disabilities serve a narrative purpose for nondisabled characters (teaching them important life lessons, perhaps) and then are cured or whisked offstage. Instead of relying solely on "narrative prosthesis," as so many disability studies scholars have done, Fraser animates Mitchell and Snyder's term "disability ensembles" (of which *Buddies/Colegas* is his best example), which was introduced in their 2006 book *Cultural Locations of Disability* in reference to "new disability documentary" (175). And as you'll see in the pages that follow, those disability ensembles of people with Down syndrome have begun to assemble.

I say this not for the too-cute slant-rhyme of *ensemble* and *assemble* but because I am struck (in a good way) that Fraser did not turn instead to the term "assemblage," with the obligatory tip of the hat to Deleuze and Guattari (*agencement* in the original French). I have nothing against assemblages myself, but it seems as if they are turning up everywhere in the humanities, mobilized for a wide array (an assemblage?) of tasks whenever someone wants to claim that a group or a concept consists of loosely aggregated and associated things rather than a single unified substance. A single unified substance would be essentialist, and no one wants that. Seriously, whenever we speak of a genre of things—or something like "global Down syndrome culture"—we shouldn't have to work ourselves into a sweat trying to show that all the things in the group are essentially the same. "Ensemble" seems more appropriate than "assemblage" for a theatrical or cinematic form of representation; or, perhaps, we could turn also to Wittgenstein's idea of "family resemblances," which he illustrates, in *The Brown Book*, by way of an analogy to rope made up of overlapping fibers none of which extends for the entire length. Down syndrome ensembles, I'm suggesting, might also be assemblages—but are perhaps more productively thought of as matters of family resemblance.

Fraser doesn't use the Wittgensteinian term here, but his argument about cinematic representations of Down syndrome pairs well with it. For Fraser points out, quite rightly, that there is no such thing as "disability drag," in Tobin Siebers's sense (that is, when nondisabled actors portray people with disabilities), when it comes to Down syndrome: "It is patently not possible to be a person without Down syndrome and play a person with Down syndrome in a mainstream film. The reverse also holds." No two people with Down syndrome are alike, of course, any more than two neurodivergent people would be: as the truism has it, when you've met one person with autism, you've met one person with autism. But people with Down syndrome are indelibly *people with Down syndrome*, and their strand in the human rope involves an identifiable genetic marker—trisomy 21. They have commonalities, and the most important of these is locatable in DNA, the rope of life itself. That understanding of the character of Down syndrome subtends every aspect of Fraser's analysis of the cinematic representation of characters with Down syndrome, and undergirds his claim that we are witnessing an emergent culture of Down syndrome—a culture, I suggest, that has been built on recognizable family resemblances.

I'll close this brief foreword by turning to chapter 4, "Where Is Down?," whose title is inspired by an English-language T-shirt worn by the dancer José Manuel Muñoz in Mateo Cabeza's film *Que nadie duerma* (Let no one sleep). Fraser riffs brilliantly on the shirt:

> While the "what question" ("What Is Down?") might suggest merely an ontological frame, the "locative question" ("Where Is Down?") moves beyond ontology, thus beyond the matter of mere existence.

The phrase "Where Is Down" itself requires one to adopt an attitude of curiosity, to be willing to consider something new rather than just rest on current knowledge. Just as the question itself is underdetermined, neither is the answer to that question fully clear. Does this question suggest that Down syndrome is in the environment, a social construction? Or does it wink at the notion that trisomy 21 is "located" in the body? Is the point that Down syndrome is elusive in some respect, invisible socially or visible only in certain ways? Is "Where Is Down?" the prompt for a silly spatial joke, one that might end with a firm finger pointed toward one's feet? Or could one answer that Down is not a direction but instead a relation that takes place somewhere, at a location?

The answer to these questions, I think, is pretty clearly yes. Down is all these things, and Down is everywhere, all over the globe, in a stunning ensemble of representational forms. And for my part, I know that for most of my three-decades-and-change as a parent of a person with Down syndrome, I used to say that there isn't a "Down syndrome culture" in the sense of "Deaf culture"—or, for that matter, Brazilian culture or Spanish culture. Now, thanks to Ben Fraser's compelling and convincing arguments here, I'm not going to say that any more. Down syndrome culture is all around us, and it is a whole way of life.

Introduction

People with Down syndrome possess a culture. They are producers of culture. We might refer to this idea as the concept of a Down Syndrome Culture. Importantly, it must be recognized, this culture is increasingly a global phenomenon.

The book you are reading is a call to see Down Syndrome Culture—which I will sometimes abbreviate as DS Culture or just DSC—not as a concept but as a reality, since people with trisomy 21 are today achieving the highest levels of cultural visibility. Isabella Springmühl is an internationally recognized fashion designer from Guatemala City, Guatemala, whose creations graced runways at London Fashion Week in 2016. Bryan Russell Mujica ran for Congress in Lima, Peru, in 2019 and continues to advocate for human rights. In 2022, *puertorriqueña* Sofía Jirau became the first Victoria's Secret model with Down syndrome. Tonet Ramírez works in the municipal government of Lleida, Spain, and starred in the Galician-Catalan coproduced film *A síndrome Cacareco* (The Cacareco syndrome) (2011). People with trisomy 21 have become increasingly visible within the wider cultural sphere, and within mainstream film. Narrative fiction films have cast actors with Down syndrome in highly visible roles. In Spain, for example, one thinks of Pablo Pineda, in *Yo, también* (Me too) (Antonio Naharro and Álvaro Pastor, 2009); and of Gloria Ramos, in *Campeones* (Champions) (Javier Fesser, 2018). In the United States, that Spanish film was remade as the English-language *Champions* (Farelly, 2023), starring Kevin Iannucci, Madison Tevlin, and Matthew Von Der Ahe; and of course there is Zak Gottsagen's performance in *Peanut Butter Falcon* (Tyler Nilson and Michael Schwartz, 2019) to consider. One does not have to look very far to find other examples.

The chapters of this book emphasize the central role of people with Down syndrome in contemporary cultural production. As a researcher in the humanities, I am interested perhaps most of all in narrative and documentary films, but I also pay attention to life writing (autobiography and cobiography). Andy Trias Trueta is a writer, speaker, and board member of the Federació Catalana Síndrome de Down (Catalan Down Syndrome Foundation) in Barcelona, who has published the critical autobiography *Ignorant la SD: Memòries i reflexions* (Ignoring DS: Memories and reflections) (2018). Also from Barcelona, Olga Espinàs is the person at the center of the much-translated book *El teu nom és Olga* (Your name is Olga) (1986), which takes the form of a series of letters written by her father concerning the life they shared. The central social actors of the documentary *Los niños* (The children, released in English as *The Grown-Ups*, 2016), Ana Rodríguez, Ricardo Urzúa, Andrés Martínez, and Rita Guzmán, attend the Coocende school in Santiago, Chile. As captured in the documentary *Que nadie duerma* (Let no one sleep) (2017), Jaime García and José Manuel Muñoz are dancers with the company Danza Mobile in Seville, Spain. In a variety of fiction films from Argentina, Mexico, and Brazil, actors Alejandra Manzo (*Anita*, 2009), Paco de la Fuente (*El alien y yo* [The alien and me], 2016), and Ariel Goldenberg, Rita Pokk, and Breno Viola (*Colegas* [Buddies], 2012) deliver performances that challenge ableist understandings of disability in nuanced ways.

By focusing on Down syndrome in particular, this book centers intellectual and developmental disabilities within the academic project of disability studies. By discussing cultural production in the Iberian and Latin American world, it pushes beyond the traditional anglophone borders of the field. Its main contribution is to center the lives, cultural work, and representations of people with trisomy 21 within an international context.

Why Down Syndrome?

Pushed toward an academic interest in disability studies by my relationship with my brother in-law—who is a person with Down syndrome, and who is also named Ben—I have been gravitating more and more toward a focus on Down syndrome in particular. This book is the first that I am aware of to systematically center Down syndrome in the disability studies project in the humanities. It highlights the representation of trisomy 21 in Iberian and Latin American cultures and continues to dialogue with the cognitive turn in disability studies. My previous books on disability—*Disability Studies and Spanish Culture* (Liverpool University Press, 2013) and *Cognitive Disability Aesthetics* (University of Toronto Press, 2018)—argued that intellectual and developmental disabilities have been relatively invisible in the historical, theoretical, and cultural fields.[1] However, a book of this sort, one singularly focused on artistic and social representations of Down syndrome, does not exist.

One of the most important reasons to strengthen and diversify the focus on people with Down syndrome within humanities disciplines is that, to date, the cultural work of people with trisomy 21 has been largely ignored. Or else it has been celebrated as a "rare" manifestation. A case in point is Judith Scott (1943–2005), who is one of the most internationally known artists with Down syndrome. Much attention has already been directed toward her wrapped-object mixed-media sculptures, which now form part of the permanent collections of numerous international museums—from MoMA to the San Francisco Museum of Modern Art, as well as others in Chicago, Dublin, Paris, and Lausanne, Switzerland. Article- and book-length studies of her artworks abound. Most notably, there is John MacGregor's *Metamorphosis: The Fiber Art of Judith Scott* (1999), a richly illustrated oversized text that allows readers visual access to her many large works and to her creative process. The image of Judith Scott appears on the cover of *Touching Feeling: Affect, Pedagogy and Performativity* (2003), the scholarly monograph by queer studies pioneer Eve Kosofsky Sedgwick, where the artist's arms are wrapped around one of her sculptures. Scott's life and work have even been explored on the screen as the central subject of a compelling feature-length documentary made by Lola Barrera and Iñaki Peñafiel (Spain), titled *¿Qué tienes debajo del sombrero?* (What's under your hat?, 2006).

Judith Scott's fame proved to be disruptive within the wider art world. The response by some critics was to preserve the notion of an artistic canon, by situating her works comfortably within a relatively minor category (outsider art, or art brut). However, disability studies pioneer Tobin Siebers celebrated her work without the need to preserve ableist privilege. In the introduction of his book *Disability Aesthetics* (2010), he wrote:

> The work of Judith Scott challenges the absolute rupture between mental disability and the work of art and applies more critical pressure on intention as a standard for identifying artists. It is an extremely rare case, but it raises complex questions about aesthetics of great value to people with disabilities. . . . Her work is breathtaking in its originality and possesses disturbing power as sculptural form. The sculptures invite comparisons with major artists of the twentieth century and allude to a striking variety of mundane and historical forms, from maps to the works of Alberto Giacometti, from Etruscan art and classical sculpture in its fragmentary state, to children's toys.[2]

The central point of Siebers's book is that "disability has a rich but hidden role in the history of art."[3] Its chapters move far beyond the example of Judith Scott to address a range of visual, cultural, and even literary practices from many movements, periods, and locations. One must wonder, however, why Siebers makes the observation that the Scott's work is "an extremely rare case." That is, part of the need to underscore her exceptionality seems to stem from the systematic lack of social attention and cultural import given to intellectual and developmental disabilities in general, and to Down syndrome in particular. What happens when people with Down syndrome are no longer regarded as exceptions in the worlds of art and culture? Now is the time to find out.

Down Syndrome Culture envisions the contributions and representations of people with Down syndrome as an integral part of the fabric of art and culture. It moves far beyond the "extremely rare case" model of cultural production that Siebers invoked in discussion of Judith Scott, and it arrives at a time of heightened visibility for people with trisomy 21. Today, people with Down syndrome are not merely hypervisible in cultural production, they are also hypervisible as a perceived threat to able-bodied normalcy under the guise of prenatal testing. At the same time, a specific disability identity has been emerging that expresses pride in being a person with Down syndrome as part of an affirmation of disability rights. In his book *Disability Theory* (2008), Siebers takes steps to underscore the importance of a disability identity, writing that such an identity need not be conceived as a "liability" but is instead an "epistemological construction" possessing what Manuel Castells calls "a collective meaning."[4] What has not been explored to date in the academic project of disability studies, however, is where a more specific Down syndrome identity might fit within this notion of a generalized disability identity.

In the first chapter of this study, titled "Down Syndrome Culture," I look to disability theory as a way of establishing Down syndrome identity as a potential strength for community, coalition building, advocacy, and rights-seeking activities. This approach underscores, as does Siebers, the necessity of identity politics in contemporary society. Here I address various tensions that are ongoing in the field of disability studies that relate to the social and the medical models of disability. For example, if one acknowledges the material specificity of embodied experiences of Down syndrome, does that mean that one accepts all of the reductive and disempowering understandings of disability that permeate ableist society? Would this mean that disability is now understood to be solely "in" the person and not at all in the social environment? To think that way would surely be a mistake. For that matter, if one approaches Down syndrome as solely existing in the social environment, does that negate the material and embodied experience of being a person with trisomy 21? Or is it possible that one can pay attention to the genetic, physiological, medical, and cognitive dimensions of being a person with trisomy 21 and still understand disability identity as an epistemological construction that takes shape within an ableist society? These sorts of nuanced questions have been expressed within the field of disability studies for decades, but have been receiving renewed attention in contemporary writings. In *The Biopolitics of Disability* (2015), for instance, David T. Mitchell and Sharon L. Snyder wonder whether it is time for a return to the notion of impairment, and, in a posthumously published essay contribution to *The Matter of Disability* (2019, edited by Mitchell, Antebi, and Snyder), Tobin Siebers argues that strong constructivist approaches to disability have focused on the social environment to a degree detrimental to the material body.[5]

It is possible to approach Down syndrome as a sort of limit case within the academic field of disability studies. It is best situated betwixt and between the social and medical models, and it thus poses the question whether a biologically based disability identity can coexist with a strong constructivist understanding of disability as a social relationship. Chapter 1 of this book thus deals with how attending more carefully to the specificity of Down syndrome can help disability studies scholars from across the wider field of inquiry to think productively about these and other tensions. It offers a way of navigating the key tensions that exist in the field of disability studies today: between individual and collective responses to ableism, between the scholarly tools developed as advocacy for people with cognitive and with physical/sensory disabilities, between the critique of social constructivism and the material relevance of impairment discourse, and between biological/genetic and social/cultural markers of identity. If the notion of DS Culture I advance there cleaves too closely to the steady glow of the promise of human rights and to the warm community ideal of minoritized politics, it is because I continue to believe that these concepts—and the concept of a disability identity in particular—remain crucial tools for the empowerment of people living in today's ableist, neoliberal society.[6]

Why Iberian and Latin American Culture?

By attending to Iberian and Latin American spaces, *Down Syndrome Culture* responds to the persisting need to globalize the academic discipline of disability studies. A call to globalize the discipline was formalized in two editorials from the *Journal of Literary and Cultural Disability Studies* in 2010 and has been bearing fruit.[7] More recent contributions to the University of Michigan's Corporealities book series (edited by David T. Mitchell and Sharon L. Snyder) by Susan Antebi (2021) and Wei Yu Wayne Tan (2022) have focused on Mexico and Japan, for example. Disability studies scholarship carried out by faculty working in the languages and literatures other than English has, already now, a relatively long history—whether we look to Departments of Hispanic Studies, Romance Languages, Modern Languages, or other similar academic organizational structures. The pioneering work of Encarnación Juárez-Almendros was featured in the early volume *Disability Studies: Enabling the Humanities* (MLA, 2002), and her impact in the field has continued through her recent monograph *Disabled Bodies in Early Modern Spanish Literature* (2017). Susan Antebi's *Carnal Inscriptions: Spanish American Narratives of Corporeal Difference and Disability* (2009) and her volume *Libre Acceso: Latin American Literature and Film through Disability Studies* (2016b), coedited with Beth Jörgensen, have been similarly pathbreaking. In truth, the last decade in particular has seen a surge of interest among scholars working in the area of Iberian and Latin American disability studies.[8]

There is reason enough for researchers in the anglophone world to look toward Iberian and Latin American contexts. Although social barriers and systemic inequalities persist in Spain and Latin America—it seems necessary to insist that such challenges are not absent from life in these United States—what some readers may not know is that, in some ways, these geographic areas have a relatively strong record on disability. Take, for example, the United Nations Convention on the Rights of Persons with Disabilities. Spain signed and ratified the Convention in 2007, and in 2008 committed to developing its fifty articles within the Spanish legal system.[9] This commitment echoed also in the cultural sphere. For instance, specific articles of the Convention were adapted into televised spots as part of a systematic campaign by organizations, including Down España, to promote rights for people with intellectual disabilities. It is of interest that the TV spot dramatizing Article 19, which asserts the right to live independently and to be included in the community, featured an actor with Down syndrome playing the role of a son who moves out of his mother's house.[10] The fiction film *Yo, también*—notable for the performance of its protagonist Pablo Pineda, who is an actor with Down syndrome and in real life the first university graduate with trisomy 21 in Spain—can be seen in part as a filmic representation of the commitment to Article 27 of the UN Convention, the right of people with disabilities to work, subject to the same conditions as others. For their part, Latin American nations also strongly supported the UN Convention. One reads in the book *Human Rights in Latin America* (2010) that "one-third of the countries that ratified the convention are in Latin America. Only two countries in the Americas have not signed or ratified the convention to date (Venezuela and the United States), placing the region at the forefront of global support for the treaty."[11] It is unacceptable that the pace of such large-scale change tends to be slow everywhere, just as it is frustrating that there remains such a noticeably large gap between a stated commitment to social change and the reality of its implementation. While I give a nod to some ways in which rights- and identity-based models have been challenged by contemporary disability theory in chapter 1, I continue to believe that disability identity, human rights, legislation, and of course implementation—along with cultural production—are all part of ensuring the continued strength of Down syndrome communities over time.

In Spain, disability rights were largely stifled during the widespread oppression and violent ideology of the dictatorship of Francisco Franco (1939–1975), but began to move forward in 1982 with the passage of the Law on the Social Integration of the Disabled.[12] This preceded other landmarks, such as the creation of the Catalan Down Syndrome Foundation in 1984 and the formation of Down España in 1991. Chapter 2 ("Down Syndrome Life Writing") returns to such historical landmarks in the context of exploring the two books by Espinàs (1986) and Trias Trueta (2018). Because both the temporal and the cultural distance between these two prose narratives about the experience of Down syndrome in society is considerable, my hope is that their juxtaposition will prompt the reader's reflection on the slow pace of social change. On the other hand, there is much to celebrate in Trias Trueta's autobiography, which at the time of this writing is available in Catalan, Spanish, and English. This is a compelling first-person narration about the embodied and social experience of Down syndrome, where the author shares individual joys and sorrows while advancing a strong critique of twenty-first-century ableism. This exploration of Trias Trueta's life and work also points readers toward the tangible benefits that organizational models of disability support and advocacy can offer individuals, families, and communities.

Antebi and Jörgensen's introduction to *Libre acceso* covers several moments in the rich history of disability advocacy in Latin America. The scholars mention the sheer number of organizations promoting disability rights in Mexico a decade into the twenty-first century (more than 160, "many of them were created by and for people with disabilities"), the formation of the Organization of Disabled Revolutionaries in Nicaragua in the 1980s, and widespread criticism of the Chilean government's inadequate support for people with disabilities following the 2010 earthquake and tsunami.[13] Certainly, as they also write, "It is nonetheless true that stigma and exclusion continue to define the status of many disabled people in the region."[14] It is not that this seeming contradiction is at all unique to Latin America, or Spain for that matter. The point of this book is not to essentialize "what disability is" or "how disability is" in Iberian and Latin American contexts.[15] Yet by attending to such diverse geographic spaces, we do gain an appreciation of how commonly uneven the social textures of modernity are, as well as how much work remains to be done everywhere. Human rights and disability advocacy are intertwined issues, and cultural production has a role to play in pushing these global conversations forward.

Rather than attempt an encyclopedic or totalizing approach to Down syndrome in either Latin American or Iberian spaces, the remaining chapters of this book analyze specific films and performances as a way of tracing key issues in disability studies from the small to the large scale. Chapter 3 ("Disability Ensembles"), for instance, turns to a Chilean film that presents viewers with everyday scenes from the real lives of four adults with Down syndrome in the country's capital of Santiago. Chilean director Maite Alberdi's documentary *Los niños* allows viewers to assess the gap between the commitment to disability rights and the reality of insufficient implementation. Also included in chapter 3 is Marcelo Galvão's *Colegas*, which is a fictional film set outside of São Paulo. The film centers three actors with Down syndrome: the trio manages to escape from their residential institution, steal a car, and embark on a lengthy road trip. Both films foreground themes of independence, sexuality, and autonomy, these being topics of great interest to contemporary disability studies scholars.

Antebi and Jörgensen caution that "those who seek evidence of disability studies, or what they consider to be disability studies, in the Global South may have to adjust their expectations, critical tools, and avenues of research."[16] Yet, as they also point out, Latin American scholars and activists have also been "in some cases, in dialogue with Anglo-American intellectual traditions."[17] What is noticeable today is the degree to which the disability movement and the academic project of disability studies together continue to influence contemporary Iberian and Latin American contexts.

Take, for example, the work of disability scholars Melania Moscoso, who is currently based in Spain, and Jhonatthan Maldonado Ramírez, who is currently based in Mexico. These disability studies researchers are in dialogue with key issues of importance to anglophone disability studies, as can be observed in their numerous publications where references to theorists such as Robert McRuer, Sharon Snyder, David Mitchell, Simi Linton—not to mention also Michel Foucault and Judith Butler—are not uncommon.

In the essay titled "La discapacidad más allá del relato" (Disability beyond narrative) (2020), Melania Moscoso introduces a special issue titled "Política tullida: Identidad, cuerpos abyectos y discapacidad" (Crip policies: Identity, abject bodies, and disability). Beyond introducing the issue's contents—seven articles and a translated piece by Robert McRuer—the scholar also stresses connections with the disability rights movement of the 1960s, the Americans with Disabilities Act of 1990, and the work of a number of disability studies scholars of the 1990s. Chief among these are McRuer, whose book *The Queer Renaissance* (1997) marked "la extensión de la teoría queer a las personas con discapacidad" (the extension of queer theory to people with disabilities), and also Sharon Snyder and David Mitchell, whose documentary film *Vital Signs* (1997) deserves to be understood as "una intervención política que presenta a los discapacitados como un colectivo con su propia identidad y cultura" (a political intervention that presents disabled people as a collectivity with their own identity and culture).[18] In her work published with coauthor R. Lucas Platero, Moscoso draws attention to the way in which disability rights are systematically undermined by legal and medical systems in Spain. Moreover, even when legislation intends to ensure services for people with disabilities, the authors stress, its conception and implementation can be problematic.[19]

Jhonatthan Maldonado Ramírez's daughter Marthié is a person with Down syndrome—a familial disability connection that the scholar references while exploring various themes that are at once central to disability studies as a whole. In the article "Sexualidad y syndrome de Down: ¿Crees que ellos no quieren tocar y ser tocados?" (Sexuality and Down syndrome: Do you think that they don't want to touch and be touched?) (2018), he explores the ways in which ableist ideology and its appeals to social, moral, medical, and legal argument negatively impact the sexuality of people with Down syndrome.[20] In "¿Quién habla por? La semiótica de representación en la ventriloquial capacitista" (Who speaks for? The semiotics of representation in ableist ventriloquism) (2017), Maldonado Ramírez blends personal experiences with anthropological theory and epistemological investigations to denounce how social and legal norms regularly reduce the voices of people with Down syndrome to *ruidos* (noise), *gruñidos* (grunts), and *una carencia* (a lack).[21]

One can see the documentaries and fiction films discussed in this book as complements to arguments made by Maldonado Ramírez and Moscoso, as well as to the work of others in the diasporic community of disability studies scholars. It should not be "rare" or "exceptional" that audiences see people with Down syndrome speaking in their own voices and expressing their own desires—whether in the art world, on the screen, or in society at large. If the cultural products discussed in this book are any example, perhaps it no longer is.

Why These Cultural Products? Plus Chapter Summaries

The longer narrative arc of this book reflects various positions that can be taken by minoritized cultures within the larger social stage. That is to say, Down Syndrome Culture can—and perhaps must—approach the process of identity construction in creative ways. By moving from chapter 3 to chapter 4, readers thus get a sense of how Down syndrome disability identity can be either fixed or fluid, depending on circumstances. That is, the struggle for human rights can often require fixed or static understandings that present identity as ontologically given and inherently knowable. On the other hand, as a minoritized identity position, disability identity is at once highly malleable, subject to change, and ultimately unknowable.

The films by Alberdi and Galvão analyzed in chapter 3 address Down syndrome disability rights much as a fixed subject position, as social actors (from the documentary) and characters (from the fiction film) confront themes of independence, labor, sexuality, and autonomy head-on, each in their own way, articulating an inclusive vision for social change. Chapter 4 ("Where Is Down?"), on the other hand, adopts a more skeptical position regarding disability representation. Perhaps more than any other cultural product discussed in this book, Spanish director Mateo Cabeza's documentary *Que nadie duerma*—and its behind-the-scenes look at Danza Mobile's[22] performance *En vano* (In vain) (2016)—questions the idea of a fixed or static Down syndrome identity. It is as Alison Kafer writes in *Feminist Queer Crip*, that it is preferable to see "disability as a site of questions rather than firm definition."[23] In the end, however, even this questioning serves to reinforce the notion of Down Syndrome Culture, in the sense that the identity politics required by representational democracy are a practice that is simultaneously material and discursive. We must remember how Siebers stressed disability identity as an "epistemological construction" with "a collective meaning."[24] Moving from chapter 4 to chapter 5 ("Interdependence and Individualism"), readers encounter fiction films that engage with Down syndrome representation and identity in a different, but equally unconventional way. In *Anita*, by

Argentine director Marcos Carnevale, the main character's family ties to the Jewish community serve as a prompt to examine broader themes of intersectional urban marginality. And in *El alien y yo*, Mexican director Jesús Magaña Vázquez imagines the move of Down Syndrome Culture from the musical margins to the pop culture mainstream in ways that are both radically inclusive and also, at times, quite problematic.

The prose writings, documentaries and fiction films selected for inclusion in this book are of interest to readers from a wide variety of disciplinary areas. With the exception of chapter 2's brief look back at a life writing text from 1986—which serves as a comparison with a more recent autobiography from 2018—each chapter emphasizes cultural products from the twenty-first century (ch. 2, 1986, 2018; ch. 3, 2012, 2016; ch. 4, 2016, 2017; ch. 5, 2009, 2016). What struck me most as I did the research for this book was the sheer social novelty of these representations of Down syndrome across Iberian and Latin American popular culture. Two decades ago, I would not have been able to imagine putting together a similar corpus of texts. Today, however, researchers and instructors in the humanities disciplines and even specialists in Iberian and Latin American cultures find at our fingertips all the materials necessary to launch a lengthy film series, or a semester-long college course, for that matter. This volume's contents are proof that there is a kind of sea change taking place, in cinema in particular, but perhaps also within a global DS Culture.

One looks back at Martin Norden's classic study *The Cinema of Isolation: A History of Physical Disability in the Movies* (1994) and finds the current state of affairs hard to believe. Norden was quite accurate in his condemnation of "the mainstream movie industry's penchant for constructing warped social imagery."[25] His book chronicled the numerous—offensive, ableist, and at once tired, unimaginative—tropes of disability as filmed over the course of the twentieth century. Such warped imagery is, of course, hardly unique to the English-language mainstream. It would be possible to write a similar book about Iberian and Latin American cinema over the course of the twentieth century, for example. Disability is everywhere in film, in the same broad way that Siebers emphasized the ubiquity of disability in visual art.[26] Still, many times disability is not "noticed" by spectators—as editors Sally Chivers and Nicole Markotić remarked in their introduction (2010a) to *The Problem Body: Projecting Disability on Film* (2010b), and as Evelyn Mogk also underscored in her editor's introduction (2013b) to the collection *Different Bodies: Essays on Disability in Film and Television* (2013a).[27] The films selected for analysis in chapters 3, 4 and 5 stand out well against this sort of warped cinematic history. These dispense with the filmic convention of what Siebers called "disability drag"[28]—where non-disabled actors play the roles of people with disabilities. Here, disability cannot but be noticed. Representation matters, and it continues to be one of the key tools used by minoritized cultures to affirm a group identity and claim political agency.

In chapter 1 ("Down Syndrome Culture"), I set the stage for this book's analyses by cultivating a space within existing disability theory for the academic study of Down syndrome in particular. Looking at the ways in which disability scholars have approached the relationship between the social and medical models of disability, I emphasize the recent return to theorizations of the materiality of the body. Because disability theory is such a wide-ranging project, it is worth asking where the material experience of Down syndrome fits within various trajectories of humanistic or post-humanistic thinking. Each of the chapters that follow documents the emergence of a twenty-first-century Down syndrome disability culture in a range of geographic spaces and through a variety of cultural products.

In chapter 2, I rely on the work of disability scholar G. Thomas Couser (2002, 2009, 2011, 2013), who has concentrated on disability and contemporary life writing, to explore both autobiography and the concept of co-biography in Barcelona, Spain. By juxtaposing two key life writing texts, from 1986 and 2018, we can gauge what has changed—and what has not changed—for populations with Down syndrome living in this capital city of Catalunya. Famed literary author, singer, and even artistic director of the Concèntric record company, Josep M. Espinàs wrote a series of letters addressed to his daughter, an adult with Down syndrome with whom he shared a life. Published in 1986 as *El teu nom és Olga*, this book was subsequently translated to numerous languages and has been reedited continuously up until the present day. Andy Trias Trueta, who is a person with Down syndrome, wrote a series of memories and reflections called *Ignorant la SD* (Ignoring DS) in 2018 that are at once personal and political. The convergence and divergence of the accounts painted in these two forms of memoir are situated against the background of organizations and programs in Catalunya and surrounding area that, since the 1960s, have sought to improve life and work conditions for people with Down Syndrome: Aspanias, ASDA, ASTRID 21, the Fundació Catalana Síndrome de Down, and Èxit21.

In chapter 3 ("Disability Ensembles"), I draw on David T. Mitchell and Sharon L. Snyder's (2010) emphasis on disability ensembles in what they term the "new disability documentary cinema" to analyze the representation of Down syndrome in two films from Latin America, each of which centers on a group of friends. Maite Alberdi's documentary *Los niños* provokes viewers even from its title, which is a derogatory phrase used in ableist society to infantilize people with Down syndrome. Alberdi's connection with her aunt, a person with Down syndrome, has motivated her to follow four social actors who, now in their 40s, still attend the Coocende school programs in Santiago, Chile. The director calls upon the traditions of the Chilean social documentary to capture Anita, Rita, Ricardo, and Andrés as they navigate work, friendship, love, and family, with a consistent focus on themes of social inequity and human rights. The film ultimately contributed to a push for improved minimum wage and inclusive work legislation in Chile. Brazilian director Marcelo Galvão's fictional film *Colegas* (2012) is no less provocative, but it tackles the notion of inclusion in a more spectacular way. Here the ensemble is formed by Stalone, Aninha, and Márcio, who set out on a *Thelma and Louise*–style road trip after stealing the car of their Institute's gardener, a flashy red Karmann Ghia. Just as in *Los niños*, their dreams and aspirations take center stage—for example, Aninha wants to get married, and Márcio wants to fly—but the film achieves its critique by placing actors Ariel Goldenberg, Rita Pokk, and Breno Viola in roles uncommon for people with trisomy 21 on-screen—that of petty criminals. Adopting the premise of the road movie genre is itself a challenge to the way in which populations with Down syndrome still lack autonomy in ableist society.

In chapter 4 ("Where Is Down?"), I analyze a challenging documentary film with reference to the inclusive theater performance that serves as its point of reference. Mateo Cabeza's *Que nadie duerma* follows selected members of the Danza Mobile company from Seville as they prepare for a performance titled *En vano* (2016). Here, Jaime García and José Manuel Muñoz are two dancers with trisomy 21 who feature along with Manuel Cañadas and Arturo Parrilla as they prepare for the performance. Analysis of the film's scenes and representational strategies is carried out in tandem with an exploration of Danza Mobile and the critical literature on dance, disability, and inclusion (Hartwig 2018, 2019, 2021; Checa Puerta 2021). A key article by Sharon Smith and Kieron Smith (2021), published in the *Journal of Literary and Cultural Disability Studies* and titled "Down Syndrome as Simulacrum," is introduced, explored, and then applied as a way of making sense of the way that *Que nadie duerma* defamiliarizes the social image of Down syndrome held by viewers.

In chapter 5 ("Interdependence and Individualism"), I explore two films from Latin America that address the image of people with DS as dependent in very different ways. Jesús Magaña Vázquez's *El alien y yo* is based on a short story by Carlos Velázquez ("El alien agropecuario") and centers on musical performance. A punk band is stagnating but reinvigorates its sound by changing musical styles and incorporating keyboardist Pepe, played by Paco de la Fuente. The film goes further than the story in celebrating what Pepe brings to the group, moving beyond the merely decorative and exploring further an amorous relationship between Pepe and Rita, broaching the topics of both sexuality and reproduction more explicitly as a part of full social inclusion. Marcos Carnevale's *Anita* does something quite unusual in disability fiction film by placing its central character, played by Alejandra Manzo, in the position of synecdoche for the entire Argentine Jewish community. The deadliest anti-Semitic act in Latin America's recent history occurred on July 18, 1994, when the Asociación Mutual Israelita Argentina (AMIA) was bombed in Buenos Aires, killing eighty-five people and injuring some three hundred. It has proven tempting to see the film as portraying the solitary wanderings of a "childlike protagonist" in the aftermath of the bombing. Yet rather than infantilize Anita, rather than see in her performance the tired trope of the isolated disabled person as analyzed by Martin Norden (1994), it is her connection to the Jewish community that displaces these readings. This is not disability as a "narrative prosthesis" in the sense explored by David T. Mitchell and Sharon L Snyder (2000), as the film's symbolism is not metaphorical, but instead metonymical, ultimately reaffirming the connective urban tissues of Anita's victimhood through the bond that tragedy and suffering creates for a much wider, (inter)national community.

The brief conclusion to *Down Syndrome Culture* takes the pulse of an international disability community on the way to greater visibility in the arts, in politics, and in everyday life. Given that so much of the coverage of these individuals with trisomy 21 has emphasized the notion of being "first" in a given cultural or geographical sphere (i.e., the first university graduate, the first international fashion designer, the first political candidate . . .), it is desirable to look forward to a time when such language is no longer applicable. There is a momentum, a strong sense of community, and an expansive global geography implied in what people with trisomy 21 are achieving in the twenty-first century. Together these aspects of Down Syndrome Culture reveal a sea change taking place regarding the visibility of a disability identity that is inseparable from wider notions of family, culture, society, and human rights.

One

Down Syndrome Culture

Tobin Siebers wrote that "disability is not a physical or mental defect but a cultural and minority identity."[1] Even so, some may be reticent to acknowledge the existence of Down Syndrome Culture. In that case, maybe it is better to echo a remark made by disability studies scholar Joseph Straus in his essay "Autism as Culture," from *The Disability Studies Reader*, and instead see "Down Syndrome *as* culture."[2] Perhaps those seeking more distance from John Langdon Down's 1866 description will prefer "*trisomy 21* as culture." Biological, developmental, and yes, medical, understandings are never far away where people who have a third twenty-first chromosome are concerned. Yet these understandings all miss something crucial. In the twenty-first century, it is now impossible to ignore the cultural impact of people with Down syndrome (DS). This chapter seeks to situate the study of Down Syndrome Culture (DSC) within existing disability theory. It first covers—concisely but, I hope, also meaningfully—the historical strengths of the social model of disability as well as contemporary shifts within that model. Its later sections explore the theoretical promise of posthumanism, the ways in which some posthumanist thinking is mismatched to account for the material experience of Down syndrome in society, and the continuing importance of humanistic approaches.

Down Syndrome and the Social Model

The focus on a global Down Syndrome Culture proves to be a way of engaging with questions central to the evolving discipline of disability studies. There are two key questions that have routinely been asked. Is disability a social construction, the product of a disabling environment, as many pioneers of disability studies asserted? Or is disability a trait possessed by an individual, an integrated, embraced, and perhaps even fundamental part of identity? An emphasis on Down syndrome suggests its own set of coordinates by which to chart a course through these and other related questions.

It is not uncommon for scholars to situate Down syndrome at the intersection of tensions surrounding how we understand disability identity. In his book *The End of Normal*, Lennard J. Davis turns to Down syndrome for rhetorical support in his argument "that disability is an identity that is unlike all the others in that it resists change and cure"—"It is patently not possible to be born a person with Down syndrome and become someone who does not have Down syndrome," he writes.[3] Here we encounter the idea of Down syndrome as a hard material fact; from this perspective, DS is not a social construction, but rather an essential way of being human. Also, Rosemarie Garland-Thomson, in her book *Staring: How We Look*, discusses Chris Rush's painting *Swim II*, in which "we recognize a face we have never seen in a portrait . . . the distinct features of a person with Down syndrome."[4] Her analysis of this painting follows in the tradition of her many analyses of photographs throughout her book. One can apply what Roland Barthes called the ontological assertion of photographic representation to the analysis of Rush's painting. Here is a life lived. (Garland-Thomson reminds readers that "Rush's drawings are studies from life done at a facility for disabled people where he volunteers.")[5] That the unnamed model is a person with the "distinct features" of Down syndrome is an essential part of that life, and consequently, of that painting's value and of discussions that emerge in its surround. In drawing nuanced awareness to socially determined patterns of seeing and not seeing (the "how we look" of her book's title), Garland-Thomson strikes a balance between what staring creates and what it reveals. What staring creates is ultimately a mixed bag, and the theorist carefully thinks through both its ableist legacy and its emancipatory potential. Underlying any negotiation between starer and the object of the stare is a person, an embodied material experience. To stare at *Swim II* and not see a person with Down syndrome is either a lack of familiarity, a lack of understanding, or an erasure. This simple and self-evident idea sometimes gets pushed aside in theorizations that adhere to a strong constructivist model of disability.

Let us dwell with this idea at greater length. It is common for disability studies to theorize the perceived tension between appearance and essence, between the material world and the social understandings and cultural representations that inform our collective experience of material being. Two divergent understandings of disability that have emerged thus far from these theorizations will be familiar to many readers: the social model and the medical model. The social model of disability seeks to critique the social stigma surrounding disability and ultimately to destabilize the notion of ableist normalcy. Opponents of the medical model of disability explain that it errs by locating disability in the individual body rather than in the social environment. Proponents of the social model say that the individual does not "have," does not "possess" a disability. Instead, it is frequently argued, disability is the product of an exclusionary society in which some people are not valued. They may be stared at, but they are not seen. There is an undeniable truth in the social model's critique of ableism. Yet the hard contrast between the social and medical models hides as much as it reveals. There is no reason that we cannot critique the social environment and at the same time recognize the value of discussing function. As Michael Bérubé puts it in *The Secret Life of Stories*, "The point is not to try to pretend that all disabilities are purely a matter of social stigma; the point, rather, is to insist that 'function' can never be a meaningful measure of human worth."[6] Overemphasizing the distinction between the social and the medical models overlooks the way in which disability identity can be simultaneously social and medical, both cultural and material, imposed from outside and at the same time embraced from within. Here there may seem to be a paradox. In the case of people with Down syndrome in particular, biological/genetic factors bearing strong links to scientific and medical understandings can in fact be considered one of the cultural markers that signal membership in a disability community. In this way, the borders between the social model and the medical model of disability become blurred in any exploration of Down Syndrome Culture.

This chapter insists that biological/genetic factors have a cultural resonance, and that in the case of Down syndrome disability identity, what might otherwise be considered relatively autonomous areas of embodied experience are in practice quite difficult to disentangle. As a point of entry into these matters, it is useful to briefly adopt a historical perspective on disability activism and advocacy. This is an area that of course has a long history, which is made up by numerous voices, tactics, and approaches. Disability activism and advocacy have unfolded both in the broader sociopolitical arena and in a more narrowly inscribed and scholarly register. This is to reaffirm the twinned nature of what Lennard J. Davis called the political and academic project of disability studies.[7] There is no reason to favor one set of practices in relation to another. It is clear that the gains made by the disability movement that emerged in the 1960s, including the Americans with Disabilities Act of 1990, owe much to the strength of the social model, which has rightly called for equality, advocacy, autonomy, self-determination, and the removal of both the tangible and the less tangible barriers erected by an ableist society. A grassroots organization strategy and a participatory ethos were tied to the emerging disability movement's trenchant critique of exclusionary practices and were embedded in the slogan "Nothing about us without us"—a phrase later adopted by James Charlton (1998) as his book's title. Still, the notion of this "us" is quite heterogeneous. In its most capacious form, it must include people with physical, sensory, and cognitive disabilities. As Sharon Smith and Kieron Smith (2021) point out, DS spans cognitive and physical understandings of disability: "While Down syndrome is primarily a cognitive disability, it is a unique condition as it is frequently recognized due to its physical characteristics (facial characteristics, short stature, etc.)."[8] I argued in *Cognitive Disability Aesthetics* for attending to the (in)visibility of cognitive difference in the realms of disability history, culture, and theory. I remain interested in exploring the particularities of those pathways for social, cultural, and political participation available to people with intellectual disabilities, especially those who are nonverbal, less verbal, or who communicate in ways that do not match the normative expectations for able-minded, independent, neoliberal subjects.

The tension between the social and the medical models might seem more or less settled to readers encountering disability studies work from the 1990s, where physical and sensorial disabilities received much attention. Important books such as Rosemarie Garland-Thomson's *Extraordinary Bodies* (1996), *The Body and Physical Difference* (edited by Mitchell and Snyder, 1997), and the *Disability Studies Reader* (edited by Lennard J. Davis, 1997), critiqued the medicalizing gaze in favor of the constructivist perspective imbued in a social model of disability. This strategy, of course, remains an important tool for disability activists and disability studies scholars alike. In books as diverse as *Crip Theory* (McRuer, 2006), *Disability Theory* (Siebers, 2010), *The End of Normal* (Davis, 2013), and *Feminist Crip Queer* (Kafer, 2013), twenty-first-century disability theorists continue to unmask the way in which the very idea of normality is constructed, and they examine the colonizing effects of an ableist society's predatory construction of disability as a problem in need of a solution.[9] Still, something of the tension between the social and the medical models persists, in one form or another, in today's disability studies. It is especially important to stay close to that tension when discussing the lives of people with Down syndrome. If we can become less reticent to discuss medicine and genetics, more willing to acknowledge cognitive difference and even impairment, we can better understand the set of values that undergird this global DS Culture and thus continue working on barrier removal with a commitment to creating a radically different disability future.

Medicine, biology, and genetics are a part of the formation of a global DS community, just as they are a part of the lives of all who live in contemporary society. A capacious understanding of social supports recognizes that those considered able-bodied and able-minded are also socially dependent for their well-being. Instead of speaking about dependency as a deviation from the ideal of the self-sufficient subject, we might accept interdependency as the rule of human societies. That is, if we move beyond what Eva Feder Kittay called "the myth of the independent, unembodied subject," we can better understand contemporary DS Culture itself as a collaborative pathway, one forged by people with Down syndrome themselves, in tandem with allies drawn from families and organizations.

As Mitchell and Snyder suggested in their book *The Biopolitics of Disability* (2015), "Perhaps it is time to return to the scholarly suppressed topic of impairment."[10] Early on, they write, it was important to distinguish between the issue of impairment and the issue of barrier removal. The social model seems to have definitively preferred the latter to the former. Thus diagnoses, pathologized states, specialized terminologies, and medical interventions have tended to be associated with the medical model. As a consequence, these scholars write, the notion of impairment has been "left on the other side of the boundary."[11] Still, they suggest that there has always been room for nuance in the field of disability studies. They note that the discussion of "impairment effects" was pushed forward by feminist disability studies scholars in the 1990s such as Susan Wendell, Carol Thomas, and Jenny Morris.[12] Carefully considering landmarks of the prior decade, they add that "disability studies scholarship continues to tug at the impaired body/social model divide."[13] Mitchell and Snyder recognize the fundamental importance, for disability studies, of attending to both "barrier removal and bodily limitations on public participation." As they put it on their book's first page, "Both of these analytical interventions have played a crucial role in disability studies as the twin pillars supporting the field's politics and research." This insight is particularly crucial for understanding new directions in the disability studies scholarship of the past five years, just as it is the formation of a Down syndrome disability identity and the contemporary emergence of DS Culture.

Note that, in many ways, the idea of marking a hard distinction between the social and the medical models—between the issue of the removal of social barriers and the issue of impairment, or "bodily limitations on public participation," as Mitchell and Snyder would have it—represents a false choice for people with DS, just as it does for many others. Sustaining a radical social constructivist approach to Down syndrome has never proven to be fully convincing in this respect. In part, this is due to the general idea that this move would require disavowing what Carol Thomas called "real bodily limits."[14] I have elsewhere referred to this concern by underscoring the material experience of disability, so as to include within that umbrella term, as relevant, experiences of intellectual disability or cognitive difference as well.[15] But applying a radically constructivist approach to populations with Down syndrome, in particular, also ignores the specifically genetic nature of this disability identity. To return to and adapt Bérubé's language, the point is not to pretend that DS is purely a matter of social stigma, but to acknowledge that the genetic basis of DS can never be the measure of human worth.

The fact that DS has been mapped to a genetic marker has undoubtedly brought unwelcome attention from today's eugenicists. Eugenics is not science, it is not medicine, but a violent ideology that lingers on in the push to screen for Down syndrome in the early stages of pregnancy. At the same time, the "racial atavism"[16] inherent in John Langdon Down's original classification has been identified and critiqued, and today the term "Down syndrome" has been embraced in many circles. One sees its resonance in various flourishing regional, national, and international organizations and conventions, not least of all the World Down Syndrome Congress. It may certainly be the case that, for some, the diagnosis of Down syndrome itself is an uncomfortable reminder of the colonizing effects of the medicalizing gaze.[17] Yet, for others, it has stuck as an identity moniker, and it even manages to convey a strong sense of disability community. If the fictional character Daniel, played by actor Pablo Pineda in the Spanish film *Yo, también* [Me too] (2009), tells his love interest, "Yo soy síndrome de Down de los pies a la cabeza" [I am Down syndrome from head to toe], it is to express a sense of pride in his body—and through it, his disability identity—and to claim membership in a disability community.[18] The opportunity is to understand this contemporary usage as being akin to the way in which other formerly derogatory terms have been reappropriated and reclaimed (e.g., "punk," "queer"). Some readers may find preferable the alternative designation for DS, "trisomy 21," which removes the association with a specific scientific figure, John Langdon Down, while substituting for it a genetic alternative. Throughout this book, I tend to alternate between these terms ("Down syndrome," shortened to "DS"; and "trisomy 21").

It is neither possible nor desirable to set aside the genetic nature of DS and its related health consequences. To consider why that is, let us look briefly at the book *Fables and Futures: Biotechnology, Disability, and the Stories We Tell Ourselves* (2019), written by George Estreich, a professor of writing at Oregon State University. The author begins by recounting the birth of his daughter Laura, who in 2001 was "diagnosed with Down syndrome."[19] While his introduction launches his scholarly monograph with a common trope of disability memoir written by parents—the "aftermath" of the child's diagnosis—Estreich quickly shifts gears to signal his interest in themes of "intellectual disability and society . . . the complications of prenatal testing, human gene editing," and the dangerous narratives of so-called preventable conditions.[20] Though Estreich writes of his parental realization that "the chromosome mattered less than the context," it is clear from his own account that the chromosome also matters; what he describes as "Laura's appearance, her heart defect . . . heart surgery and a feeding disorder," for example, are linked to this chromosomal difference, and are medical conditions that are hardly uncommon in the early life of many people with trisomy 21.[21]

If the notion of impairment has been suppressed in disability studies scholarship, as Mitchell and Snyder wrote in *The Biopolitics of Disability*, it has nonetheless always been present, as their book also conveys, in the embodied material experience of living as a person with disability in an ableist society. A constellation of diagnosable conditions is associated with those who have trisomy 21, from intellectual disability to heart problems, and the prevalence of Alzheimer's dementia with an earlier onset of disease. "People with Down syndrome, to be sure, face an increased probability of a range of health difficulties, the most common being heart defects (40%) and gastrointestinal disorders. (They also have a greatly reduced risk of solid tumors, including lung cancer, breast cancer, and cervical cancer.) . . . people with Down syndrome have a life expectancy of around 60 years."[22] Consideration of bodily difference, of which individuated genetic circumstances are a part, is an important consideration—perhaps even an identity marker—and is not irreconcilable with social understandings of disability.

DS is associated with a number of phenotypical traits that are highly visible across times and cultures. Estreich writes that "we stigmatize what we can see, and people with the condition are instantly recognizable at two levels of magnification: their features are distinct, and chromosomes are easy to see under the microscope. The people have absorbed stigma in the way chromosomes absorb stain, but the expression of stigma reflects time and place."[23] The relational dance between the hard materiality of genetics and the constructed meaning mapped to it by a given set of social circumstances is complex. People with DS are not immune from the scrutiny, categorization, and disabling effects of the ableist social imagination. The relationship between microscopic and macroscopic levels that Estreich describes is always subject to place and time, thus to the intangible character of the social imaginary.[24] Without a doubt, it is the social meaning given to chromosomal difference and its visible, now also conceived as genetic, expression, that matters.

But there is also something quite interesting at work in DS Culture's direct reappropriation of genetics. Estreich's phrase, "The people have absorbed stigma," suggests the complex way in which people with trisomy 21 are neither reducible to nor separable from genetic traits and risks. Take a look at the T-shirts being sold online: "Down Right Perfect," "I'm Downright Fabulous," "Love My Homie with the Extra Chromie." Chapter 4 includes discussion of another specific Down syndrome T-shirt as it appears in documentary from Spain. It is as Frantz Fanon put it in *A Dying Colonialism*, in discussing the colonial French presence in Algeria: "To the colonialist offensive against the veil, the colonized opposes the cult of the veil."[25] Something not entirely dissimilar is at work in disability communities—yet, here, such cultural resistance is grounded also in genetic identity. Leaning into genetics has become one path to combating the ableist ignorance and dehumanization that people with DS experience in society. One can say that chromosomes are part of who people with trisomy 21 are, while the stigma they face is social—but neither aspect of this complex duality is dispensable.

Down Syndrome and Posthumanism

The tensions between social and what are alternately genetic, biological, or material factors have never been settled in disability studies. Nor should they be. Those doing the most exciting work in disability studies today have found nuanced ways to bridge critique of ableist environments and discussion of individuated impairments, bringing together aspects of the social and the medical models, forcing us to confront the ableist world we live in now, and to imagine the disabled futures to come.

One example of this exciting work is the collection titled *The Matter of Disability: Materiality, Biopolitics, Crip Affect* (2019), edited by Mitchell, Antebi, and Snyder. The editors are themselves unsatisfied with the tendency toward radical constructivism that tugs at the strings of the social model of disability. In their introduction, they make clear that they are seeking to address "something amiss in social constructivism itself."[26] They are matter-of-fact about the existence of "bodily variations" and "even severe impairments,"[27] and they are committed to realizing the more radical potential of disabled lives. Beyond mere inclusion, they want to see "nonnormative and nonhuman embodiments as a source of insight."[28] Most interesting is their assertion of "the ways in which the materiality of impairment opens up new worlds of potentiality"—adapting Lynn Huffer's argument regarding queer lives, they are interested in the "ethical frame" that "disability alternatives make available."[29] DS lives can be, in the social arena—and in cinematic representation, I would argue—similarly suggestive of just such an "ethical frame."

The result of Mitchell, Antebi, and Snyder's efforts is a compelling reconfiguration of the social model, one that from the outset recognizes and values the material experience of disability, but not the way in which this has been—one could say always, already—coded by the ableist imagination. It is easy to find, in the editors' return to the material body, to the embodied mind, a course correction offered up for disability studies as a whole. The editors employ a posthumanist approach as the vehicle for this course correction. But the metaphor of a course correction is perhaps inadequate to explain their aim, which is much more provocative, indeed. The goal of *The Matter of Disability* is a radical displacement of the disabling structures of the ableist imaginary in favor of a new way of seeing, one that arguably has not yet come into being at a large scale anywhere in the world. The posthumanist thinking at the center of the volume is emblematic of the very best that the academic project of disability studies has to offer. The editors' command of the field is as pathbreaking as ever, and their prose is nimble: "Over the past two decades," they write, "theorizations of posthumanism and neomaterialist philosophy have begun to radically reshape our understanding of what counts as materiality. Matter itself begins to take on a complex, interactive role in the configuration of knowledge and the world, and is in turn shaped by that universe of interactions."[30] Far from being the passive object of contemplation, matter has generative potential, which is to say that it can produce meaning. This (re)theorization of matter asserts what social constructivism glossed over or, arguably, minimized—that is, the materiality of bodies, the dialectical relation between body and mind, and what I would say involves the material imbrication of consciousness.

Hallmark insights associated with the social model that have become foundational aspects of disability theory live on in this new posthumanist disability approach: "It is no longer possible in this formulation to see disability as a deviance from able-bodiedness. Instead, posthumanist disability theory actively avoids thinking about disability as some preexisting, external force that throws instability into a stable pattern or code."[31] Instead, they offer a dynamic model. "Disability, then," they write, "is matter in motion."[32] This mobile model entails a rejection of static forms, a rejection of "materiality as a stable baseline of limited plenitude," and ultimately, too, a rejection of staid binaries such as able-bodied/disabled: "Within able-bodiedness's parasitism exists a disability host. One cannot exist without the other, but to yield only to exposés of this interdependency of binaries further erodes disability's material promise."[33] Because able-bodied society is so thoroughly saturated through the binaries that the editors mention—a situation that brings disability studies into a productive relationship with postcolonial studies, for one example—they want to challenge readers to think outside of categories, to imagine a way of being that is either beyond, or before, or instead/in place of. Putting aside questions regarding the degree to which posthumanism is a recalibration of long-standing philosophical insights surrounding the fundamentally interconnected nature of matter and consciousness, this posthumanist disability approach is valuable because it allows us "to encounter disability more viscerally as an active participant" in the world.[34] This does not mean abandoning the social model, but rather deepening its critique through recalibration of a sort, recovering the agency of people with disabilities, and decolonizing both able-bodied society and also, if this is not too much to say, part of the complex legacy of disability studies—which is to again stress their proposal that the simple social model is insufficient.

As the editors of *The Matter of Disability* point out, this radical recalibration of the social model can be attributed to Tobin Siebers, whose own essay, appropriately titled "Returning the Social to the Social Model" (2019), has been posthumously included as the first chapter of the collection. Siebers's unfinished essay anticipates and inspires the central premise of the collection's introduction. His critique of the social model is clearly laid out. The main problem, as he saw it, is that constructivism's characteristic emphasis on the social environment had effectively ignored the material body. Moreover, the social model risks objectifying disabled people, who are now reduced to being the targets of disabling environments, and it denies agency to disabled people, as a consequence of an overemphasis on constructivism. Siebers wanted to "rebuild the social model" so that "the body and environment are seen as mutually transformative."[35] He wanted to attend to "the knowledge being gathered and exercised by disabled people," to foment the use and application of this knowledge, and to conceive of disabled people as active subjects.[36] Part of what Mitchell, Antebi, and Snyder have done is to draw powerful lessons from Siebers's formulations, extending their relevance to a wide range of geographic spaces, literary and cultural expressions, and disabled lives.

An important question remains. What of readers hoping to understand the place of Down syndrome in posthumanist disability theory? In principle, there is nothing more fitting than to think Down syndrome through a posthumanist lens. One may certainly think of people with DS when reading of what Antebi calls "the lived materiality of nonnormative and precarious embodiments"; and trisomy 21, denigrated via the ableist ideology that adheres in discourses over prenatal testing, also confirms that "disability materiality circulates as a public threat, shadowed by its own potential disappearance."[37] Similarly, when, in the final chapter, Mitchell and Snyder build on their own idea of "peripheral embodiment" with the concept of "low-level agency,"[38] one may be thinking of intellectual disability in general or of DS specifically. What, they ask, "do we do with people who do not, or are incapable of, performing in the role of the robust, sturdy, minority, rights-seeking citizen? . . . What of those who do not perform their opposition openly or even with a working knowledge of themselves as oppressed?"[39] There is an immense amount of variation to take into account when considering the social participation of people with intellectual disability in general, and people with DS in particular may fall into any one or another of these many descriptors.[40] People with Down syndrome may be more or less verbal, more or less performative in the role of rights-seeking citizens, more or less interested in a formalized or "working knowledge of themselves as oppressed." But whether they may exercise "low-level agency" or in fact embody the very ideal of "sturdy citizenship"—we will observe the latter in chapter 2's discussion of Andy Trias Trueta's autobiographical text—either way, their movements through the world, material existence, and everyday activities are already speaking.

It may be more difficult to see where people with Down syndrome fit in other invocations of posthumanistic thinking. For example, Stuart Murray's *Disability and the Posthuman: Bodies, Technology, and Cultural Futures* (2020) extends a certain tradition of posthumanism that can be traced back to the critique of liberal humanism found in N. Katherine Hayles's text *How We Became Posthuman* (1999). Murray explores "where ideas of humanity, humanism wholeness, body and mind might reside when we bring them into dialogue with disability and the various questions of technology, augmentation and the future that cluster around the figure and the idea of the posthuman." He wants to comment on a "digital age . . . in which the physical and the cognitive . . . are subjected to ever more sophisticated technological developments that advance year upon year."[41] As with other neomaterialist approaches—we have just considered Mitchell, Antebi, and Snyder's above—acknowledging the body is fundamental for Murray. In the largest sense, this is an equally welcome revision of the social model. Murray's technological present and imagined future are, of course, concerned with ethical questions, just as they are also with Robert McRuer's desire to create "worlds capable of welcoming the disability to come."[42] But considered in light of Down syndrome, specifically, a certain contradiction emerges.

Murray's intention to mobilize "a frame in which disability is understood to mean difference and not deficit"[43] relies on the humanistic concept difference and the social model's skepticism of deficit thinking, but it glosses over the reality and the material experience of impairment. This seeming contradiction becomes more noticeable in those moments where Murray's posthumanism edges toward transhumanism. That is, not all of the "potential assistive tools and skills, from smart prostheses, exoskeletons, care companions and inclusive design to pharmacological interventions and neurological enhancements"[44] will be of use to people with DS. It is against those parts of Murray's argument that deal with hardware, prostheses, and tech enhancements that the material experience of Down syndrome pushes back with the full plenitude and potential of humanistic thinking.

Readers are wise to remember Davis's warning that "some cosmetic surgeries to normalize the faces of people with Down syndrome are available, and now drug therapies are being researched to improve cognitive skills."[45] When does posthumanistic thinking slide into transhumanistic thinking? When does it entail the erasure, and not simply the modification, of a way of being in the world, of a person? Here the genetic aspects of DS are a factor that potentially complicates our reading. Murray takes on the problems with transhumanism directly, and certainly understands that there comes a time when we must denounce what Estreich, in his own book, calls "transhumanist fantasy."[46] For their part, Mitchell and Snyder are unequivocal in their similar denunciation of "the disastrous effects of transhumanist (read: eugenicist) approaches to rid society of the 'burden' of people with disabilities."[47] Many will agree that transhumanism is not posthumanism. Yet one lingering question for readers of *Disability and the Posthuman* is whether the ideas about "replacement and reformatting, adaptation, augmentation and extension along with the reconfiguration of bodies and their stories" are indeed posthumanist, as Murray argues they are.[48] And if they are, then a second question concerns whether such posthumanist approaches are well suited for understanding the location of DS Culture.

Down Syndrome and Humanism

The lucid contrast between disability studies and posthumanism that Murray advances in his book can help us to understand some potential limitations of posthumanistic thinking, or at least certain varieties of it, as well as the importance of what might be called humanism, plain and simple, for an understanding of DS Culture. He writes, "For the most part, disability studies has argued for a need to ground theoretical reflection in an understanding of the lived experience of people with disabilities, while much scholarship on posthumanism is wary of the identity politics that might result from such politics of location."[49] This next part is fundamental: quoting from the work of Tobin Siebers, Murray underscores that we cannot dispense with identity politics. In *Disability Theory* (2008), Siebers wrote that "identities, narratives and experiences based on disability have the status of theory because they represent locations and forms of embodiment from which the dominant ideologies of society become visible and open to criticism."[50] If minoritized identity politics and the potential challenge they present to the exclusionary logic and obsession with normative productivity driving neoliberal societies can be considered humanist, then I believe that it is important to affirm the continuing value of humanism. Murray himself writes "that concepts such as rights, autonomy and agency" can be of continuing importance in posthumanistic thought.[51] These are implicitly the very concepts that drive the remainder of this book's chapters, and they receive some direct attention in chapter 3.

If we are willing to see posthumanism as a reconfiguration of humanism, rather than its opposite, then there are indeed aspects of Murray's posthumanism that are instructive for present purposes. He critiques the ableist imagining of a future where disability has been eradicated. In this, he is echoing other scholars—for example, Alison Kafer,[52] whose work figures prominently in his book's second chapter. In line with the disability studies work that has explored nonproductive labor as a perceived threat to neoliberal accumulation, Murray writes that "disability aesthetics unlock what can appear to be the remorseless logic of work cultures and their seemingly inevitable insistence on greater productivity."[53] This issue is also explored, perhaps more directly, in Robert McRuer's *Crip Times: Disability, Globalization, and Resistance* (2018), which is cited, of course, in Murray's bibliography. McRuer does not engage explicitly or at length with posthumanism here (though I return to one brief aside as an example in a quotation below). Instead, he is interested in demonstrating "that the absolute centrality of disability to a now-global politics of austerity has rarely been theorized explicitly or comprehensively, even if increasing numbers of disabled activists and artists globally are recognizing and calling out the disproportionately negative impact of austerity on disabled people."[54] This text and McRuer's earlier book, *Crip Theory: Cultural Signs of Queerness and Disability* (2006), range far and wide in their concerns, exposing those seemingly invisible forces that are taken for granted in an ableist, advanced capitalist society.

In both books, McRuer's emphasis on matters of labor, attention to neoliberal economic strategy, and analyses of cultural narratives and texts reveal the outline of that storied invisible hand of the market so theorized in Marxist and post-Marxist thought, just as they reveal and challenge the "invisibility of compulsory heterosexuality and able-bodiedness."[55] His focus on "claiming disability in and around queer theory"[56] can be seen as a way of both recognizing a coalition, a collectivity, in theory and practice, and of also of denaturalizing the dehumanizing relationships that structure and threaten queer lives, disabled lives, and others situated at the economic and cultural margins of neoliberalism. Regarding the "global economic crisis," McRuer writes that "*Crip Times* crips this crisis by specifically adding crip and queer perspectives to studies that are seeking to analyze the cultural logic of neoliberalism and the austerity that is now part and parcel of it."[57] McRuer's approach is itself dynamic and interdisciplinary, and he seeks to forge an original and novel understanding rather than adhere to the hard lines of established disciplinary boundaries or -isms. Yet for me, at least, the ideal of humanism nonetheless persists throughout *Crip Theory* and *Crip Times*, even though it may take the form of a variegated, rather than a homogeneous, universality.

McRuer's *Crip Times* (2018), the essays collected by Mitchell, Antebi, and Snyder in *The Matter of Disability* (2019), and Stuart Murray's *Disability and the Posthuman* (2020), all make strong contributions to disability theory. That said, thinking beyond these specific texts to consider the wider field, I have often wondered whether there is room in disability studies for approaches that look at specific disability identities. If disability theory has seldom mentioned Down syndrome specifically, for example, is that because the genetic visibility of Down syndrome makes it less appealing as a scholarly topic for a discipline in which the social model still remains a strong and viable tradition? Does the reality that people with DS may arguably already enjoy a relatively strong disability identity have an impact? Is the shared sense of (global) community—what I am calling the idea of DS Culture—a factor that suggests it is better addressed by practical action in the sociopolitical sphere? Or are we really dealing with a special case? Is there something about trisomy 21 that makes it less well suited for an articulation with posthumanist approaches? Or is this just an oversight to be corrected by future research? Yes—a bit of each of these, perhaps. The idea of Down Syndrome Culture is thus offered here merely as one more way of folding the academic project of disability studies into the political project of disability studies—to return to the terms offered up by Lennard Davis in the first edition of *The Disability Studies Reader*.

Posthumanism is valuable as a critique of the many failures of neoliberal capitalist societies: failure to remove physical and social barriers to participation, failure to secure meaningful inclusion for minoritized peoples, failure to fulfill the (certainly unfulfilled) promises of universal equality and access. It offers a convincing indictment of the way in which inclusion has been tied to the creation and reconfiguration of consumer markets and strategies of accumulation, in which it has been reduced to the accumulative logic of spectacle. It reveals and rejects the myths—always fascist in nature, I would argue—on which modern nationalisms and their supposedly uniform, unproblematic histories have been narrated: a population singularly inscribed on territory, bounded, internally homogeneous, and sharing a history that is continuous through time.[58] If traditional humanism still believes (has ever believed) in "unified subjects" or "a unified citizenry," if it has presumed a "a logic of control and capability,"[59] then it is certainly forfeit. Though an objection arises: one might attribute these expectations not to humanism but instead to nationalism, distinguishing between humanism and the historical project of the Enlightenment, and attributing these failures to specific state forms. Mitchell, Antebi, and Snyder draw on Carol Thomas and Asma Abbas to point out that "an idealization of citizenry neglects the lives of those who must labor to scrape out their needs on a daily basis, those bodies who, by definition, do not promise transcendence to a transhumanist overcoming, but rather are fully posthumanist in their composition, behaviors, and tactical alternatives of living."[60]

Posthumanism is valuable if it can help us cast off some of the fixations of previous disability scholarship—thereby effecting a course correction in the field, so to speak. Chief among these fixations, the expectation that every individual, every group, must speak up for themselves—itself a long-standing contrivance of neoliberal democracy through which inclusion is offered in trade for assimilation, ensuring the perpetuation of existing power structures. I am thinking of the point made by McRuer regarding the problematic nature of "a limited identity politics that incorporates some identities while positioning others . . . as inadmissible or *incomprehensible*."[61] Consider the statement by Mitchell and Snyder: "Unlike many biopolitical theories of the human, posthuman materialism does not strictly adhere to models of resistance embedded in the agency of 'politically sturdy citizens' . . . , persons who exercise their rights with a fictional idea of full, self-present, and coherent subjectivity,"[62] Here there is the potential of a posthumanist viewpoint to challenge the basis of ableist society. People exercising what Mitchell and Snyder call "low-level agency"—I return to my characterization of those who are nonverbal, less verbal, or who communicate in ways that do not fit the image of the able-minded, independent, neoliberal subject—are speaking, are exercising their rights, with their bodies. We might refer to this as "the matter of disability"—not just the topic of disability, but the physical, material, ontological existence of disability and its everyday force in the world.

Let us then understand humanism as a matter in motion. It is thus not an outdated model that should be discarded, nor a failed historical project, but an ideal that can and should be continually updated. From this perspective one sees that posthumanism is in fact this very updating of humanism, or that it is a complement, a partner to humanistic thought. It is a challenge to humanism, and at the same time its radical intensification and extension. Posthumanism is the long revolution, and humanism is the near revolution, posthumanism a radically different future, and humanism a better tomorrow. What is one without the other?

What deserves further consideration is that there are concrete ways in which posthumanist approaches have underemphasized or mischaracterized pathways to participation that are still crucial for people with DS. One glaring example can be found in Cary Wolfe's book *What Is Posthumanism?* (2010), where he writes that posthumanist thought "opposes the fantasies of disembodiment and autonomy inherited from humanism itself."[63] Murray follows suit when he writes that the "overwhelming fantasy of modern disability identification is that disability is a knowable, obvious and unchanging category. Such a fantasy permeates all levels of discourse regarding disabled bodies and minds."[64] Understandings of Down syndrome are certainly subject to changing social circumstances, but it is the perception regarding its "knowable, obvious and unchanging" status that underlies not just its perceived threat to able-bodied normalcy, but also the disability identity that has forged in response to the latter. Unlike Wolfe—and paraphrasing what Tobin Siebers wrote in *Disability Theory*[65]—I am unwilling to abandon the generative potential of disability identification to the dustbin of history or to adopt a perspective that denies socially constructed concepts the material force of the real. I am similarly unwilling to abandon certain core issues that have been advanced through reference to the social model, including autonomy, inclusion, agency, interdependency, and human rights, however imperfect they might be judged to be. If it is a return to humanism to put effort and hope into the idea of human rights, then let it be so. These ideas remain extremely important, even if the substantial change they promise has so often been truncated in practice.

A noticeable frustration with rights talk has emerged within twenty-first-century disability studies. Mitchell, Antebi, and Snyder make a good point by suggesting that "by idealizing the rights-slinging alternative, we miss what these lives that matter have to teach us."[66] Still, after all, lives can teach at the same time that rights can be slung. Similarly, it is reasonable for McRuer to invoke a Marxist critique that sees rights as an "insurance policy for the established order,"[67] given the fact that rights talk can, sometimes in practice, foreclose more radical, systematic, and meaningful change. But to draw the line so clearly between meaningful social change in the short term and radical social change in the long term is a false opposition. This is not an either/or situation, but rather an opportunity to think both/and. One can explore the lessons offered up by disabled lives through an ethical frame and also speak of human rights. One can engage in rights talk and also look more closely at "nonnormative and nonhuman embodiments as a source of insight."[68] Rights are never guaranteed. But they are worth fighting for. In this sense, the situation has not changed much since the 1990s. Activists (and scholars) are still fighting (and writing) for the recognition of "alternative ways of being human."[69] There is still "no room for actual lives, or for the idea that Down syndrome is a form of human variation, an acceptable way of being in the world."[70] Those who would question rights talk have the responsibility to advance the "argument for the acknowledgement that those with disabilities, like other groups subject to marginalisation, have been contained within histories of prejudice that leave their present (and future) as a space where rights and justice are meaningful and beneficial (if all too frequently absent) terms, where indeed they may well save lives."[71]

As long as the fundamental reality of interdependence is not acknowledged or addressed by neoliberal society and its ableist drive toward austerity, there will be a place in disability studies for rights talk and disability identity. Until this acknowledgment of interdependence as a baseline for understanding human societies has a demonstrable and, even more important, definitive impact on the lives of people with disabilities through enforced policy, there will be a place in disability movements for rights talk and disability identity. The fact that people with disabilities "have not as yet been included"[72] as equal citizens need not by itself dispense with the promise of inclusion in the short term. It is Tobin Siebers who put it best, commenting on his intention in *Disability Theory*: "The dossier represents a deliberate act of identity politics, and I offer no apology for it because identity politics remains in my view the most practical course of action by which to address social injustices against minority peoples and to apply the new ideas, narratives, and experiences discovered by them to the future of progressive, democratic society."[73] The innovation of the present book is merely to apply the spirit of Siebers's insight to a specific disability identity through the exploration of DS Culture.

Two

DS Life Writing

As signaled by Joseph Straus, narrative is an important discursive tool for individuals with IDD and their communities, who together forge a disability culture through the culture they produce.[1] The stories that disability communities tell about themselves, and the stories of the individuals who comprise these communities, are critical to enacting social change. Such stories circulate and are shared in the cultural, social, and political arenas. They necessarily intersect with other, often conflicting, narratives about disability produced and consumed by an ableist society. This chapter hinges on a specific form of narrative, of disability storytelling, that can be considered a popular genre: life writing. Life writing is a term that can be said to include many variations: biography, autobiography, and co-biography. Underlying this chapter's analyses of such written texts are important questions concerning whose stories are told and consumed, as well as who has the right to tell these stories. Perhaps most important is the matter of what these stories tell us about the ongoing work to secure rights for populations with Down syndrome.

Though books are undoubtedly products in the consumer market, the publishing industry cannot be reduced to crass consumerism, nor can readership be isolated as an area of its own. In theory, life writing might be conceived as part of a relatively autonomous cultural sphere, but in practice we find it is deeply embedded in broader social and political networks. As discursive practices, biography, autobiography, and co-biography are difficult to separate from sociopolitical narratives and circumstances. By considering two life writing texts that narrate the material experiences of individuals with Down syndrome, readers thus at once gain insights into the historical, political, and social circumstances that shape DS disability culture in Barcelona. First is *El teu nom és Olga* (Your name is Olga) (1986) by Josep M. Espinàs, who writes from his perspective as a father about the life he shares with his daughter,

Olga, who is a person with Down syndrome. Second, there is *Ignorant la SD* (Ignoring DS) (2018), written by Andy Trias Trueta, with a prologue by his sister and an afterword by his mother. Trias Trueta is himself a person with Down syndrome who became independent in the year 2000, got married in 2015, and serves as president of the Assembly on Human Rights in La Fundació Catalana de Síndrome Down (Catalan Down Syndrome Foundation). Placing these two life writing texts in dialogue, this approach accomplishes three goals pertinent to disability studies: it focuses attention on the lives of individuals, people with DS, who are not always visible in social life, nor in the academic studies of disability more generally speaking; it highlights the formation of a disability community in Catalunya, one that has seldom received scholarly attention, neither in English, nor in Spanish or Catalan; and it at once insists on the diversity of individual experiences within that larger DS community.

DS Storytelling and the Family

Despite the differences that emerge from a study of these two disability narratives, they both work in service of the communitarian intent to affect and change the ableist base of society. Adapting the idea put forth by Joseph Straus's essay "Autism as Culture," it is possible to see these Down syndrome life writing texts as an alternative to the way in which IDD is constructed by medicalizing discourse. Straus writes, "Within a medical model, autism is constructed by professionals—psychiatrists, psychologists, educators—in their articles, books, and clinical practices. Within a social model, autism is constructed by autistic people themselves through the culture they produce (including writing, art, and music), and its shared features give it cohesion and a distinctive identity."[2] To the medicalized account of disability, such cultural texts juxtapose a social account. By producing culture—that is, by writing about their lives and experiences, and by becoming themselves the narrators of disability stories—people with Down syndrome (and their families) are reinforcing the social and cultural elements of a collective identity. Keeping in mind that populations with Down syndrome are heterogeneous, thus internally differentiated in a number of ways, there is nonetheless a cohesive and distinctive identity emerging here just as there is with Straus's understanding of autism identity. Adapting that model to a new context, the idea here is that Down syndrome is constructed by people with Down syndrome themselves through the culture they produce, to which this chapter suggests a possible caveat.

This caveat deals with the way both texts considered here emphasize the family as a part of this distinctive DS disability identity. The structure of the texts by Espinàs and Trias Trueta, that is, the way in which they both presume a shared familial dialogue, testifies to the supporting role that family members may have in helping to carve out a discursive space in ableist society for individuals with Down syndrome. This assertion should present no conflict whatsoever with the hallmark values of self-expression, self-advocacy, and self-determination as articulated by the disability rights movement since the 1960s and that now form the foundation of contemporary disability identities. The disability rights slogan "Nothing about us without us," as explained in the book by James I. Charlton that employed this phrase as its title, emphasized "self-representation and control over the resources needed to live a decent life."[3] Both slogan and book have affirmed core principles of the movement, namely "independence and integration, empowerment and human rights, and self-help and self-determination" for populations with disabilities.[4] The context and the deployment of these valued principles, however, should be considered more carefully, particularly as they relate to people with intellectual and developmental disabilities.

Charlton himself acknowledges that a drawback of his book is that it does not deal as substantially with cognitive disabilities. In a candid reflection on his own text, he writes,

> The absence of people with mental and cognitive disabilities is especially notable because these disabilities combine to make up the largest disability "category." Although I have incorporated some material from U.S. sources, it is sketchy. Still, I received almost universal confirmation from disability rights activists that people with mental illness are the most discriminated against and the most isolated in their respective countries. This is a significant finding.[5]

This drawback of Charlton's book is at once broadly representative of an earlier period of scholarship in disability studies. The call for further work on cognition has been echoed in theoretical texts from David Mitchell and Sharon Snyder's *Narrative Prosthesis* (2000) through Licia Carlson's *The Faces of Intellectual Disability* (2010) and Alison Kafer's *Feminist Queer Crip* (2013), and without a doubt this call is being answered in contemporary work.[6] Still, the matter of what self-representation and independence may mean for populations with intellectual and developmental disabilities may differ somewhat from the way these terms have been employed by cognitively abled disability communities.

Any consideration of disability rights must simultaneously entail a deep understanding of social, political, and economic context. It can be helpful here to return to *The Biopolitics of Disability*, in which Mitchell and Snyder advocate for disabled populations while focusing on how neoliberal capitalism places conditions on inclusion. In practice, the ideal of full integration, inclusion, and participation, they argue, is routinely constrained, weakened. Thus, they are critical of what they call the "weak strain of accommodation" or the "weakened strain of inclusionism extant in neoliberalism," concluding that "neoliberalism holds out a false promise of inclusion."[7] The histories and the battles fought by disability rights movements provide insights into how the neoliberal state requires self-advocacy, and how inclusion offered to a given minority group is so frequently weak, conditional, context dependent, or even ephemeral, destined to wane over time. As Mitchell and Snyder compellingly explore, inclusionism can sometimes result in superficial social improvements while working against more permanent, large-scale or long-term changes.[8]

Even in principle, the idea of representational democracy is predicated on ensuring individual rights for members of a given community through an assimilationist minority identity model, an idea critiqued also by numerous other scholars. For instance, Robert McRuer writes of "identity and state-based appeals," concluding that these "may nonetheless remain indispensable—necessary but simply and always insufficient."[9] Together, McRuer and Anna Mollow push us to "ask difficult questions of the minority group model and about the ways that model moves through history and through authoritative institutions."[10] There is the reality that neoliberalism requires individuals and groups to speak for themselves. This has been an obstacle for communities with intellectual and developmental disabilities who may not have the social resources to self-organize as a community nor pursue the position of the self-advocate as defined by the state. Anticipating Straus's concerns in "Autism as Culture," McRuer asks, "How does 'the group' grapple with those figures who do not, or cannot, or will never 'constitute themselves as a minority identity'?"[11] Underlying the normative expectation of self-advocacy is what feminist theorists such as Eva Feder Kittay and Licia Carlson, for example, have called the myth of the independent subject. While the independent subject may be an ideal of representational democracy, it is already ableist. Instead, they argue, we are all "inevitably dependent."[12] A central tension thus emerges between an individual and a social view of disability. On the one hand, putting focus on the material experience of disability possessed by an individual or a group of individuals is often a necessary step for self-organization in the assimilationist model of inclusion. Whether one talks of social services, health care, or work/educational accommodations, individual members of a group must necessarily claim status within a minority identity model constructed by ableist society in order to recoup rights they have been denied.

The idea that disability is something embedded in the individual bodymind, instead of being a social relationship, hides much, and has deservedly been critiqued by the disability rights movement and the academic project of disability studies. For some, this individualizing of disability may seem to excuse or to legitimize the ableist society that constructs disability as a lack, something less than the constructed notion of normality.[13] If this individual view is equated with a medical view of disability, with social stigma, with the negation of personhood, with the abrogation of human rights, then it is forfeit. Yet the individual or bodily view of disability does not have to be synonymous with the medical view. Mitchell and Snyder effectively suggest a way out of this false dichotomy. There is the potential offered by "new materialist approaches," which "offer an enrichment of the way alternative cognitions/corporealities allow us to inhabit the world as vulnerable, constrained, yet innovative embodied beings rather than merely as devalued social constructs or victims of oppression."[14] The phrase "innovative embodied beings" is of crucial importance, as it squares with Straus's insistence that disability identity emerges through cultural production. By innovating in their lives and works, people with Down syndrome are producing a cultural disability identity with social, economic, and political consequences. More to the point, Mitchell and Snyder's way of putting things suggests that one does not have to choose between contesting the social constructs that devalue disability experience and the material experience of disability. Here there is a productive resolution of the tension between individual experience and social context.

A similar resolution of this tension can be found in the work of Michael Bérubé. His is one of the academic voices most committed to exploring the situation of people with trisomy 21 in the anglophone world.[15] As a disability studies scholar and the father of Jamie, his adult son with Down syndrome, Bérubé has, over the course of decades, written publications that attend to the narrative representation of cognitive disability.[16] Understanding that Bérubé's contributions to disability studies are varied and nuanced, here we can explore further a few ideas from his book *The Secret Life of Stories* (2016a). The purpose of that book was, in his words, "to find in fictional modes of intellectual disability a way of imagining other ways of being human that expose and transcend the limitations of our own space and time."[17] This endeavor suggests that the reader grapple, at once, with inequities, racial anxieties and nationalist ideologies, practices of institutionalization, sterilization programs, and other pseudoscientific justifications for conditions and social relationships "that affected people with a wide variety of conditions from Down syndrome to epilepsy."[18] Bérubé is attending to the almost diffuse and abstracted way in which social construction of intellectual disability is made manifest in narrative. Yet this does not prevent him from offering, too, some direction on the central tension implied in Mitchell and Snyder's new materialism.

On the first page of his book Bérubé writes, "Representations of disability are ubiquitous, far more prevalent and pervasive than (almost) anybody realizes. Not because of the truism that we all become disabled in one way or another if we live long enough, but because disability has a funny way of popping up everywhere and without announcing itself *as* disability."[19] This is a crucial point that cuts to the core message of the social model of disability studies: disability is a social relationship, not something possessed by the individual. As a social relationship, it is inseparable from aesthetics and more diffuse shared social understandings that reveal themselves through notions of taste and enjoyment, through entertainment, and art, and that have a great deal to do with social bonds, reactions, communities, and histories. The scholarly disability studies project—in many cases pioneered by individuals working in or adjacent to Departments of English, of Women's and Gender/Sexuality Studies, perhaps also History, Anthropology, and others—has traced the breadth of these social understandings and their role in aesthetic projects precisely as a way of drawing attention to their seeming inconspicuousness, the way that certain assumptions about disability become ingrained in us all, given that we live in a predominantly ableist society. This explains, in part, why one of Bérubé's concerns in this work lies with the way in which disability "pops up" in modernist literature, popular literature, and film without announcing itself as such. Popular characters can represent or suggest disability without introducing it as such (from Dumbo to the X-Men, for example), able-bodied and cognitively abled actors feign disability (what Tobin Siebers has called disability drag), and narration itself can convey what Bérubé calls "narrative deployments" of disability even without resorting to representations: that is, "that disability in the relation between text and reader *need not involve any character with disabilities at all.* It can involve *ideas about* disability, and ideas about the stigma associated with disability, regardless of whether any specific character can be pegged with a specific diagnosis."[20] He wants to "broaden" how disability is handled in literary criticism,[21] and he certainly does so. Other examples of this broadening include, in a different way, the work of Tobin Siebers and Joseph Straus, both of whom he mentions as inspirations, and that of still others who are working on not merely the representation of disability but the aesthetics of disability.[22]

Yet *The Secret Life of Stories* is not an escape from the material experience of intellectual disability to a world of floating signifiers and abstract representations. Far from it. Despite the book's focus on fictional tales from Don Quixote to Harry Potter, and despite Bérubé's own insistence that "literary characters are not real people,"[23] these two distinguishable realms are complementary, and intimately connected in the scholar's estimation. A few pertinent digressions in his disability scholarship serve to reinforce the individual, material experience of disability while critiquing its medicalization. One example appears in the article "Disability and Narrative" (2005), where he writes that "the dynamics of disability compel us to recognize that there will always be among us people who cannot represent themselves and must be represented."[24] This latter statement may read as controversial to those hoping to apply the concept of self-advocacy, with little modification, to populations with intellectual disabilities. But it is at once an affirmation of a material reality with which relatively few cognitively abled people in society have sufficient familiarity. Bérubé's view is a direct product of his fatherly experience advocating for Jamie. It is also an implicit condemnation of the consequences that neoliberal democracy's expectation of self-representation raises barriers to full inclusion for populations with cognitive disabilities. As Mitchell and Snyder have also argued, the disability rights movement's distinction between impairment and the social construction of disability need not lead us to ignore the material experience of impairment altogether.[25]

A distinction Bérubé makes with regards to literary narrative is, I would argue, also useful in the areas of social narrative and life writing. He suggests that there are two ways of approaching the presence of cognitive disability in literature, writing of these two ways as if they were two alternatives, even two "worlds":

> In one world, cognitive disability remains irreducibly alien, and self-representation depends on one's capacity to distinguish oneself from those incapable of self-representation; in another world, cognitive disability is part of a larger narrative that includes an indeterminable number of characters, only some of whom have the capacity to narrate but all of whom shed light on the mechanics of narrative and narration.[26]

In literature, Bérubé argues, self-representation is not the only pathway to narrating disability. Taken at this general level, the same can be said of social representation. Outside of the literary text, the heterogeneity of material and social experiences of cognitive disability requires an acceptance of both self-representation and collective representation. The point is not to force a false choice in social terms, not to require individuals to narrate themselves in all cases, but to see that collectives can be made up of a number of individuals, "only some of whom have the capacity to narrate," as Bérubé writes in the literary context. In the realms of social narration and life writing family members can sometimes—not as a rule, of course—make important contributions. That is, part of the move toward recognizing the material experience of disability entails underscoring the role of family, where this family is also an important part of this material experience of disability. Two of Bérubé's own books written for English-reading audiences—*Life as We Know It: A Father, a Family, and an Exceptional Child* (1996) and *Life as Jamie Knows It: An Exceptional Child Grows Up* (2016b)—use memoir as a way of affirming deep connections between family, social justice, and advocacy for people with Down syndrome. The two works of life writing from Barcelona examined here prompt further reflection on the potential role of family in the lives of people in the DS community.

G. Thomas Couser and the Varieties of Life Writing

One of the most significant scholars working in the area of life writing is G. Thomas Couser, who has written that "autobiography warrants study not just as all too rare first-person testimony about disabling conditions but also as potentially powerful counterdiscourse to the prevailing discourse of disability."[27] Couser's interest in life writing has had both direct and indirect influence on disability studies in Iberian and Latin American contexts.[28] In the words of Susan Antebi and Beth Jörgensen, "a consideration of disability in the construction of individual identity and consciousness as expressed in autobiographical discourse" is one important point among many others in the panorama of "globalized biopolitical readings."[29] As Joan Ramon Resina describes it in the introduction to his book *Inscribed Identities* (2019), the person who writes an autobiography participates in the activity of self-realization: the act of writing can be understood "not only as writing about the self, but also as the subject writing itself, and in so doing giving itself an identity."[30] One cannot underestimate the impact of autobiographical contributions that reclaim discursive power in contradiscursive form: the individual who speaks, who is defined in neoliberal society and who thus demands recognition and sustained attention. As Mitchell and Snyder have explored, the discourse of inclusion, which is a fundamental part of liberal democracy, requires self-advocacy, for better and sometimes also for worse—perhaps even, in the last instance, as a way of reinforcing the general rule of exclusion in the long term.

At the same time, life writing must be approached from a broader perspective, as an expression not only of the individual who experiences disability in society but also of a disability community. For Couser, "Autobiography reveals a distinctive culture"; "Written from inside the experience of disability—and in some instances from inside a distinct disability culture—autobiography may represent disability in ways that challenge the usual cultural scripts."[31] The two texts introduced to English readers in this chapter function as challenges, each in its own way, to the cultural and social values that affect their production and dissemination. Thus, what makes this challenge possible is the focus on identity rather than embodiment. As Couser has said, "When the new disability memoir is written by someone with a congenital or early acquired impairment, the narrative may be concerned with issues of identity more than with embodiment per se."[32] In the most general sense, Down syndrome without a doubt pertains to such a classification, and the texts explored do indeed emphasize identity.

At the same time, we do well in adopting a capacious, cultural, and community understanding of identity, rather than seeing it as something that is a purely individual marker. From the point of view outlined by Sidonie Smith (2019), it is important to approach the idea of life writing and its connection to identity from a perspective grounded in the concept of assemblages, a notion of clearly Deleuze and Guattarian inheritance. We must admit what she calls "the myriad entanglements of identities and autobiographical inscriptions." She adds, "I hope to attach to identity increasing density, dynamism, and elasticity and to give autobiographical inscription not only its particularity but also its history of being swept up in large social and material and semiotic and affective currents, ranging across the globe and across time."[33] This wider perspective is quite important if we are to talk about a DS community in the process of formation.

We limit the two texts by Espinàs and by Trias Trueta if we conceive of them as individual stories or isolated products, separated from their wider familial patterns and community contexts. Already in 1982 the Llei d'Integració Social del Minusvàlid (Law of Social Integration of the Handicapped) (LISMI) was approved in Spain, and in 1984 La Fundació Catalana de Síndrome Down (FCSD) was created, with the constitution of the European Down Syndrome Association following in 1987 ("de la qual la FCSD n'és membre fundador" [of which the FCSD is a founding member]).[34] LISMI was a watershed moment for a country that had lived through the violence and death of the Spanish Civil War of 1936–1939, and whose dictatorship led by Francisco Franco was equated from its early years with starvation, exile, imprisonment, and oppression.[35] Approved on April 7, 1982, LISMI became Article 49 of the Spanish constitution of 1978. In a commemoration of the thirtieth anniversary of the law, Spain's Comité Español de Representantes de Personas con Discapacidad (Spanish Committee of Representatives of Persons with Disability) reflected that "por vez primera en un texto constitucional de nuestro país establecía un mandato a los poderes públicos para amparar especialmente los derechos de las personas con discapacidad" (for the first time in a constitutional text of our country it established a mandate for the public powers to especially support the rights of people with disability).[36] It may be also interesting for readers to learn, as Andy Trias Trueta explains in his autobiographical book, that "el meu pare era una de les persones que, juntament amb altres persones, havia fet la llei LISMI, més coneguda com a llei [Ramon] Trias Fargas" (my father was one of the people who, along with others, had created the LISMI law, also known as the [Ramon] Trias Fargas law).[37]

Josep M. Espinàs was not connected with LISMI, but as a famous and even popular *cantautor* (singer-songwriter) in his own right, and as the artistic director of the Concèntric record company of Barcelona, he was already enjoying public attention when he began to write about the topic of disability in the 1960s.[38] In 1965 he published the article "Els nens que sempre seran nens" (The children who will always be children) in the illustrated magazine *Cavall Fort* (issue 53, October). The title certainly reads as dated, if not offensive, by today's standards. However, his article was a strong call to de-invisibilize people with trisomy 21 at a time when images of and public knowledge about Down syndrome were scarce, and it is still receiving attention in the twenty-first century. One such contemporary critical reflection states: "Hi introdueix una reflexió social a l'època de les paraules improcedents per parlar de la síndrome de Down. I l'aportació d'Espinàs és definitiva quan el 1986 publica *El teu nom és Olga*, un llibre de cartes a la seva filla amb síndrome de Down" (There he introduces a social reflection using words that, at the time, were unprecedented when talking about Down syndrome. And the contribution made by Espinàs was definitive when in 1986 he published *El teu nom és Olga*, a book of letters to his daughter with Down syndrome).[39] His book—translated into numerous languages, including, for example,

Czech[40]—was soon infused into the wider European consciousness and culture through radio programs produced at the BBC in London.

Espinàs's book was thus not written in a complete vacuum, but rather in the context of accelerating interest in Down syndrome, and in disability rights and disability community, which bore fruit in the 1980s. Soon after the initial publication of *El teu nom és Olga* (1986), the organization ASTRID21 was formed in Girona, north of Barcelona. In the year 1989, "The association's objectives are already clear: to sensitize society, to support families, to improve the children's quality of life through their integration into educational and social life, and to create services. The name of the association is ASTRID21, formatted thus: AS, for association; TRI, for trisomy (three chromosomes on the twenty-first pair); the D is the initial of 'Down,' the scientist of the discovery [of Down syndrome]."[41] Today, comment Anna Galdon and Sergio Ruiz, "It is estimated that in Spain—there are no exact data—there are some 34,000 people with Down syndrome. Based on this figure it can be calculated that in Catalunya there are some 5,400."[42] If it is true that "en la història de la síndrome de Down, Catalunya hi té una aportació notable" (within the history of Down syndrome, Catalunya has made a notable contribution),[43] this is because organizations like the FCSD (www.fcsd.org/ca) continue to offer innovative programs like Èxit 21 (www.exit21.org). "Èxit 21 is the first digital medium that serves as a loudspeaker for people with intellectual disability and has as its objective to provide a channel for those to whom society has denied a voice and, above all, to influence directly the way in which the general media represent disability and Down syndrome."[44] Today one can find additional titles for sale in the online bookstore of the FCSD.[45]

It is necessary to insist that the "cultural scripts" regarding Down syndrome, to use Couser's words, were significantly changed between the 1980s, when Espinàs was writing, and the year 2018, in which Andy Trias Trueta was writing. Some contemporary readers might object that the writings of Espinàs run the risk of being read as slightly problematic—the trope of the father who speaks "for" his daughter instead of "with" her. Olga Espinàs died in 2019, and we are thus reading of her life only indirectly. On the other hand, the expectation that Olga—or that any given person who experiences cognitive disability in society, for that matter—embodies what Mitchell and Snyder refer to as "sturdy citizenship"[46] is itself a problematic way of thinking. It is important that Espinàs structures his work by emphasizing the absence of the voice of his daughter, in the form of a one-sided conversation, the responses to which we must imagine. Thus, the idea that he is speaking for her is denied by the construction of the text itself, which

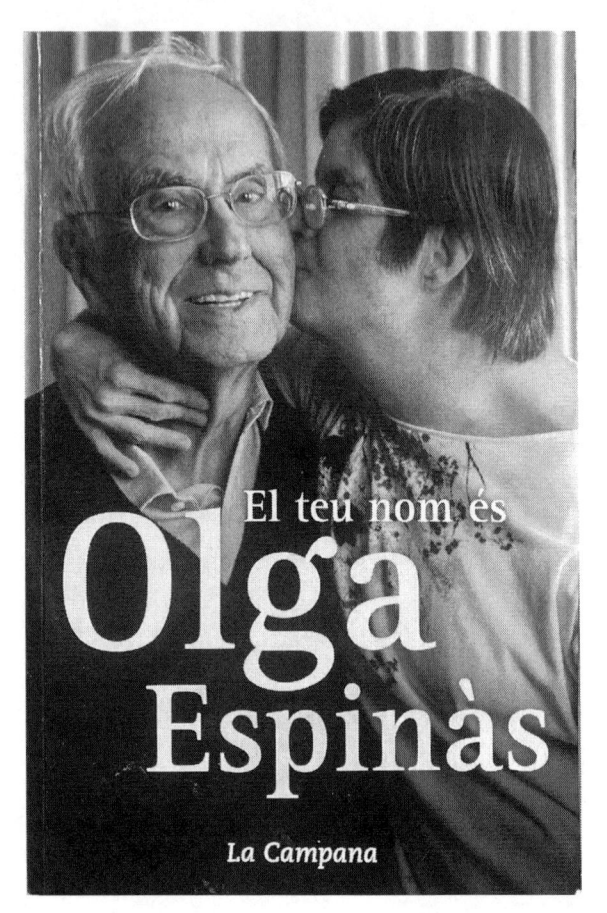

Figure 2.1: The cover of the 41st edition of *El teu nom és Olga*, originally published in 1986. Author and father Josep Espinàs poses with his daughter Olga Espinàs. Barcelona: La Campana, 2016.

foregrounds her absences and generates a space in the mind of the reader for her response, even if it is to remain unknown. He speaks to her about the life they share. One might argue that this one-sided conversation is at once already infused with her voice—conversations between father and daughter, shared experiences—reflecting not an outsider but an insider perspective on her material experience of disability. This is not a complete biography, but rather an incomplete co-biography, a book that announces its incompleteness, its partial perspective. If, in their reading of the text, contemporary readers apply the expectation of a society that requires disabled individuals to speak for themselves, this will be at the expense of two foundational contexts: the history of the formation of disability organizations and the history of the specific social barriers that have disabled people with cognitive difference.

For his part, neither has Andy Trias Trueta produced a conventional auto-

Figure 2.2: The covers of the Catalan and Spanish versions of *Ignorant la SD/ Ignorando el SD* by Andy Trias Trueta. Barcelona: Fundació Catalana Síndrome de Down, 2018.

biography, but instead a text that functions as a treatise and that diverges from the text by Espinàs in important ways. While Olga Espinàs may not have pursued the model of what Mitchell and Snyder call "sturdy citizenship," Andy Trias Trueta certainly has. In his book *Ignorant la SD* readers will find the very model of this sturdy citizenship, one that for many may have seemed incompatible with intellectual disability. This idea of a seeming incompatibility is, of course, itself the product of an ableist society. Trias Trueta's autobiographical book reflects on its author's life experiences and at once contests the dehumanizing and disabling conditions and ideologies that people with Down syndrome must confront. Even though the author uses his individual voice to construct a powerful and intellectually critical autobiography as a person with Down syndrome, the result is not an individualist text, but rather one that underscores the connections between an individual and both his family and an organization, the FCSD, that did not exist when Espinàs wrote his own book.

It may be possible to characterize these two examples of life writing as pertaining to the social world of the Catalan elite. It is evident that such a claim is a description or an acknowledgment rather than a judgment. The fact is that Olga Espinàs had a father whose fame in the cultural sphere certainly influenced the wide distribution of the book about her. Andy Trias Trueta's father was also famous in the political sphere, as noted above. But in neither case is this a reason to discount the impact of their life stories, which are shared both indirectly and, respectively speaking, directly. The notion of assemblage theorized by Sidonie Smith suggests a broad framework in which we conceive of the "I" of (auto)biographical writing as a relational construct of identity. Identity, as Smith reminds us, has a social meaning; it is historically contingent.[47] Both texts have enjoyed widespread popularization, and both seek to forge a social dialogue that goes beyond a single individual's story.[48] In this way, they avoid what David Mitchell called the "dangers in the autobiographical turn that also need to be critically addressed."[49] Although Mitchell has written that "disability life writing tends toward the gratification of a personal story bereft of community with other disabled people,"[50] these two prose representations of DS presume and affirm a disability community in formation in Catalunya, one that is not narrowly defined. They signal the existence of a shared DS Culture with internal differentiation, one that presumes strong familial relationships as well as links with a wider regional—and potentially even global—DS community identity.

Co-biography: *El teu nom és Olga* (1986) by Josep M. Espinàs

Upon first glance, one might classify this book as autobiography, given the fact that Espinàs has intended it to be received as a "confessió pública" (public confession) written by the father of a daughter with a disability ("la trisomia 21").[51] Still, it is more accurate to call it a form of shared biography (co-biography), one that presents one perspective on a life shared by two people, both father and daughter.

The idea of co-biography and its application to populations with intellectual disabilities has not, to my knowledge, been explored in depth—in fact, it is difficult to find articles centered on this topic.[52] In the area of the comic/graphic novel, for example, there is the case of Miguel and María Gallardo: the father, a famous comics artist from 1980s Barcelona, and the daughter, a person with autism and his coauthor. Here there is an instructive comparison to be made, perhaps more so the more one is familiar with the tradition of autobio comics and the confessional mode of comics narration.[53] In *María y yo* (María and me) (2007) and *María cumple 20 años* (María turns twenty) (2015), readers are presented with everyday scenes of the life that father and daughter share, with drawings made by María herself taking up greater space in the second volume.[54] Although it is a work in prose rather than a comic, the content of *El teu nom és Olga* explores quite a similar quotidian terrain.

Espinàs emphasizes the value of Olga's autonomy, he reflects on her personality traits (e.g., her "memòria visual" [visual memory], "la teva notable discreció" [your notable discretion], "no ets gens possessiva" [that you are not at all possessive], "Em sembla que res és capaç d'amargar-te" [It seems to me that nothing can embitter you]), and he comments on her idiolect.[55] Olga, it becomes apparent, has "una certa creativitat verbal" (a certain verbal creativity), and Josep very much likes to include details. Thus, we read from time to time of examples of Olga's preferred expressions: "Hi ha d'haver pau entre les persones i a tot el món" (There should be peace among all people and all over the world), "La gent s'ha d'estimar" (People must love one another), "Les persones que no són bones no són persones" (People who are not good are not people).[56] Those sections where Josep elaborates on "El que tenim en comú . . ." (What we have in common) (the title of chapter 9), and where he discusses the looks that he does not like to see from people, for example, have their inexact complements—these connections are too similar to ignore—in *María y yo* and *María cumple 20 años*.[57] Here, just as in those comics, the emphasis falls on a shared life, lived together, father in relation to daughter and vice versa, which demands a frame of understanding broader than either autobiography or biography can provide. The idea of co-biography speaks to this middle ground.

The epistolary structure of *El teu nom és Olga* leaves empty spaces that resound throughout the work. With each chapter, each letter that we read, we realize that Olga is not absent—Josep incorporates her voice, approaches it, encircles it. Moreover, it is significant that he reflects explicitly on the many ways in which she has influenced him, in which she has changed his manner of seeing the world. The idea is that the letters that constitute the book describe, not an individual being—either Josep or Olga—but instead a material experience of disability that is ensconced within a familial relationship. Olga was born in the 1950s, and died in 2019 at the age of sixty-four.[58] Considering the historical reality that people with disabilities tended to be institutionalized or else hidden away from society, the image of the family that emerges in Josep's telling provides a great contrast to such normative social practices.

There are, certainly, aspects of the work that we read today that might be considered problematic. It is a plus of the reedited work that this is now swiftly, if indirectly, pointed out in the formatter of the forty-first edition: "La situació dels discapacitats ha evolucionat socialment des que aquest llibre va ser publicat per primera vegada ara fa trenta anys. Però les successives reedicions permeten creure que les idees que s'hi troben continuen sent vàlides" (The situation of disabled people has evolved socially since this book was first published thirty years ago. But its successive reeditions suggest that the ideas found in it continue to be valid).[59] Valid, yes. Still, among the problematic aspects we find the use of a few antiquated and offensive concepts and terms. Today, for example, the concept of the "supercrip"—the person with a disability who triumphs over one's limitations—is widely criticized by anglophone disability studies, seen as being in service to the medical model of disability, which divorces disability from its social construction and isolates it in the individual body as a lack of function, most often physical. The concept appears in exactly this way—in relation to physical disability—in the book. The situation is that Olga had a leg operation when she was young, and the language used by her father without a doubt fits this mold: "Però la teva voluntat va esdevenir 'supernormal' i només tu deus saber com vas aconseguir caminar altre cop, començant lentament a assajar les passes agafant-te entre dues cadires" (But your will became "supernormal," and only you know how you managed to walk again, beginning slowly to practice your steps while supporting yourself on two chairs).[60] Today's readers will have to decide how they see this usage of language, certainly an outdated relic.

The effect produced by this usage of "supernormal" is interesting both for the way that Down syndrome is treated and for the marked reference to cognition. That is, when the text reflects upon the social, psychic, intellectual, and mental aspects of Olga's life, those discussions are characterized by nuance and are not at all reductive. Josep distinguishes between the concept of intelligence and intellectual capacity[61] and thus keeps the medical model at a distance:

> A mi no em sembla gens que tinguis una ment infantil, i estic segur que barrejar el *coeficient intel·lectual* amb l'autèntica *edat mental* és un disbarat. Tu estàs incapacitada greument per a l'aprenentatge de moltes matèries que constitueixen el tradicional ensenyament escolar, però la *ment* és una altra cosa, i la teva ment funciona tan correctament en determinats aspectes–aspectes que jo valoro molt, des del punt de vista humà–que jo la trobo tan adulta com ho és el teu cos.[62]
>
> It doesn't at all seem to me that you have a child's mind, and I am sure that confusing IQ with an authentic *mental age* is nonsense. You

are seriously incapacitated in learning many subjects that constitute traditional school teaching, but the *mind* is something else, and your mind functions so correctly in determined aspects—aspects that I value greatly, from a human point of view—that I find it is as adult as your body is.

One can observe in these words a correction of the author's earlier article "Els nens que sempre seran nens," and in fact later Espinàs does write about that contribution to *Cavall Fort*: "La intenció era bona, i potser va ser útil, però han passat anys i tu m'has demostrat que aquell títol era equivocat" (The intention was good, and perhaps it was useful, but years have passed and you have showed me that the title was wrong).[63] The decoupling of the all too narrow concept of IQ and the more expansive concept of mind seems to hint at a more contemporary model of cognition that would be more in line with the social model of disability. Josep in fact frequently approaches this social model of disability, shifting the focus to society rather than medicine, criticizing the lack of social supports for people with disabilities ("No ni ha els equipaments i serveis socials adequats, perquè la societat—no els malalts—és inhumana" [There are not adequate facilities and social services, because society—not those who are ill—is inhumane]), and questioning the concept of normality in an explicit way ("¿És 'humana' de debò, la vida dominada per l'obsessió dels diners, per l'egoisme petrificat, per . . . ?" [Is it truly human for life to be ruled by the obsession with money, by an entrenched egotism, by . . . ?]).[64]

Normality becomes a concept overdetermined by ableist society, which prefers to render populations with disability invisible:

Per això m'imagino el drama dels pares que no han gosat treure aquests fills de casa—durant tants anys hi ha hagut deficients de tota mena que eren "invisibles" . . .—i que no podien suportar la idea de sotmetre's juntament amb els infants, a la curiositat pública. En amagar el fill amagaven també la seva inseguretat, la seva por. Hem de comprendre-ho perquè aleshores la societat era més cruel, i més injusta, perquè estava menys informada.[65]

This is why I imagine the drama of the parents who have not dared to bring these children out of the house—for so many years there have been people of all kinds who were 'invisible' . . .—and who cannot bear the idea of submitting themselves, together with the children, to public scrutiny. By hiding their children they were also hiding their own insecurity, their fear. We must understand this because at the time society was more cruel and more unjust, because it was less informed.

In chapter 3, "Uns pares normals . . ." (Normal parents . . .), he inverts the application of the concept completely. He suggests a definition of non-normal parents: those who, instead of integrating the son or the daughter into their life, cease to have a life altogether, sacrificing everything in the name of the son or daughter. Josep uses the example of those people who told him that he should stop his singing.[66] Populations with disabilities have the right, he says in this third chapter, to have normal parents, and the reality is, he writes, that there aren't that many of these. A similar effect is produced in those moments where he inverts the concept of minority, for example. Instead of talking about "noies com tu, Olga" (girls like you, Olga) as a minority, he deconstructs the idea of a majority: "Cada u de nosaltres és una existència menor en el conjunt de l'especie" (Every one of us is a minor existence in the whole of the species).[67] These are a few of the book's many "valid" moments, while the use of the word "subnormal" and, worse, the "m"-word[68] serves as a quite uncomfortable reminder of how the discourse of disability was shaped in the Spain of the 1980s.

One of the strengths of the book lies in its insistence on diversity. Readers soon learn that "no existeix el deficient arquetípic, ni tan sols la síndrome de Down com a patró uniformitzador" (the archetypal deficiency does not exist, nor does Down syndrome [exist] as a unifying pattern), and the message is repeated with frequency: "Entre els subnormals—deficients mentals, caracterials, etc.—hi ha tanta diversitat com entre els normals" (Among those who are subnormal—mentally or behaviorally deficient—there is as much diversity as there is among those who are normal); "Sabem què és la síndrome de Down, però no podem arribar a saber com és cada una de les persones que han nascut amb la síndrome de Down" (We know what Down syndrome is, but we cannot know who each of the people who are born with Down syndrome is).[69] This diversity translates into the need to recognize multiple paths in life narrative. If *El teu nom és Olga* represents a model of co-biography, that in its time was noteworthy, the book by Andy Trias Trueta marks a milestone that better reflects the tenets and the international reach of the contemporary disability rights movement as it has developed since the 1980s. In shifting from one to the other, we see the family take a supporting, rather than a leading, role: advocacy and representation become self-advocacy and self-representation; co-biography becomes autobiography. Family continues to be a crucial constitutive part of this disability narrative, but it is distinguished from self-representation in a clear preface and afterword, rather than permeating the entire book as occurs in the text by Espinàs.

Autobiography: *Ignorant la SD* (2018) by Andy Trias Trueta

What G. Thomas Couser writes about North America is equally applicable to Europe: "Whereas in the 1970s it was difficult to find *any* representation of most disabling conditions today one can find *multiple* representations of many conditions. Equally significant, and more remarkable, one can find *autobiographical* accounts of conditions that would seem to preclude first-person testimony altogether—for example, autism, locked-in syndrome and early Alzheimer's disease."[70] The book by Andy Trias Trueta stands out in this regard. Its existence—its simultaneous availability in Catalan, Spanish, and English—illustrates Couser's remark that "with particularly severe or debilitating conditions, particularly those affecting the mind or the ability to communicate, the very existence of first-person narratives makes its own point: that people with condition 'X' are capable of self-representation."[71] To move from the book by Espinàs to the book by Trias Trueta is to travel from the 1980s to the second decade of the twenty-first century. This journey through time carries with it a change in perspective, effecting a crucial shift in who is telling the story of DS Culture in Barcelona.

The book's subtitle, "Memòries i reflexions" (Memories and reflections), signals a change in narration as compared to *El teu nom és Olga*, and it is clear that there are both similarities and differences to acknowledge. Among the thematic similarities are discussions of abortion, while *Ignorant la SD*'s emphasis on love and marriage are innovations.[72] Regarding memories, Trias Trueta incorporates scenes of youth, and of infancy, along with episodes from his adult life. As a newborn, he "tenia un buf al cor" (had a heart murmur); as a child, he learned of his father's death from watching television ("Com que ell era un polític de CiU, la seva mort va sortir per la tele" (As he was a politician of the CiU [Convergència i Unió], his death was covered by the television); he became independent in 2001, "ara fa setze anys" (now sixteen years ago), and he married his wife Eva in 2015.[73] He describes his work history in chapter 8, titled "M'agrada treballar" (I like working). Yet all of these memories are at once reflections. The book's subtitle is not merely a reference to the past, but instead communicates an authorial intention. He is the interpreter of his past, integrating it into a carefully shaped narrative of who he is today ("Ara tinc quaranta-cinc anys" [I am now forty-five years old]).[74] Moreover, he addresses multiple constituencies and conveys the way in which disability intersects with the family, work, society, and politics.

Regarding reflections, *Ignorant la SD* is simultaneously a statement or declaration of self-definition and an advocacy project in the name of a community of disabled people. Andy Trias Trueta wants to "ajudar a obrir els ulls i a formar les famílies" (help to open people's eyes and to form families), and he strives for "la nostra integració social i laboral" (our social and work integration).[75] He calls for "una societat més solidària, més voluntariosa, més amable, més afectuosa, més cordial, més còmode, amb més gust i més oberta i integradora, que apostés per ser cada vegada més inclusiva i que tingués més interès a aprendre realment com som nosaltres" (a society that is more supportive, more willing, more kind, more affectionate, more cordial, more comfortable, more tasteful, and more open and inclusive that strives to be more inclusive over time and that is more interested in really learning about us).[76] As he writes toward the end of the book, "L'arma més poderosa que tenim és la nostra veu" (The most powerful weapon that we have is our voice).[77] He lends this voice in service of a community, and even though he is not the first to do so—nor will he be the last—his book is a unique and moving call to action. Perhaps its most convincing contribution, from the point of view of the struggle for human rights in the area of disability, is that this voice reflects upon itself and upon its colonization by an entire society that is defective due to its reliance on exclusion. Trias Trueta adopts an inclusive position in his discourse:

> Jo, en totes les conferències que he arribat a fer al llarg de la meva vida, sempre he dit que la SD és un cromosoma de més i que nosaltres hem nascut així. La societat d'abans ens deia mongòlics o subnormals, ara pel que veig, vivim encara en una societat que ens ignora, que ens aparta d'ella i que ens vol excloure. Estem en una societat que ens discrimina i que, fins i tot, no ens deixaria néixer, pel sol fet de ser com som.[78]

> I, in all the conferences that I have given in the course of my life, have always said that DS is one more chromosome and that we have been born this way. Society used to call us mongoloids or subnormal people; now, as I see it, we still live in a society that ignores us, that pushes us away, and that wants to exclude us. We are in a society that discriminates against us and that would not even let us be born, just because of how we are.

Nor is Trias Trueta content with this alone. He also reflects upon the practice and the purpose of such a definition.[79] And he reflects on moments from the past when he himself ignored DS, when he did not want to relate with people with DS, or when he felt a strong depression and the social relationship known as shame. "Va ser en aquella època quan jo vaig saber que tenia la SD (Síndrome de Down). Sentia impotència, ràbia, tristesa i un buit dintre meu" (It was during that time that I realized I had DS [Down syndrome]. I felt impotence, rage, sadness, and an emptiness inside); "Jo no volia saber com era jo ni ho valia acceptar. Dies, nits setmanes, mesos i anys amb un fort disgust, amb ràbia i em sentia humiliat, plorava com un desconsolat" (I didn't want to know how I was nor to accept it. Days, nights, weeks, months, and years with a strong disgust, with rage, and I felt humiliated, I cried and was inconsolable).[80] But he also reflects on the possibility that the notion of ignoring Down syndrome might also have a positive aspect: "Tenir la SD no és una raó que ens impedeixi fer la nostra vida tal com la volem nosaltres" (To have DS is not a reason to prevent us from living our lives as we choose to).[81] One can argue that these moments strengthen the book's call to action.

Most significant is the matter of who is launching this call to action. In Couser's words, "Disability autobiography should be seen, then, not as spontaneous 'self-expression' but as a response—indeed a retort—to the traditional misrepresentation of disability in Western culture generally."[82] In this vein, chapter 1, "Qui soc jo" (Who I am), is followed by chapter 2, "Com som nosaltres" (Who we are), and he explains clearly: "Per aquesta raó he posat per títol *Com som nosaltres?* És una manera de presentar-nos davant la societat" (For this reason I have chosen the title "Who We Are." It is a way of presenting us to society).[83] This response—which is directly prompted by what Couser calls "the traditional misrepresentation of disability"—is something forged in the community and many times in the family, whether we are speaking of Espinàs's era or that of Trias Trueta. In this way, one avoids the dangers of focusing solely on individuals as they were described by Mitchell.

That the prologue is written by Katy Trias Trueta, the author's sister, emphasizes the value of family for people with DS.[84] For that matter, the epilogue is written by Trias Trueta's mother, Montserrat Trueta i Llacuna. There is a crucial difference here with respect to the narrative form of the book by Espinàs, wherein Olga's family seemingly structured her experiences. Those chapters functioned as windows through which readers could catch a glimpse of her individuated life, and the episodic format kept the readers centered on her own family structure. Here, however, Andy's voice is not presented in the same way. For him, family does not interrupt his narrative but rather informs it. It frames and bookends his chapters. It is merely one further support, certainly an important one, that is present in Trias Trueta's life just as in his narrative. His sister Katy had a great impact on him and exercised a very productive role in his life and his disability community. As she conveys in her preface, "Vaig anar als Estats Units . . . a veure experiències de vida independent allà on ja feia més de vint anys que es practicava. Era l'any 1999. Vam conèixer en Jay Klein. I després vaig importar i adaptar el projecte americà a l'estil de vida de la nostra cultura, per tal fer-lo factible al nostre país" (I went to the United States . . . to see experiences of independent living there that had already been practiced for more than twenty years. It was 1999. We met Jay Klein. And afterward, I imported and adapted the American project to our culture's lifestyle, thus making it feasible in our country).[85] Andy himself writes on the second page of his narrative about the United States, "És així que la meva mare va conèixer la Val Dmitriev i, a través d'ella, va conèixer el que era llavors l'Estimulació Precoç i que avui es coneix com a Atenció Primerenca" (That is how my mother met Val Dmitriev and, through her, learned what was then called "early stimulation" and that today is known as "early care").[86]

There are other social supports that he acknowledges explicitly. Trias Trueta moves away from the medical model of disability while reinforcing the need for access to health care.[87] But it is clear that the greatest importance is given to the Fundació Catalana Síndrome de Down, where he exercises the role of president of the foundation's Assemblea dels Drets Humans (Assembly on Human Rights).[88] The author relates his parents' role in establishing the foundation and the special significance it has for him: "La FCSD és com si fos la meva segona casa" (The FCSD is like a second home to me), and it should not surprise readers that he dedicates an entire chapter to it ("Qué és per mi la FCSD" [What the FCSD means to me]).[89] As president of the Assembly on Human Rights, he addresses a wide public, emphasizing that "tots som iguals, tots som diferents" (we are all equal, we are all different) (the title of chapter 9), that independent living with a successful working life is possible (in chapter 13, "Som com som: Les persones amb la SD que vivim independents" [We are how we are: We the people with DS can live independently]), and that people with Down syndrome have "el dret a formar la nostra pròpia família" (the right to form our own families) (the title of chapter 15).[90] He has traveled and delivered lectures in "Lió, Dublín, Orlando, Andorra, Brasil i Galícia, etc." (Lyon, Dublin, Orlando, Andorra, Brazil, Galicia, etc.].[91] He is also editor of the Èxit 21 team: "És la revista digital que ha creat la fundació on escrivim articles d'opinió i entrevistes a persones mediàtiques perquè ens ajudin a donar-nos a conèixer a la societat" (It is the digital magazine that the foundation has created where we write opinion pieces and publish interviews with people from the media to help us become known to society).[92]

The social and cultural distance between the texts by Espinàs and by Trias Trueta is significant. The connection with disability is contextual/familial in the first instance (Espinàs), and immediate/personal in the second (Trias Trueta). The structure of the book by Espinàs seeks to leave a unique imprint, its contribution falling somewhere between epistolary literature, poetic prose, and testimony. Trias Trueta's book, which is equally unique, offers an even sharper sociopolitical critique in addressing wider conversations surrounding disability. To return to Couser's words, *Ignorant la SD* can be seen as emphasizing identity over embodiment.[93] To this it must be added that these conversations of course have their roots in the Catalunya of the 1980s: for example, in the formation of groups and organizations like the FCSD and ASTRID21, if not also others like Aspanias.[94] But if *El teu nom és Olga* has left its mark, then *Ignorant la SD* has left one even greater. It is doubly notable in its own context, because it brings to light both what has changed in the interim, and what still remains to be changed. If it is true that there was not much information about Down syndrome circulating in the 1980s in Spain, as Espinàs pointed out, the situation is nonetheless similar today, as Trias Trueta puts it, "perquè hi ha poca informació i molt desconeixement" (because there is little information and a great lack of understanding).[95]

Placing these two texts side by side, we encounter a disability culture in the process of achieving greater social visibility. This is a DS Culture, one that is constructed by individuals with DS—arguably, with the support of their families. To return to and adapt the words of Straus, this DS Culture's participants become visible "through the culture they produce (including writing, art, and music), and its shared features give it cohesion and a distinctive identity."[96] One can argue in favor of the inclusion of Espinàs's book in this definition of DS Culture, given Couser's affirmation that "the autobiographical act models the agency and self-determination that the disability rights movement has fought for, even or especially when the text is collaboratively produced."[97] Everything is a question of whether we can accept that Andy Trias Trueta's autobiography, with the contributions made by Katy and Montserrat, just like the co-biography of Josep Espinàs, with the implicit contributions of Olga, might be able to break from the limits of medical diagnoses and forge an expansive and inclusive DS Culture. Just as important, in Barcelona, part of the basis for this DS Culture is made up of the writings published by the authors who write for Èxit 21, who of course share a wonderful anchor in the magnificent book published by Andy Trias Trueta. There is the need to acknowledge an increasingly diverse cast of authors writing from and about the material experience of Down syndrome in Barcelona. Considered together (including also Josep and Olga Espinàs, I would argue), "They address membership in a larger community or culture of disability," as Couser writes: "They reflect the growth of disability consciousness."[98]

Three

Disability Ensembles

The academic project of disability studies is increasingly drawing the attention of scholars of Latin American cultural studies.[1] Nevertheless, further effort is needed to apply the insights of this interdisciplinary formation to the full range of artistic products, cultural practices, and social realities spread across the discipline's uneven geographies. This chapter takes on the presence of people with Down syndrome in a Chilean documentary—as social actors—and a Brazilian fiction film—as narrative film actors—as a way of continuing to expand the geographic and linguistic boundaries of disability studies.[2]

These analyses stay true to the general push of this book in asserting the lived experience and cultural representation of trisomy 21 as itself a viable subject of disability research.[3] Indirectly, of course, the hope is to contribute to a broader conversation regarding the social struggles over autonomy and rights in Latin America and across the globe. Just as canonical work in disability studies has strongly suggested, readers do well in adopting a critical stance regarding the idea that those labeled disabled even want access to the privileged category of normality. Nonetheless, caution is in order, as the choice between radical social change and tangible gains for disabled populations—between the long-term goal of equity and the short-term goal of inclusion, to put it crudely—is not a zero-sum game.[4]

As explored in the first chapter of this book, debates within the field of disability studies continue to reassess the relationships between biological and social markers of disability, medical and social models, and the nuanced and divergent approaches to physical, sensory, and cognitive disabilities and their social and cultural representations.[5] With these concerns in mind, the representations and social/human rights of people who experience disability in society must be approached in a nuanced way. In particular, people with

Down syndrome deserve consideration on their own terms given the way in which factors that are both biological and social, both physical and intellectual, play into their lived experience and cultural representation.

The specific cinematic representations of trisomy 21 that viewers encounter in Chilean documentarian Maite Alberdi's *Los niños* (The children, released in English as *The Grown-Ups*) (2016) and in Brazilian filmmaker Marcelo Galvão's fictional film *Colegas* (Buddies) (2012) provide evidence of a global Down Syndrome Culture in the process of formation. Alberdi's social documentary allows the words, actions, and material experiences of a group of forty-somethings with Down syndrome to speak through the screen to viewers, who are now pushed to think through issues of autonomy, inclusion, and human rights that are of extreme importance for this disability community. Galvão's fiction film demonstrates perhaps more playfully the value of inclusion and autonomy in its choice of a road movie format, but it also uses both its central characters and a large number of secondary characters who are people with Down syndrome to stress the sheer diversity of this disability community.

Disability is hardly an absent category in the Chilean documentary, but historically speaking it appears to have been seldom, if at all, approached on its own terms. This state of affairs within the industry has been carried over to the scholarship on the documentary genre itself. As Jacqueline Mouesca put it bluntly in her book *El documental chileno*, scholars have generally had to work against the perception that documentary is "el hermano chico" (the younger brother) of fiction film.[6] The themes of political violence, trauma, and historical memory have proven to be mainstays of the scholarship on Chilean documentary, with Patricio Guzmán's three-part masterpiece *La batalla de Chile* (1975–1979) easily becoming one of the most commented films to date. In their introduction to *Latin American Documentary Film in the New Millennium* (2016), María Guadalupe Arenillas and Michael J. Lazzara conveyed a concise summary of the concerns that, since the 1990s, have motivated such scholarship:

> transitions to democracy; truth commissions; persistent socioeconomic inequality; continued battles over memory and justice; struggles for gender equality, sexual rights, and equal access to education; as well as the return to power of leftist governments and political actors who just two decades earlier were brutally persecuted. These phenomena coexist with the entrenchment of neoliberalism in the region, which, next to bodily and psychological violence, is perhaps the greatest legacy of the recent wave of Latin American dictatorships.[7]

As Mitchell and Snyder explored in *The Biopolitics of Disability: Neoliberalism, Ablenationalism and Peripheral Embodiment* (2015), such concerns cannot be regarded as distinct from those that ground the methodological approach of disability studies. As both a political project and an academic formation, it shares with other academic approaches a general focus on human rights as the driver of social change. Disability studies has long been concerned at once with the social construction of inequality—the stigmatization of such constructs as "the disabled body" and "the disabled mind"—and the social construction of power through the concepts of normality and the normate.[8] These concerns are intimately compatible with those more broadly social themes listed by Arenillas and Lazzara. Moreover, they are deeply relevant to Maite Alberdi's reinvigoration of the social documentary in Chile, a generalized tradition upon which she draws in her filmmaking as a way of centering the lives of people with trisomy 21 in particular, as discussed below.

In Brazilian filmmaking, where disability representations have markedly increased during the twenty-first century, the situation appears to be different. One can argue that cinematic representations of Down syndrome specifically have achieved a high level of visibility. Both Mirjam Leuzinger and Ana Cristina Bohrer Gilbert have situated this trend in historical perspective. Since Brazil ratified the Convention on the Rights of Persons with Disabilities in 2008, "Se observa en la industria cinematográfica de Brasil un interés tímido, pero constante y creciente por considerar y representar la discapacidad en sus múltiples manifestaciones" (One observes in Brazil's movie industry a trepidatious, but constant and increasing, interest in considering and representing disability in its multiple manifestations).[9] As Leuzinger maps out carefully in her book chapter, titled "¿Hacia un séptimo arte inclusivo? El cine brasileño a través del prisma de los *disability studies*" (Toward an inclusive seventh art? Brazilian film through the lens of disability studies) (2020), people with Down syndrome, specifically, have become a particularly visible reflection of this trend. She cites from Bohrer Gilbert's study to explain that, in Brazil, the community of people with DS is "um dos símbolos da diversidade humana" (one of the symbols of human diversity).[10] Bohrer Gilbert goes even further than Leuzinger in tying cinematic representation to a history of disability legislation. She insists on the relevance of the Constitução (Constitution) of 1988, the Política Nacional para a Integração da Pessoa Portadora de Deficiência (National Policy for the Integration of People with Disabilities) of 1999, and the Política Nacional de Saúde de Pessoa com Deficiência (National Health Policy for People with Disabilities) of 2002—all of which, as she notes, follow in the wake of the disability movements of the 1960s and

1970s in the United States and the United Kingdom.[11] To a certain extent, then, the legal, social, and cultural visibilities of the DS community in Brazil have evolved in tandem.

Both scholars examine a similar set of films and pull from disability theorists. While Bohrer Gilbert examines the period from 2003 to 2013, Leuzinger traces the trend further. We have not only two different documentaries about a plastic artist with DS named Lucio Piantino (one by director Evaldo Mocarzel, the other by Rodrigo Paglieri), but three more about the DS community to consider (one by director Gilca Maria Motta de Silveira and two by Renata Sette).[12] Bohrer Gilbert underscores the heterogeneous character of this DS community, noting that there are nevertheless both somatic/bodily (thus material/genetic), but also sociopolitical similarities among its members.

> Fala-se, também, de memórias e experiências que se referem a um grupo específico, uma paisagem biológica na política vital contemporânea, que, apesar das particularidades individuais, compartilha aspectos comuns que vão desde as semelhanças somáticas provocadas pela presença de um cromossomo 21 extra até os significados gerados pela proliferação dos discursos.[13]

> One talks, also, about memories and experiences shared by a specific group, a biological landscape within a vital and contemporary politics that, despite individual particularities, has common aspects that range from somatic similarities caused by the presence of an extra twenty-first chromosome to the meanings generated by discourses.

This wider trend of social interest in DS in Brazil invites a certain set of questions introduced earlier. Why is it that DS, and not another disability community, has become "um dos símbolos da diversidade humana" (one of the symbols of human diversity)? Why is it that perceptions (and perhaps also misperceptions) regarding the features of DS seem to have made it uniquely suited for cinematic representation? More important for this chapter, it is the leap of DS Culture from documentary to fiction film in Brazil that is of interest—Marcelo Galvão's *Colegas* (2012) is credited with being "o primeiro filme brasileiro protagonizado por atores con síndome de Down" (the first film from Brazil to have people with Down syndrome as protagonists).[14]

What *Colegas* and Maite Alberdi's *The Grown-Ups* have in common is that they resist the tendency, present in other films, to treat the individual person with disability as an isolated case study.[15] That is, the "lone figure" trope of disability representation is common to both documentary and fiction films featuring cinematic portrayals of Down syndrome. For example, the documentary *Praying with Lior* (2009), filmed in a Jewish community in Philadelphia, and the fictional drama *Peanut Butter Falcon* (2019) can both be critiqued to some degree for their use of an individual disabled character as what David T. Mitchell and Sharon L. Snyder (2000) call narrative prosthesis. In the latter case, the disability of a lone individual is employed as a plot vehicle to push forward the development of neurotypical central characters, and in the former case, it seeks to evoke a more transcendent consideration on the universalized themes of religion and spirituality.

Other films with DS protagonists have sought a middle ground of sorts, keeping the focus on a single individual but including other DS characters. The portrayal of artist Judith Scott, who was a deaf person with Down syndrome, in the coproduced Spanish-US documentary *¿Qué tienes debajo del sombrero?* (2006, dir. Lola Barrera and Iñaki Peñafiel) also includes an ensemble of other non–DS disabled artists working at the Center for Creative Growth in San Francisco. Spain's fictional drama *Yo, también* (Me too) (2009) also included elements of ensemble thinking, despite its central focus on a single protagonist with Down syndrome.[16] Yet against the backdrop of Latin American fiction films featuring individual characters with trisomy 21—for instance, in Mexico, *El alien y yo* (2016), directed by Jesús Magaña Vázquez; and in Argentina, *Anita* (2009), directed by Marcos Carnevale, as discussed in chapter 5 of this book—*The Grown-Ups* and *Colegas* are unique in that they employ an ensemble approach that centers multiple protagonists with trisomy 21.

In their chapter titled "Body Genres: An Anatomy of Disability in Film," Sharon L. Snyder and David T. Mitchell outline what they called the "new disability documentary cinema" and emphasize the genre's emphasis on disability ensembles. Films deserving of inclusion in this category may have most frequently appeared in what the authors elsewhere call "in(ter)dependent" disability film festivals,[17] given the way in which ableist tropes of disability still attract the attention of wider audiences:

> One could argue that the primary convention of the new documentary genre is the effort to turn disability into a chorus of perspectives that deepen and multiply narrow cultural labels that often imprison disabled people within taxonomic medical categories. . . . While disability documentary films *do not seek* to repress, suppress, or erase the

fact of differing biological capacities and appearances (as is sometimes charged in critiques of disability studies), they *do* seek to refute pathological classifications that prove too narrow and limiting to encompass an entire human life *lived*.[18]

Despite the fact that one is a documentary and the other a fictional narrative, the films by Alberdi and Galvão both offer the "chorus of perspectives" and "the portrayal of disability *ensembles*" signaled by Snyder and Mitchell.[19] Against the "lone figure" type of disability representation that continues to be a "staple and contrivance of popular genre filmmaking,"[20] the filmmakers draw attention to the social dimensions of a much larger issue, thus participating in a broader conversation surrounding DS Culture.

Alberdi centers her documentary film on four protagonists with DS: Anita, Andrés, Rita, and Dani. Anita's story, and her relationship with Andrés—and to a lesser degree Rita's story and relationship with Dani—foreground the rights of people with Down syndrome as they relate to love, marriage, and sex, while Ricardo's story draws attention to needed improvements in a minimum wage and access to a form of social normality that includes work, bill paying, and financial independence.[21] The director's use of disability ensembles in her film thus ensures that each individual story effectively evokes a larger social struggle faced by people with Down syndrome, while sustaining an emphasis on the "biological capacities and appearances" of people with trisomy 21. One might venture that Alberdi accomplishes, in the realm of international documentary film, something similar to what the popular television show *Born This Way* (2015–2019) accomplished in a more mainstream American media context.

Galvão crafts a fictional story that centers on three protagonists with DS named Stalone, Aninha, and Márcio. Taking the idea of ensemble thinking to a welcome extreme, he also includes a supporting cast of some sixty other people with Down syndrome in the film. Here too, questions of rights, autonomy, inclusion, and social integration are explored in the plot's central conceit. The trio of protagonists escapes from an institutionalized life to claim the freedom of a life of petty crime on the road. The director's choice of the road movie genre is itself a decision that foregrounds notions of inclusion and integration in a sense that goes beyond representation. Is there not a form of social and artistic exclusion at work in the idea that people with Down syndrome can only be cast in certain kinds of stories? Still, as the road movie reaches its conclusion, it does not fail to bring up the subject of social and human rights: among them, "o direito de vivenciar a sexualidade" (the right to experience sexuality)[22] and the right to marry. This ensemble approach allows Galvão's actors to engage with quite an impressive range of social critiques.

Autonomy, Inclusion, and Human Rights: Maite Alberdi's *Los niños* (2016)

Although she has been making shorts and feature-length films since 2004, Maite Alberdi Soto (b. 1983) is a Chilean documentary filmmaker whose international recognition has increased substantially in just a few short years. *La Once* (Tea time) (2015), which was nominated for Spain's Goya award for Best Iberoamerican Film, is a study in aging that chronicles the monthly meetings of a group of seventy-year-old women who have been friends since high school. *El agente topo* (The mole agent) (2020), which was nominated for an Oscar for Best Documentary Feature, embraces the genre's penchant for creativity in its central conceit—an unassuming elderly man is sent into a nursing home to record and report back on the treatment of its patients. Sandwiched between these two films is *The Grown-Ups* (2016)—which was also released under the original Spanish title, *Los niños* (The children), and the French title, *L'ecole de la vie* (The school of life)—which itself added four lines to the director's long list of recognitions and awards: the Spirit Award at the Festival EIDF 2017, Best Film at DocsBarcelona 2017, the Zeno Mountain Farm award at the Miami Film Festival 2017, and the award for Best Female Director from the Alliance of Women Film Journalists in 2016.

Themes of autonomy and inclusion are threaded throughout Maite Alberdi's documentary *The Grown-Ups*. The Chilean filmmaker has crafted a story centered on Anita, Rita, Ricardo, and Andrés, four people in their midforties with Down syndrome who attend a private school program in Santiago (the Centro Educacional Especial y Laboral Coocende). The coproduced documentary film brings further international attention to the human rights of people with Down syndrome, a theme whose treatment by Alberdi includes several intriguing formal touches. She chooses "the portrayal of disability *ensembles*" over the disabled individual, shows a preference for leaving the images of neurotypical people blurred or out of frame (with their speech often left "in-off"), and at times adapts the speech of central characters to narrative voice-over through editing. Foregrounding themes of autonomy, aging, love, sex, parenthood, marriage, work, vocation, minimum wage, and income, *The Grown-Ups* contributes to the diversity of representations that characterize Mitchell and Snyder's call the new disability documentary cinema.

Alberdi's gravitation toward themes of aging and community in *La Once*,

Los niños, and *El agente topo* should be taken as a statement on our status as a species being. That is, against "the myth of the independent, unembodied subject," the director's empathetic point of view and relational storytelling assert the undeniable fact of our interdependence as human beings.[23] If we are to dismantle oppressive legal structures and more systematically support inclusion efforts and social services for people experiencing disability in ableist societies, it is important to recognize that we are all dependent on others.[24] While some may see autonomy as a synonym for independence, the term is not used that way here. Autonomy and in(ter)dependence are not, in truth, incommensurable ideas. Autonomy looks very different when it is considered, not through the individualist and ableist paradigm of neoliberalism, but against the notion of interdependence as the ground of all human experience. Under the right social conditions, people can be interdependent and still exercise autonomy in their own lives. What makes *The Grown-Ups* such a powerful film is that it shows how people with trisomy 21 are routinely denied this autonomy. While the social actors in the documentary may live in Santiago, it would be a mistake to understand their struggles solely through the lens of national cinema or national policy, as the fact remains that people with Down syndrome face similar obstacles to their own autonomy across the globe.

Thematically speaking, Alberdi's documentary shares much with the director's other two major films as it, too, is a meditation on the larger issues surrounding aging and community. Anita, Rita, Ricardo and Andrés are people with Down syndrome in their mid-forties, and the viewer is to understand that they have been attending the Centro Educacional Especial y Laboral Coocende (Coocende Special Education and Work Center) in Santiago, Chile for decades. Here there is more of a parallel with *La Once* than some viewers might initially think, given the current life expectancy for people with trisomy 21. As Alberdi makes clear in interviews accompanying the DVD of the film, today people with Down syndrome are expected to live some sixty years—rather than the twenty-five years that was commonly expected during the 1980s. Even with this improved metric, to be forty-five years old as a person with trisomy 21 suggests a relative age similar to that of the septuagenarians in *La Once*. This is an instructive comparison, as it points to the film's core messaging regarding how elusive autonomy proves to be for populations with Down syndrome—in Chile, across Latin America, and by extension around the world.[25] To wit, the international scope of the film's coproduction—it is a joint effort crossing organizations in Chile, Colombia, France, and Holland—further emphasizes the film's global resonance and the broad applicability of its critique of ableist social attitudes and policies.

The original Spanish-language title of the film is *Los niños*, which works on two levels. On one hand, it accurately reflects the entrenched cognitive ableism that persists in contemporary societies. Anita, Rita, Ricardo, Andrés, and others are reduced to the social status of children through routine discourse, normative legislation, and forms of discrimination that have long been embedded in tropes of charity, pity, and benevolence.[26] The director has explained: "We have an understanding of Down syndrome as something that affects children. In Latin American countries everyone calls them *Los niños*, even when they're in their 50s. So for me it became important to understand this disability in adults."[27] The title thus reflects a documentarian's urge to capture and screen the textures of everyday experiences of marginalization. The sense of social disparagement it conveys is captured equally, if differently, in the choice of *The Grown-Ups* as the English-language title—since the latter is an infantilizing phrase that tends to be used only with subjects who show pretensions of growing up, but who cannot yet be considered adults. On the other hand, Alberdi's choice of *Los niños* is meant to call this infantilization into question. It should not be lost on viewers that the director herself has a family connection to Down syndrome through her aunt, about whom she talks in the accompanying interviews.[28] She wants viewers to reflect more deeply on the attitudes behind the normative ableism the term carries with it. Here the ableist term in use in Chile (*Los niños*) is foregrounded precisely because it is objectionable. By comparison, the French-language title selected for the film, *L'ecole de la vie* [The School of Life], is far less nuanced, and may perhaps even be considered controversial because of this key omission. By erasing the original Spanish-language title's reference to social stigma, the French title merely suggests that school is a universally held, lifelong value. As a consequence, it thus fails to mimic and thus criticize the ableist slur of *Los niños / The Grown-Ups*.

From the title onward, it is important that Alberdi arrives at the discourse of universal human rights for people with disabilities[29] by confronting inequities and marginalization in the lives of specific people with Down syndrome head-on. Actualizing the legacy of socially committed Chilean documentary filmmaking in the twenty-first century, her approach emphasizes interdependency, not dependency, and touts autonomy and access over the closed world of the sheltered workshop often modeled for people with disabilities.[30] By presenting what Snyder and Mitchell have called "disability ensembles," she crafts a formally ambitious artistic and social representation that diversifies viewers' understandings of people with Down syndrome and emphasizes that the struggle for human rights must continue.

In interviews Maite Alberdi has discussed her desire to diversify the representations of adults with Down syndrome, that is, to recognize the diversity of faces, of goals, of struggles, of interests within the community, rather than simply juxtapose a single individual against the group that, unmarked, goes by the name general population. Each of the protagonists she selects for deeper portrayal has an individual set of desires and struggles, which contributes to a greater critique of ableism as a social problem. The resulting choral presentation moves viewers beyond the individualistic and ableist idea of disability as an obstacle to be overcome. In truth, this goal of diversifying cinematic representation in order to bring attention to social marginalization has a long history in Chile.

Maite Alberdi has herself reflected critically on the social commitment that has helped shape Chilean documentary filmmaking as coauthor of the book *Teorías del cine documental chileno, 1957–1973* (Theories of Chilean documentary cinema) (2007, along with Pablo Corro, Carolina Larraín, and Camila van Diest). In the book's introduction—note that authorship is not individuated to specific chapters of the text—the four coauthors invoke Dziga Vertov and the social commitment of the documentary form in historical context to characterize advances carried forth in Chile from 1957 to 1973. They show how films produced during these years—in connection with the Instituto Fílmico (Film Institute) and the Escuela de Artes de la Comunicación (School of Communication Arts) of the Pontificia Universidad Católica de Chile, as well as the Centro/Departamento de Cine Experimental at the Universidad de Chile—define the scope and sharpen the focus of contemporary documentary cinema.[31] These are documentaries that "representan un desplazamiento de la inteligencia cinematográfica chilena desde la escenografía y las coreografías de la acción edificante hacia las zonas intersticiales de la inacción" (represent a displacement of Chilean cinematographic intelligence from the scenography and choreography of edifying action toward the interstitial zones of inaction).[32]

Historically speaking, attending to these margins has led documentarians to delve into sociopolitical and economic factors that shape the lives of workers, that are revealed in the activities of organizing and manufacturing, and that reinforce poverty, limit access to housing, and propagate alcoholism, among other themes.[33] There is a "retórica didáctica" (didactic rhetoric) in play here that functions through the screening of the bodies of "ancianos, niños, mujeres, borrachos, enfermos mentales, cesantes, inválidos laborales, los diversos sin tierra, mapuche, callamperos" (the elderly, children, women, alcoholics, the mentally ill, the unemployed, disabled people, the landless, indigenous Mapuche people, people in low-quality housing).[34] A celebrated example is the Chilean short film *Testimonio* (Testimony) (1969), by Pedro Chaskel and Héctor Ríos. The filmmakers' portrayal of people interned in a psychiatric hospital in Iquique, Chile, can perhaps be thought of in terms analogous to *Titicut Follies* (1967, directed by Frederick Wiseman and John Marshall). What is being screened in *Testimonio* is effectively the idea that normality is withheld from certain populations, that is, "normalidad entendida principalmente bajo los códigos del sistema político y económico: pagar impuestos, sufragar, estar en los registros electorales, tener dinero, tal como se señala en el filme de Chaskel y Ríos" (normality understood principally in terms set out by the codes of the political and economic system: paying taxes, covering expenses, being registered voters, having money, as indicated in the film by Chaskel and Ríos).[35] In a general sense, the Chilean social documentary has been committed to questioning legal and social barriers that restrict full access to Chilean life. While *Teorías del cine documental chileno* is explicitly a historical reflection on the school of social documentary that thrived before Pinochet came to power in 1973—and thus also before Alberdi was born, a decade later in 1983—it speaks also to a cinematic legacy emphasizing alterity and social marginalization that was forged in the 1950s and kept alive by subsequent generations.[36] Diamela Eltit's *El infarto del alma* (The soul's infarct) (1994), for example—which was a narrative and photographic project carried out in collaboration with Paz Errázuriz documenting the lives of residents at the Phillipe Pinel psychiatric hospital in Chile[37]—can also be approached in the context of this legacy.

The Chilean social documentary's thematic focus on vulnerable populations is not uncomplicated. As Arenillas and Lazzara note, the choice of documentarians in Latin America to "represent extreme poverty, marginality or precarity" raises ethical questions about the objectification or exploitation of represented groups.[38] However, viewers must balance these concerns with the fact that "most people make the majority of their life acquaintances with disabled people only in film, television, and literature, [such that] the representational milieu of disability provides a critical arena for disability studies analysis."[39] The fact remains that in social life there is a disconnect between the assertion made by disability movements and disability studies scholars, that "el sujeto con discapacidad es un sujeto autónomo, que tiene autoridad sobre las cuestiones que le conciernen, y es defensor de sus derechos, y no un sujeto débil y dependiente de las decisiones de los otros" (the subject with disability is an autonomous subject, who has authority over the matters that concern him, and is a defender of his rights, not a subject who is weak and dependent on the decisions of others),[40] and the lived experience of disability as shaped by ableist institutions. *The Grown-Ups* is best viewed as a critique of the distance that persists between the hope represented in this assertion and the social reality of institutional experiences. In this respect, it is concordant with the goals of new disability documentary cinema, which "rather than target the body as the site of intervention . . . targets the social services, rehabilitation, and medical industries as a more appropriate site of revision."[41]

The idea of autonomy as a social condition to which not all people have equal access is fundamental in *The Grown-Ups*. As issues of aging, love, sex, parenthood, marriage, work, vocation, minimum wage, and income are brought to the screen, Alberdi emphasizes the bodies and faces of her film's social actors with trisomy 21 in order to critique social services that are unable to secure their autonomy. As the coauthors of *Teoría del cine documental chileno* explain in their third chapter regarding films of the period that assert "lo comunitario como estrategia de subsistencia" (the communitarian as a strategy of subsistence):

> Muchos de los documentales que abordan esta temática ponen énfasis en las características corporales de los sujetos pobres: fisionomías, gestualidades, posturas, vestimentas, índices de higiene. De esta manera, y cosa congruente con las capacidades dramáticas y miméticas del medio, la pobreza se expresó con evidencias físicas sobre la posesión más básica del hombre, su cuerpo.[42]

> Many of the documentaries that address this theme emphasize the corporeal characteristics of poor subjects: physiognomies, gestures, postures, clothing, indicators of hygiene. In this way, to a degree congruent with the dramatic and mimetic capacities of the medium, poverty was expressed with physical evidence about the most basic possession of a person, one's body.

Alberdi's film is consistent with the Chilean documentary tradition's legacy of emphasizing the bodily characteristics of its protagonists and similarly oriented toward the social message that the body is—or, at the very least, should be—the basic possession of those who possess little else in society.[43] This is precisely the idea expressed in the film's repeated use of the figure of a man who dances vigorously in the Coocende's central plaza—his headphones on, rhythmic body movements on display for his peers at the center as well as viewers.[44] It is not without significance that a shot of this dancer has been selected as the very last image of the film. For the duration of these brief performative segments,[45] the dancer is not a student of Coocende, or rather, he is not solely a student. The camera remains still, a mere witness to a contagious joy in his dancing that sympathetic viewers can actually feel.[46] Yet the emotional effect of such shots is nonetheless fleeting when contrasted with the larger truth the film conveys: the protagonists are not in full charge of their bodies. Decisions are made for them, by others, by the school, by their families. Thus, Anita is resentful of the ableist social system that prohibits her from marrying Andrés. Andrés, who would prefer to be with Anita daily, if not forever, must stop attending Coocende altogether when he moves in with his sister as the film reaches its conclusion. Rita shows frustration with the culinary program, but enjoys pocketing, and later eating, the chocolate scraps with which she works, only to be later transferred out of catering to the school's arts program. Ricardo yearns to make enough money to have his own place and share a life with his girlfriend, though the meager payments he receives from two jobs do not even, together, total the minimum wage in Chile.

Lingering and thus lyrical close-ups of the faces of its protagonists are one of the primary ways in which Alberdi's film screens the disabled body. While the social commitment of the Chilean documentary form leads viewers to associate each face with the marginalizations faced by the protagonist in a general sense, there is also a more specific sense in which the face here carries the physical and biological identity markers of Down syndrome. Even accounting for variations across individuals, these physical markers are instantly recognizable. Thus, it is no surprise that Lennard J. Davis, in *The End of Normal*, uses Down syndrome to insist on the biocultural dimensions of disability, or that Rosemarie Garland-Thomson has invoked Down syndrome in her exploration of how portraits grant viewers "permission to stare."[47] Here the director's presentation of the unique features of faces with Down syndrome necessarily draws from the privileged status assigned to the close-up in cinema. The human face is arguably that part of the body which has received the greatest cinematic attention. Béla Balázs wrote perceptively on the use of close-up in film, not merely on "the face of things" as they show up on the screen, but also of "the psychological effect of facial expression": "Good close-ups radiate a tender human attitude in the contemplation of hidden things.... Good close-ups are lyrical; it is the heart, not the eye, that has perceived them."[48] The cinema can be such an important and perhaps even transformative tool precisely because it brings what is hidden to our full attention—to the eye and the heart of the viewer. Susan Antebi and Beth

Jörgensen begin their volume *Libre Acceso* with the recognition that "disabled people in Latin America have traditionally been drastically marginalized, remaining isolated and hidden from view in the family home or less often relegated to institutions."[49] Given their social marginalization and isolation within the general population, people with Down syndrome illustrate this point quite well. It is because they are often hidden from view in family homes that the cinematic close-up can be such a powerful tool of representation. A case in point is Jaco van Dormael's silent, black-and-white short film *The Kiss* (1995), wherein the titular kiss is enacted by two adults with Down syndrome, their physiognomy and intense romantic connection observed in close-up constituting the core of the film's message.[50]

In *The Grown-Ups*, the close-up is not reserved solely for climactic moments, but pursued as a matter of course. It is the visual complement to the insistence on Anita, Rita, Ricardo, and Andrés as protagonists of their own stories. In a simple but quite important sense, this emphasis on the facial physiognomy of Down syndrome has the effect of giving viewers close visual access to a population with which they, quite likely, have little experience. As Rosemarie Garland-Thomson points out, there is an important distinction to be made between what Laura Mulvey, in her classic contribution to 1970s feminist cinema theory, called "the gaze," and what might be considered "the stare."[51] The disability theorist points out that "staring," when it leads to knowing, may have a "generative potential" and invite "empathy and sensitivity."[52] "Staring offers an occasion to rethink the status quo."[53] She also notes that under such conditions, persons stared at are "subjects not objects."[54] Maite Alberdi's preference for the close-up demonstrates precisely this empathetic and sensitive approach to treating her protagonists as subjects, not objects, to rethinking the status quo, and to the "generative potential" of staring. This becomes evident in considering precisely how she uses it over the course of the documentary. One must consider not merely who is depicted in close-up, but at once who is not depicted in this way, and thus who is by consequence relegated to the margins of the film. Alberdi's privileging of the faces of people with Down syndrome over the faces of neurotypical staff and family members further emphasizes the protagonism of Anita, Rita, Andrés, and Ricardo.

Early in *The Grown-Ups*, Anita emerges as the film's primary social actor. As we follow her in a day at the Cooende, she says that she is "aburrida. Y llevo cuarenta años trabajando acá" (bored. And I have been working here for forty years).[55] She goes on to explain that she wants to do other things outside of the school, that she doesn't want to work there her whole life. As she talks, the editing cuts to action shots portraying aspects of the gastronomic workshop and catering program in which she participates: a mixer is whirling, lemons are being cut, and a blowtorch is toasting the meringue on several dessert tortes. Significantly, while we hear Anita's words in this voice-over, they are not synched with images of her speaking. Instead, we see incongruous images of her, that is, shots where we see her face, but where she is not speaking: for example, she walks into the school wearing her coat and backpack; now she has changed into a white chef's garment, her facial expression exuding frustration. Later, while she perches one elbow atop a kitchen countertop, her eyes are closing, perhaps fighting off sleep, perhaps also indicating she desires to be somewhere else. This disjunction between the sound of her spoken words and the image of her weary facial expression creates the sensation that viewers are hearing her thoughts. What elevates her from protagonist to narrator of her own story is precisely the director's lyrical threading of these close-ups that reveal the depth of her world-weariness through the surface of her facial expressions. In this sequence she also effectively narrates an introduction to Ricardo, who she says gives others instructions all day, and to Rita, who has never grown up.[56] Her face brightens considerably upon seeing Andrés—"Andrés es mi novio" (Andrés is my boyfriend), she says—after which they embrace each other. A cut shows viewers an empathetic and quite beautiful—even "lyrical," to return to the work of Balázs—close-up of their two faces side by side. The fact that they are facing in the same direction and are sharing the screen connotes a common purpose and even an intimacy. By contrast with the earlier shots from the catering program, here Anita's closed eyes convey a warm feeling of love and contentment (0:03:34) that registers with the eyes and hearts of viewers.

It is crucial to acknowledge, too, that Alberdi's insistence on the faces of her film's protagonists with Down syndrome comes at the expense of other faces. Staff who work at the Coocende programs are, with very few exceptions, never shown on camera. For instance, when Miss Paty leads the "Taller Adultez Consciente" (Autonomous Adults Workshop), we hear her voice in-off, but do not see her face. The camera stays focused on participant responses, which are at times the exuberant cheers of the group ("¿Quiénes somos?" [Who are we?] followed by "¡Adultos conscientes!" [Autonomous adults]),[57] and at others the careful and reasoned explanations of an individual. In this sequence we learn that Ricardo wants to be able to "pagar las cuentas, de la luz, del gas, del agua, de la comida, de la ropa, de la casa . . . de todo" (pay the bills, for electricity, gas, water, for food, clothing, for the house . . . for everything), Anita talks of the significance of parental love and her desire to marry

Andrés, and Andrés talks of his desire to have Anita live with him under one roof.[58] When staff does appear on-screen, it is only momentarily. Viewers see mostly only the back of the head—not the face—and faces that do appear within the frame are often blurred. When the protagonists speak individually with an employee of Coocende—for instance, Rita, Ricardo, and Anita, separately, regarding their payments for services rendered[59]—the staff member's face is either cropped out of the frame or, if it does fall within the frame, kept out of focus. This is similarly the case in numerous other instances: for example, when Rita is reminded about her diet, and when she receives advice on how to stand up to Rodrigo; when Ricardo receives his "sueldo por cuidar a los abuelitos" (salary for taking care of the elderly) at the eldercare facility where he works, and when he consults with a Coocende staff member about how much money he would need to live on his own.[60]

The same can be said of the appearances of family members. This is the case when Anita—echoing the notion of autonomy espoused by Coocende staff in group meetings—tells her mom (who is not visible in the frame) that she is an "adulta consciente" (autonomous adult)[61] and that she loves Andrés, wants to marry him, and doesn't see him enough. When Andrés talks with his sisters, they are depicted either from behind or from the front but blurred. In the latter scene, the conversation is progressively drowned out as nondiegetic music rises in volume. Given the context of the discussion—that Andrés will be pulled from Coocende—these formal decisions employ editing to elicit sympathy with his situation, mirroring his disappointment as he nods along in disbelief and rubs the arm of his chair distractedly with his hand.[62]

This strategy of marginalizing the presence of neurotypical people, leaving them out of the frame, is a formal response by Alberdi to a social problem, a directorial reaction to the marginalization that affects the lives of her film's protagonists. Over the course of the film this provocation becomes quite marked for viewers. It might be understood as an artistic retribution for the errors of an ableist society. This use of visual and narrative framing, combined with the sympathetic editing described above, may also have the effect of helping some viewers to see the protagonists as interdependent but autonomous social actors, to hear their own words, to see their own actions, in a way less mediated by the institutions in which they must live, work, and love. Overall, what concerns us most are the images that appear in the frame, the way in which the protagonists are prioritized, kept in focus by the camera lens. What stays with viewers of the film most of all are the subjective reactions to the lack of autonomy they experience on a daily basis: Anita in close-up, with her hands to her face in resignation. The faces of the protagonists, their embodied subjectivity, and Alberdi's strategic use of certain close-ups and avoidance of others all lend strength to the film's political message. Filming at the Coocende center has provided the director with the opportunity to address larger questions of disability rights for a community of people with Down syndrome.

A key anchor for the storyline involving the romantic relationship between Anita and Andrés comes in the scene where the couple watches a video of a young woman with Down syndrome and a young man with cognitive disability getting married in Peru. However, viewers soon learn, along with the couple themselves, that their dream to be married is not a real option for people with Down syndrome in Chile. Andrés talks with a priest about his desire to marry Anita and asks about setting a date, only to learn that while some sympathetic churches may have a ceremony, the marriage would not be legal (the neurotypical priest's image is blurred, as per the above discussion).[63] Another moving scene shows Andrés praying that God will help him have a normal life with Anita. Earlier in the film, the idea of marriage and family are introduced in scenes such as the one where Andrés strokes Anita's head and face, asking if she wants to live with him and saying, "Vamos a tener una familia juntos, vamos a vivir siempre juntos. Yo te lo juro por tu papá y tu mamá" (We're going to have a family together, we're going to live together forever. I swear this to you by your father and your mother). Anita is shown visibly upset about the lack of legal marriage for people with Down syndrome in Chile, and asks (a blurred) staff member at Coocende why she can't marry, insisting that "Paty, estoy hablando en serio" (Paty, I am talking seriously).[64]

While love and the right to marry are frequent emphases of the film, physical aspects of intimacy and sex are discussed as well, showcasing Alberdi's acknowledgment that an ableist society systematically denies adults with cognitive disability their physical and sexual desires.[65] In one scene, Andrés and Anita ask staff for a place where they might be able to be intimate (0:59:56). Once in a room at the center that contains a bed, they get under the covers together, still wearing their chef uniforms, and talk both about making love and about how they might adopt a child (1:00:48). In another scene where they are both painting a wall together, Andrés talks with Anita about his previous intimacy with someone named Pamela (0:19:26). The fact that Anita's application of the paint with a roller becomes noticeably more aggressive during the discussion might be taken as an indication that the topic bothers her—the viewer is to presume that this is due to jealousy. Physical aspects of intimacy also receive attention in the portrayal of Rita's relation-

Figure 3.1: The group from Coocende's gastronomy program goes door-to-door to sell their baked goods. While Ricardo (not pictured) interacts with residents over their intercoms, Andrés, Anita and Rita are among those listening in hope of a purchase. From Maite Alberdi's *Los niños* (2016).

ship with Dani (0:57:55), who is discomfited by the way she kisses him with her tongue. In a scene that engages a larger group, one of the Coocende staff members asks them what they know about sex, what they might have seen on TV, and she introduces the topic of contraception.[66] The staff member affirms that "son dueños de sus cuerpos, de sus vidas, de sus sueños" (you are the owners of your bodies, of your lives, of your dreams), an explicit message that is consistent with the legacy of the Chilean documentary tradition's focus on embodiment.[67] Yet as Alberdi's film captures so well, the positive messaging espoused by the Coocende center may nonetheless be out of joint with the values of the larger normative Chilean society.

The state of national conversations on the right to minimum wage, meaningful and remunerated work, and access to bill-paying normality is similarly fraught, as depicted in *The Grown-Ups*. This theme appears also in the above storyline, as Andrés hunts for a ring for Anita only to find that he has only 5,000 pesos instead of the 50,000 he would need to purchase it.[68] Yet it is Ricardo who most demonstrates a frustration with his access to meaningful work and payment. Though he shows high achievement in the skill sets required at his two jobs, at Coocende and at the old-age home, Ricardo receives only a nominal wage. His total income is still well under minimum wage. When he asks a staff member how much he will need to save to live on his own, he is told the answer is 500,000 pesos, and that he is 485,000 pesos short.

Alberdi devotes much screen time to documenting Ricardo's skills and contributions. His leadership qualities are on display as he puts his culinary skills into practice and mentors others in the school's catering program regarding some of the finer points of preparing desserts. When the group goes door-to-door selling meringues (see Figure 3.1), he leads conversations with residents over their street-facing intercoms only to be refused time and again. This sequence is a masterful portrayal of the fact that the somewhat isolated but nonetheless meaningful community of people with Down syndrome that Coocende makes possible has its corresponding complement in the self-isolation of the larger neurotypical population. After they have been turned away several times, Ricardo gives voice to the frustration of the group, saying, "Pero no somos animales, somos personas" (But we are not animals, we are people).[69]

Beyond his work in the Coocende's gastronomy program, Ricardo spends time interacting with eldercare residents, where he is captured on film demonstrating a professional, calm, and caring demeanor even with an elderly woman who is screaming. This demeanor is also evident when he speaks with his own elderly grandmother about her pain. Even as his grandmother gets frustrated and lashes out at Ricardo, telling him to shut up, he responds calmly, "Pero ¿por qué quiere que me calle?" (But why do you want me to shut up?). The fact that her face is visible and in focus, that she shares the frame with Ricardo in a double close-up—without excessive blurring from the camera lens, as occurs regularly with neurotypical staff and family members—suggests a certain sympathy. This can be understood as an indication of the director's awareness of their common status as two socially marginalized people. When Ricardo's grandmother calls him stupid, he calmly but pointedly replies, "Y ¿por qué usa esa palabra?" (And why do you use this word?) and he strokes her face, telling her he loves her.[70]

These extended depictions of Ricardo's skills and contributions are part of a persuasive undercurrent that is palpable throughout the documentary. It should be no surprise for viewers to learn that the film has been considered "la punta de lanza" (the tip of the spear) in a movement to change minimum wage legislation in Chile.[71] Prior to the film, Article 16 of Law 18.600 allowed for payments given to individuals with cognitive disability to fall short of the minimum wage. Yet Alberdi has a deep commitment to using the documentary form as a social tool, and accordingly, as she has stated in an interview, the documentary "siempre ha tratado de movilizar al público, desde el rol social, desde el drama total" (has always tried to mobilize the public, using its social role, using all that drama can do): "Hicimos un petitorio, junto a 40 fundaciones que integran la Red Incluir Chile, a cargo de la adultez y la discapacidad, donde íbamos enviando las firmas al Congreso cada vez que se reunía la Comisión de Trabajo y Previsión Social para que se vote la eliminación de ese artículo. El resultado fue increíble" (We launched a petition, along with forty foundations that make up the Chile Inclusion Network, in charge of adulthood and disability, where we were sending signatures to Congress every time the Labor and Social Welfare Commission met so that the article would be voted down. The result was incredible).[72] This incredible result to which the director refers is that the Chilean Senate approved the Ley de Inclusión Laboral (Inclusive Labor Law), which requires that companies and organizations with one hundred or more workers reserve 1 percent of their employee positions for persons with disabilities (as of April 1, 2019), and also, in theory, does away with wage discrimination.[73] This outcome, which is certainly a step in the right direction for Chile, is a testament to Alberdi's actualization of the Chilean documentary's commitment to social change. Yet viewers must also keep in mind that Chile had already ratified the United Nations Convention on the Rights of People with Disabilities in 2008.[74] To understand the pervasively ableist character of contemporary society is to acknowledge that there are gaps between theory and practice regarding the human rights of people with Down syndrome.

What *The Grown-Ups* does so well is present the everyday lives of its protagonists in remarkable complexity. There are moments of happiness, solidarity, and communion threading throughout the film. For example, when Andrés uncorks a bottle of champagne during a picnic scene on a bright, sunny day, he and Anita and their two guests raise a toast—their arms intertwined.[75] The lack of diegetic sound allows the foursome a private moment that viewers can witness, but not fully experience. Another joyous occasion is Rita's forty-fifth birthday party. She is ecstatic as she blows out the candles on her cake and, later, as she strikes a decisive blow to a hanging piñata, letting spill out a bounty of presents for attendees. Her happiest moment is when she opens the Barbie doll present from her boyfriend Dani.[76]

But just as frequent are moments of devastating consequences as the protagonists face their collective lack of autonomy. When Andrés tells Anita it is his last day attending Coocende, they cry and hug in one of the film's relatively long takes. A staff member informs Anita that her mom is keeping her at the Coocende even though Andrés is leaving. Just as Anita's mom makes this consequential decision for her, and against her wishes, Andrés's sisters have made the decision for him.[77] The only way that Andrés has available to him to respond with dignity in this moment is to give a characteristically poignant speech to the group. Stating that he will love Anita until the end of his life, that he will never forget his friends at Coocende, he gives hugs all around, and—wearing a tuxedo to mark the occasion—he and Anita sing a soft love ballad together. The film jumps ahead to a later time, and we see Anita clad in a vibrant red shirt, singing along to a louder song with great emotion.[78] Here she is depicted in a quite lyrical close-up as a confident and passionate woman in her forties who is working through sadness and intent on loving as much as she can in this life—despite the lack of autonomy afforded to her in contemporary Chilean society. In the end, as Maite Alberdi is fully aware, the goodwill of some families, the opportunities provided by some centers like Coocende, the UN Convention, and inclusive legislation are all steps on the way to removing all social barriers for people with Down syndrome. Yet there is much more work to be done if people with trisomy 21 are to enjoy sufficient levels of autonomy, whether in Chile or around the world.

The Scale of Ensemble Thinking: Marcelo Galvão's *Colegas* (Buddies) (2012)

Filmmaker Len Collin's contribution to the edited book *Disability and Dissensus: Strategies of Disability Representation and Inclusion in Contemporary Culture* (2020) references a host of recent fictional films that have cast people with DS in lead roles. Including his own creation, these include feature-length films from number of countries: from the United States (Evan Sneider in *Girlfriend*, 2010, dir. Justin Lerner; and David De Sanctis in *Where Hope Grows*, 2014, dir. Chris Dowling), Spain (Pablo Pineda in *Yo, también*, 2010, dir. Antonio Naharro and Álvaro Pastor), Canada (in French) (Marin Gerrier, in *Café de Flore*, 2011, dir. Jean Marc Vallée), England (Steven Brandon in *My Feral Heart*, 2016, dir. Jane Gull), Scotland (Paula Sage in *AfterLife*, 2003, dir. Alison Peebles), and last but not least, Ireland (Charlene Kelly and Kieran Coppinger in *Sanctuary*, 2016, dir. Len Collin). Still, Marcelo Galvão's Portuguese-language film *Colegas* (2012) arguably stands apart from all of these, most of all due to the radical way in which it integrates ensemble thinking into its design. This ensemble thinking permeates script, casting, and production.

As the first Brazilian fiction film with Down syndrome protagonists, *Colegas* has received no shortage of critical attention. It won awards from the Festival Paulínia de Cine, the Festival de Gramado, the Muestra Internacional de Cinema de São Paulo, the International Disability Festival, the Brazilian Film Festival of New York, and many more still.[79] After it was released, the actor Breno Viola—who plays one of the three protagonist roles—delivered a speech at the United Nations on World Down Syndrome Day in 2013.[80] The sheer scale of the film's approach to inclusion and integration is staggering, even when compared with Collin's own film *Sanctuary*, which that director described as having "five actors with Down's in the ensemble cast."[81] That is, "*Colegas* conta em seu elenco com mais de 60 pessoas com síndrome de Down, incluindo os protagonistas" (*Colegas* counts among its cast more than sixty people with Down syndrome, including its protagonists).[82] Rather than engage in a full analysis of *Colegas*, this concise discussion begins by highlighting the innovative approach of the film as seen through a few scenes, concentrating on a police interrogation scene where Galvão's ensemble thinking and cinematic vision is most pronounced.

The first image of *Colegas* is that of a cathode-ray Philips television screen displaying a black-and-white snow pattern. A color-bar test pattern soon snaps into place. As a slow zoom begins, viewers start to see the images on the Philips TV screen sift through logos associated with various sponsorships (e.g., the "Governo Federal Brasil" [Federal Brazilian Government] and the "Agência Nacional do Cinema" [National Cinema Agency]). An intentional visual effect recreates the feeling of watching an old videocassette. There are intermittent and roving, horizontal black-and-white bars spanning from one margin of the screen to the other, as well as momentary distortions and sharp jumps. If it were not for the fact that the logos remain intact and clearly visible throughout, one might take these effects to be unintentional—it would be reasonable for viewers to think that something is wrong with their playback devices. This carefully crafted introduction is not incidental but rather central to the film's message. By foregrounding the materiality of cinematic playback, and thus leaning into a metafictional element, Galvão is calling attention to our patterns of viewership, the expectations we have as spectators. We are being presented with a self-aware narrative that plays with the very idea of how we see the world. This is a harbinger of things to come. In quite innovative ways, *Colegas* consistently asks us to see differently—and thus to see disability and people with trisomy 21 differently.

That *Colegas* blends several identifiable genres of filmmaking is also a decision that plays with conventions of viewership. This is a movie positioned between and betwixt genres—not merely the road movie, but also the prison escape, and in its later parts, a detective film as well. There are also aspects of the film that resonate with higher-status cinema. For example, there are hints of the urban scamp energy found in the early films of Charlie Chaplin, perhaps, and a noticeable wink to the wry but arch tone of voice-over narration viewers may associate with *Amelie*.

The voice-over narration of *Colegas* accompanies the very first diegetic image of the film, which is a long shot of a gas station convenience store.[83] The voice—which we later discover is a grounds-caretaker character whose red Karmann Ghia sports car has been stolen by the protagonists—recalls, "Me lembro de um ator em um filme que dizia, 'O nosso destino é a gente quem faz.' Acho que é por isso que eles adoravam filmes . . . os filmes são realmente inspiradores" (I remember an actor in a film who said, "Our destiny is what we make it." I think that this is why they loved films. Films are really inspiring). This monologue calls our attention to the cinematic world as a playful place of creation where roles are acted out and anything is possible. Given the way that the introduction highlights the theme of viewership, we are coaxed into recognizing the implications of this for our noncinematic reality.

Leaning into the staple elements of fantastic cinematic entertainment—the thrill of adventure, the freedoms of the imagined road—is Galvão's greatest provocation. It is, in a sense, precisely by being completely unrealistic, or rather, by being cinematic in the purest sense, that *Colegas* achieves a message that cannot be anything but social. As Leuzinger writes, "La fuerza transgresora de la película parece residir justamente en el carácter hiperbólico y humorístico de esta anormalidad" (The transgressive force of the film seems to reside precisely in the hyperbolic and humoristic character of this abnormality).[84] This is a disability film where an escape to a realm of pure representation aspires to the same social critique as more realist film or even documentary realism. Galvão has said in an interview that Down syndrome is not mentioned in the film.[85] But it need not be mentioned, as people with DS are visible on-screen throughout. If Maite Alberdi's documentary film *The Grown-Ups* showed us what planned, institutional life can look like on a daily basis for people with trisomy 21—as a way of getting viewers to think differently about disability—*Colegas* accomplishes the same thing by way of its inverse. In the case of Galvão's film, what is most interesting is how the sheer scale of the visible, material presence of a DS disability community is shaped by various techniques of cinematic representation.

The first scene of the film depicts a robbery. The trio's stolen sportscar screeches to a halt just outside of that aforementioned gas station convenience store. Each member of the crew is wearing striped pajamas, a pattern that seems also to mark their status as escapees. The scene is constructed using a mobile frame, tight angles, and chaotic jump cuts. The camera stays close to the three protagonists, but never lingers too long on their bodies or the clown masks they use to disguise their faces.[86] Viewers hear a pat phrase voiced in English rather than Portuguese: "Everybody be cool. It's a robbery,"[87] a likely reference to *Pulp Fiction*. The clerk stays still, watching with a quizzical eye. A gun is flashed. A stuffed teddy bear is liberated. Candy is swept off a shelf. As urine drips down onto the floor beneath a scared customer's pant leg, one of the robbers takes a moment to give him the hug that he presumably needs. Intertitle frames gradually introduce us to the names of the actors starring in the film, with visual reference to the canon of American and Hollywood films and genres: the western, the spy movie, the superhero film, the princess fairy tale, even *The Godfather*. Grabbing a pornographic magazine from a rack near the door, the lead robber quotes Arnold Schwarzenegger from *Terminator* on his way out: "Hasta la vista, baby!"

From this first scene it is clear that Galvão has cast three actors with DS in the time-honored role of the folk hero, outsiders who seek to live beyond the confines of an unjust society, those who simply seek to live life on their own terms. This is most certainly a provocative break with the ways in which people with Down syndrome have been cast in films. Galvão fashions them in the roles of grifters with a heart, who must turn to a life of crime in order to survive, but who do not act out of greed or the will to power. In a later scene, as the protagonists are portrayed mid-robbery, two small children in a parked car watch what transpires and wave at them in admiration or awe, or perhaps just out of friendliness, plain and simple. The inclusion of this shot signals the trio's folk-hero status and evokes sympathy for the band of outlaws.[88] Such outlaw characters have not yet lost their moral compass, but it no longer corresponds to normative social expectations. They have only the clothes on their backs, their stolen vehicle, and their dreams. As the DVD cover informs viewers, "Stalone (Ariel Goldenberg) quer ver o mar, Márcio (Breno Viola) quer voar e Aninha (Rita Pokk) busca um marido pra se casar" (Stalone [Ariel Goldenberg] wants to see the sea, Márcio [Breno Viola] wants to fly, and Aninha [Rita Pokk] is looking to marry a husband). Even beyond the explicit intertitles of this sequence, there is very much a Hollywood echo that resounds throughout the film: one thinks of Bonnie and Clyde. Galvão's ensemble thinking begins by casting this trio of adventurers in a tale that would normally focus on a lone wolf outlaw—but it rests atop a much more profound series of social strata. These are not lone figures but a part of a much more expansive DS community.

Hollywood films of petty crime, grifting, escape, and adventure often inspire pathos in the viewer through an implicit or explicit denunciation of restrictive or even harsh social norms. Deviation from norms is often explained as a reaction against impersonal and cruel conditions. The initially puzzling 'decapitation' of parking meters at the beginning of *Cool Hand Luke*, for example, carries largely symbolic weight for a personal struggle that Luke Jackson (Paul Newman) has waged against social institutions, one that then recapitulates itself in Luke's responses of to the harsh and dehumanizing conditions of incarcerated life. In *Colegas*, the pathos stems from the explicit denunciation of the institutionalized lives from which Stalone, Márcio, and Aninha are escaping. It is not too much to imagine that the striped pajamas worn by the trio in a number of early scenes also mark them as convicts. Galvão spends time presenting and denouncing the residential institution from which they have escaped. The scenes that take place inside the institution emphasize normative expectations of behavior through shots of numerous institutionalized people with Down syndrome wearing identical costuming, walking in single file, and entering the cafeteria at the same time every day.[89] Their lives are controlled and highly regimented. We also learn a bit about why the characters have been institutionalized—for example, Aninha has never met her parents, who presumedly gave her away after learning of her disability.

Part of seeing differently, of seeing people with Down syndrome differently, involves seeing this disability community as internally heterogeneous. As Collin writes, "Two persons with Down's are not necessarily equal in their abilities, or impairments, either physically or mentally."[90] Seeing difference across or within a given, delineated, population of people reinforces the idea that humanity as a whole is also heterogeneous. This complex endogamous view recapitulates the complex exogamous view. Said another way, difference is revealed to be, not a trait that is possessed by an individual group or person, but rather a quality of all life at the largest scale of contemplation. At its best, ensemble thinking positions itself to look both within communities and across communities. It faces both inward and outward. By contrast, in its carefully contrived individualism, the "lone figure" trope of disability representation critiqued by disability studies scholars looks only inward. It encourages narrow thinking, of the kind that is active in stereotypes. No doubt, there is an ableist ideology at work in any production of the cinematic "lone figure" with a disability, but this ideology itself hinges in part on a process of isolation. The isolated figure is a clinical contrivance—individuals are removed from social networks and approached as potentially illuminating case studies. Ensemble thinking disrupts this approach and its conclusions by asserting a collective material presence in the face of social and ideological isolation. There is something quite simple about this correction. The greater the number of bodies, the greater the evidence of DS community and shared DS Culture.

Beyond insisting on the centrality of Stalone, Márcio, and Aninha, for the narrative, Galvão pushes ensemble thinking to an extreme unparalleled in any other fiction film viewers are likely to have seen. Additional actors with Down syndrome do not merely appear as extras in the scenes depicting the stultifying life in the institution mentioned above—lining up for breakfast in single file, for instance—they also have minor, but significant, acting and speaking roles. For example, when an attractive male singer visits the institution, a number of additional female actors take part in a scene with Aninha. They are shown smiling and dancing, and some enjoy reaction shots of their own, before Aninha finally gives in to her amorous feelings and jumps on top of the visitor.[91] It is also of interest that elements of Aninha's story—here and also toward the conclusion of the film where she and Stalone get married and "entram em um caminhão baú e consumam o casamento" (go into the back of a truck and consummate their marriage)—as well as another scene featuring Márcio, illustrate the movie's cinematic recognition of what has been called "o direito de vivenciar a sexualidade" (the right to experience sexuality).[92] Remember, from the introduction to this book, the question posed in the subtitle of Jhonatthan Maldonado Ramírez's article on Down syndrome and sexuality: "¿Crees que ellos no quieren tocar y ser tocados?" (Do you think that they do not want to touch and be touched?).

Another example of a minor but significant speaking role for an actor with Down syndrome is a scene where Giulia de Souza Merigo plays the role of Jazilma, a wonderfully stern second-in-command at the institution. We meet Jazilma when the two detectives who have been assigned the duty of tracking down the escaped trio of protagonists arrive and start asking questions. She introduces herself as the "braço direito da tia Esmeralda" (right hand of Ms. Esmeralda) and bangs on a table, commanding their attention and respect.[93] Galvão films the actor at somewhat of a distance and places the camera on the table at which she sits. As a result, the staging accentuates her authoritative delivery and reflects her position of power.

Ensemble thinking is pushed to the limit in one of the film's most striking and hilarious sequences, which also takes place at the institution.[94] The two detectives have arranged to interview anyone who might know where the escaped residents are likely to be heading. Much humor ensues as some twenty actors with speaking roles waste the detectives' time. For this sequence, Galvão selects the form of a lively montage with quick cuts. In response to

Figure 3.2: Ensemble thinking during the scene where some 20 actors with Down syndrome are interrogated by the detectives. One interviewee fires pretend bullets from behind the chair. From Marcelo Galvão's *Colegas* (2012).

the serious questions of the detectives, the numerous interviewees are largely unhelpful. When asked where Stalone has escaped to, each person names a different place: "Espanha, Japão . . . Para a selva . . . Itália . . . Holanda, México . . . Ele foi no shopping, saiu para o cinema . . ." (Spain, Japan . . . To the jungle . . . Italy . . . Holland, Mexico . . . He went to the mall, he went to the movies . . .). Or else they change the subject. Are the interviewees being difficult on purpose to impede the investigation and give their colleagues the time they need to put some distance between themselves and the institution? Or are they simply enjoying performing for the detectives, for the camera crew, for viewers, for themselves? All of the above. Galvão's filming decisions here, as elsewhere in *Colegas*, are crucial to blending the diegetic and the social meanings of all that we see on the screen. The level of narrative (the fictional situation) and the levels of production/representation (the material presence of people with Down syndrome on the screen) function in unison, discursively speaking. These interviewees/actors are controlling the conversation. Galvão's script functions as a hinge where the inclusion of actors with Down syndrome is meaningful in terms of both the film's narrative action and the film's production.

Along with the performances of these numerous actors with Down syndrome, the staging and editing of the scene are crucial to this scene's impact. Only two camera positions are used; these cut across the axis of action to show questions posed and answers given. The backgrounds for both points of view are similar-looking bookcases, suggesting an institutional library. The detectives are seated on a couch while the interviewees are captured—one at a time, though jump cuts—seated in a single chair. The frame is static. The interviewees are seated at a table and tend to be framed more closely—in mid-shot, versus the mid-long shot for the detectives, who are sometimes framed in a static close-up. The stability of the framing and distance of the camera with respect to the characters with trisomy 21 accentuates the interviewees' position of power, while reminding viewers that the visiting detectives are out of their element. Generally, no one sits down or gets up. Still, the movement of the detectives seems more restricted. Their movements are limited to shifting their weight in discomfort while seated. This discomfort is both physical and also situational, as they squirm to show disapproval of the answers they receive. The interviewees are thus comparatively more dynamic. Pressed for information, they instead perform dance moves, sing a song, talk about Michael Jackson, make a face at the camera, laugh, smile, or just stare silently at the detectives. At the end of the sequence, the detectives remain seated and thus immobile as an interviewee jumps behind the chair to fire finger pistols at them, using the chair as cover for any possible return fire (see Figure 3.2). This scene functions allegorically to convey the dynamism of a DS community in contrast with the stodgy able-bodied world whose expectations are poorly formulated.

As a consequence of these various filming decisions, the role of the detectives has been effectively instrumentalized. They are reduced to being passive vehicles for pushing the plot forward and allowing the numerous actors with Down syndrome the screen time they deserve.[95] A certain contrast is established as the scene cuts back and forth between the blank stares and immobile bodies of the detectives and the active, playful behavior of the interviewees. Leuzinger describes "las historias descabelladas de los alumnos interrogados por la policía" (the crazy stories of the students questioned by the police) as a scene "que roza lo grotesco" (that borders on the grotesque) and concludes that "los personajes con SD confirman y, a la vez, exageran los estereotipos impuestos por la sociedad" (the characters with DS confirm, and at the same time exaggerate, the stereotypes imposed by society).[96] The idea that the characters/actors are intentionally playing into stereotypes here seems plausible, but one wonders what, specifically, Leuzinger might mean by this. Another study suggests that the scene showcases the ineptitude of the police officers, which seems evident enough: "Esses policiais passaram a interrogar os jovens do instituto, demonstrando que não tinham a menor habilidade com os jovens e nem para o serviço" (These policemen then begin to interrogate the young people in the institute, demonstrating that they don't have the least skill either with the young people or in their official duties).[97] But there is more to it than that. What seems most clear—given the folk-hero narrative that has been established already in the film—is that the scene will evoke the sympathy of viewers for this group of time-wasters, whose de facto avoidance during questioning suggests a subversion of law and order and parallels, perhaps even enables, the primary narrative of the escaped trio. This is a vision of filmmaking that—for all its masterful camera work, stylized edits, and careful emplotment—is also interested in what Alison Kafer calls crip time.[98] This term implies, in part, a critique of the ableist ideology that expects the use of time to be predictable and productive. With this concept in mind, we laugh at the policemen, as their attempts to gain information are thwarted, and we laugh with those interviewed, as their playful and seemingly unrelated performances amuse and entertain. This indulgence of crip time works at the two levels already mentioned, in the narrative action and in audiences' reaction.

By way of conclusion, a statement made by Len Collin concerning writer/director Galvão's intentions is worth considering in greater detail. Discussing the practical matter of filming with actors with Down syndrome and intellectual disability, Collin writes that "*Colegas* had three main actors with Down's, though writer/director Marcelo Galvão kept action and dialogue relatively simple, relying on his non-disabled cast to drive the narrative."[99] Collin himself worked with five actors with Down syndrome for his own film *Sanctuary*, yet I cannot help but think that there is more to consider in his assessment of Galvão's project. All hinges on what one considers the narrative to be. Collin's statement makes the most sense if by narrative we understand the propulsive push of the detective story. But as suggested above, the film cannot be reduced to a single genre imprint or set of genre tropes. From start to finish, the narrative is a self-aware story about the social restrictions placed on personal dreams. It is a narrative not about escape, but about disability representation generally, and about Down syndrome specifically. The film's blending of fictional play and its social realist message is precisely what constitutes the narrative. In this sense, this interrogation scene—perhaps more than any other single scene in the film—pushes the narrative forward. Focusing on the conventional detective narrative, as do the two detectives when they meet Jazilma (the stern character played by Giulia de Souza Merigo), effectively ignores what the film is about—which is an ambitious form of, in a word, inclusion. In Galvão's words, "O nosso filme tem três protagonistas especiais e 60 garotos com síndrome de Down no elenco, mas não queremos dar nenhuma lição, mas divertir as pessoas. Essa é a verdadeira inclusão" (Our film has three special protagonists and sixty extras with Down syndrome in the cast, but we don't want to give a lesson, just to entertain people. This is the true inclusion).[100] *Colegas* is a spectacular film in many respects, but most spectacular is the scale at which Marcelo Galvão engages an ensemble thinking that transcends the film's fictional impulses in order to focus our attention on the social representations of Down syndrome.

It is true that the pair of films discussed in this chapter are of two very different types. Yet while Alberdi's is a documentary and Galvão's is a fiction film, they have much in common. Each engages a form of ensemble thinking that moves beyond the tired and unimaginative lone-figure tropes that abound in cinema. In addition, both express a confidence in the cultural representation of individuals and communities with Down syndrome. Especially in the case of the documentary from Chile, but to a large degree also in the case of the narrative fiction from Brazil, viewers are encouraged to embrace the fidelity between screen representations and social representations of disability. Whether they are cast in the role of social actors or whether they are traditional actors portraying a role, the bodies with Down syndrome we see on the cinema screen have their complements, it is understood, in the lives, struggles, and dreams of people with Down syndrome who live and work in contemporary Chile and Brazil. These filmic dramatizations of the themes of access, pay, sexuality, and marriage are dramatizations of human rights. From this perspective, *Colegas* is just as much of a social document as *Los niños / The Grown-Ups*. Both films are visual arguments against ableism and for disability rights that are in dialogue with DS identity. Despite the artful composition of Alberdi's documentary and the playful spirit that pervades Galvão's fictional narratives, spectators are in this sense right to take what they see at face value. This is not the only strategy that filmmakers have at their disposal, however. In the next chapter, we look at what happens when viewers are encouraged to adopt a more skeptical position regarding what they see.

Four

Where Is Down?

There is a gap between the material reality of disability and the social image of disability. On the one hand, there is the material, lived experience of disability. The idea is one that, at the moment, many times, gets expressed in terms of "diversidad funcional" (functional diversity), a usage is that is prevalent in certain circles in Spain.[1] The intent of this hybrid phrase, "functional diversity," is to emphasize that any discussion of function—whether cognitive, bodily, or both—cannot be severed from the social circumstances that produce impairment discourse and that code it as a deviation from an ableist norm. On the other hand, there is the image, or the representation, of disability. This refers at once to two distinguishable things. There is the diffuse and intangible general mental image of disability held by an individual, a community, or a society. This mental image may involve social expectations, stereotypes, or ableist reductions coded in either positive or negative terms (the "supercrip" and the "sadcrip," respectively). There is also the concrete image of disability, that image expressed through mimetic representation such as photography, film, advertising, and other visual media forms. Thinking through the frictions that emerge from these various understandings of disability's materiality and representation is productive for the academic study of disability, just as it is for the political project pushing for the inclusion, integration, autonomy, and human rights of people with disabilities.

One of the greatest challenges for those who are involved in the academic or political projects aligned with disability studies is how to assess and convey the distance that one encounters between the social image of disability and the material reality of disability. This can be particularly difficult in the case of trisomy 21. George Estreich has written that Down syndrome is often "a projection. Call it a huggable ghost: a vague shape, a diagnosis with a personality, a mix of sweetness and tragedy of angels and heart defects and maternal age."

People often see the projection and not the person, the image and not the reality. He writes that in the case of Down syndrome, this projection "hides the individual. The projection, the ghost, obscures" the person.[2] This social image is in principle distinguishable from the cultural image of Down syndrome one might see in a film, but is not in practice completely distinct from it. While films have often played into reductive social projections of people with disabilities,[3] this is unrelated to the narrative possibilities offered up by the medium itself, which are infinite. Disability film is in a unique position to challenge ableist understandings of disability. More than that, as Mitchell and Snyder write, it may provide "an alternative ethical map of living interdependently with each other."[4]

We have seen in the previous chapter how cinema induces different ways of seeing Down syndrome—from positions as diverse as the social documentary tradition in Chile and the genre-mixing fiction film from Brazil. The next chapter will continue to explore the representation of Down syndrome in a selection of films from Argentina and Mexico whose uncommon narratives ostensibly seem crafted to attract mainstream interest. Here, however, we are concerned with a very particular niche of DS Culture and documentary filmmaking, one that might be described as avant-garde. In contrast with Alberdi's *Los niños / The Grown-Ups*, where the Chilean director's social critique is evident in the title itself and throughout the length of the film, Spanish documentarian Mateo Cabeza's *Que nadie duerme* (Let no one sleep) (2017) is a much more subtle, but perhaps even more radical, meditation on the limits of disability representation. A discussion of this film's challenge to both the social and the cultural images of Down syndrome is the central topic of this chapter.

Using a cinematic style that the director has characterized as drawing from the observational documentary tradition,[5] Mateo Cabeza films the months leading up to a theater performance titled *En vano* (In vain). Put on by the organization Danza Mobile, the four-person team of actors performing in *En vano* includes two people with Down syndrome, Jaime García and José Manuel Muñoz, and two people without, Arturo Parrilla and Manuel Cañadas. Of the Danza Mobile theater performance of *En vano* itself, viewers of the documentary *Que nadie duerma* will catch only intermittent and fleeting glimpses. Yet from what little of the theatrical performance we see on-screen, it is nonetheless clear that *En vano* boasts only a minimalist set. Its staging centers around a large but rudimentary, movable, four-paneled frame. This frame is constructed out of tall wood squares that are linked through hinges. Through choreographed movements in, around, and through these paneled frames, the play emphasizes the materiality of bodies as they are placed in relation to each other, as they are pushed through constrained spaces. These movements suggest the trope of intangible social frames of reference for viewing such bodies and the perspectives that may result from their application. The heart of the theater performance *En vano* is thus already quite heady.

The documentary film *Que nadie duerma* builds on this invitation to think deeply about bodies, movements, and minds by emphasizing the play between abstract and embodied notions of presence and absence. As a director, Cabeza opts to conceal more than he reveals. This is true not merely with regards to the viewer's access to the intercalated play, but also in terms of the motivations, emotions, and thoughts of the two central protagonists. It is hardly an example of the "Introduction to My Disability" documentary genre discussed by Mitchell and Snyder.[6] The impact on the viewer of the film's interplay between presence and absence, of the links established between visuality and knowledge, may be intentionally perplexing. Adding further complexity are the ways in which Jaime García and José Manuel Muñoz inhabit doubled roles. They are conventional actors who are preparing to play their roles in a theatrical performance, and they are also simultaneously social actors in a documentary, wherein they are in a sense playing themselves. This is a film that multiplies the image of disability with which viewers engage. The multiplication of this image corresponds with an understanding that disability itself can be addressed at multiple levels of signification. Mateo Cabeza has layered his camera frame on top of a theater performance that is itself about framing, effectively nesting frame over frame. The result is a sort of cinematic *mise en abyme*. Stressing this conceit, the director turns the ontological question of disability into an epistemic question. This is not an "Introduction to Down Syndrome" film that answers the question "What is Down syndrome?" Instead, it is a film that asks what we might know about Down syndrome, and whether we can, in fact, know anything about it. That is, *Que nadie duerma* poses a question about the limits of knowledge, not a question about existence. Cabeza is not explicitly interested in matters of substance or identity, but instead in the ways that these matters are constructed in society. He wants to emphasize the way that social images are organized through and respond to the movements of bodies and minds—thus the way in which vision plays a role in producing knowledge, the way it becomes entangled with the act of thinking itself.

This epistemological questioning has motivated the title of this fourth chapter of *Down Syndrome Culture*. The phrase "Where Is Down?" I have selected for the title comes directly from an English-language T-shirt that the dancer José Manuel Muñoz wears in Cabeza's film. In practice, this T-shirt becomes the perfect encapsulation of the critique to which Cabeza's documentary aspires. It seems to work as a more perplexing version of the T-shirts mentioned in the first chapter of this book (i.e., "Down Right Perfect," "I'm Downright Fabulous," "Love My Homie with the Extra Chromie"). In a quite similar way, *Que nadie duerma* is a more perplexing contribution to documentary film. While the "what question" ("What Is Down?") might suggest merely an ontological frame, the "locative question" ("Where Is Down?") moves beyond ontology, thus beyond the matter of mere existence. The phrase "Where Is Down" itself requires one to adopt an attitude of curiosity, to be willing to consider something new rather than just rest on current knowledge. Just as the question itself is underdetermined, neither is the answer to that question fully clear. Does this question suggest that Down syndrome is in the environment, a social construction? Or does it wink at the notion that trisomy 21 is "located" in the body? Is the point that Down syndrome is elusive in some respect, invisible socially or visible only in certain ways? Is "Where Is Down?" the prompt for a silly spatial joke, one that might end with a firm finger pointed toward one's feet? Or could one answer that Down is not a direction but instead a relation that takes place somewhere, at a location? This way of seeing things brings to mind something that Snyder and Mitchell write in *Cultural Locations of Disability*: "We mean the phrase 'cultural locations of disability' to evoke sites of violence, restriction, confinement, and absence of liberty for people with disabilities."[7] As readers will see, tropes of restriction and confinement are quite relevant to the forms of thinking that viewers of both the theater performance and documentary are encouraged to adopt.

This chapter views the porous borders between Danza Mobile's production *En vano* and Mateo Cabeza's film *Que nadie duerma* as a contribution to (re)thinking the image of Down syndrome in society. Although the filmmaker may adopt the perspective of an observer, the film itself works actively as the theoretical level as a metacommentary on disability images. The theatrical performance and the documentary film—for our purposes here, one is nested inside the other—are critical interventions working to interrupt thought. Specifically, they work to interrupt the machinations of the ableist social imaginary through which people with Down syndrome are restricted, confined, and made absent in society. The theoretical arguments I attribute to Cabeza's film are here first anticipated by working through an article by Sharon Smith and Kieron Smith (2021) in the *Journal of Literary and Cultural*

Disability Studies titled "Down Syndrome as Pure Simulacrum." If the next section of the chapter reads as an article review, this is intentional. Smith and Smith's article contribution is, in my view, pathbreaking and deserves careful consideration and continued dissemination. Its amplification here is meant to underscore the resonance between their thinking and my own. Their argument points wonderfully toward the recognition of a Down Syndrome Culture in which the ableist social image of DS is replaced with the material, lived reality of DS. On the basis of this preparatory review of concepts, the play *En vano* and the film *Que nadie duerma* are subsequently put in context, and the theoretical contribution of the documentary film analyzed.

The DS Image: Down Syndrome as Simulacrum

Sharon Smith and Kieron Smith are the parents of a daughter with Down syndrome. In their scholarly article from the *Journal of Literary and Cultural Disability Studies* they are concerned above all else with the distance between reality and representation as it concerns trisomy 21. Socially speaking, the image of Down syndrome is, they write, dominant over the reality. That social image of DS is imbued with the hallmark signs of the ableist, "deficit model" of disability. They admit that invocations of Down syndrome have become more prevalent in society—"in advertisements, television and the press"—but they contrast this greater visibility with the lack of measurable progress for people with DS regarding social inclusion, education, and the workplace. The social image of trisomy 21 simply does not match the reality. It is, as Estreich also underscored, a "projection." Calling for "a renewed focus on the real, the material experiences of people with Down syndrome," Smith and Smith insist that such a renewed focus "is the only way that the dominant prevalent image of Down syndrome can be overcome."[8]

One can think of Down Syndrome Culture as both an academic and political project to which many different kinds of people make contributions. There are people with trisomy 21 themselves, for example, Andy Trias Trueta (chapter 2), who embodies Antonio Gramsci's notion of the organic intellectual in his position, writing, and invited, international talks. There are parents, such as Josep Espinàs (chapter 2), who reflect on the everyday life they share with an adult child who has Down syndrome, but who do so in a way marked more by a disability perspective than by the limitations of a conventional disability memoir.[9] And there are then disability studies scholars, such as Sharon Smith and Kieron Smith, Jhonatthan Maldonado Ramírez (cited in the introduction), Susanne Hartwig (cited in this chapter)—and, of course, also Michael Bérubé—who write at once both as parents of a child with Down syndrome and as scholars. Of course, there are differences between these varied perspectives, but this kind of diversity can be productive when considering that disability communities can be strengthened by allies who have witnessed the effects of ableism on a loved one. Still, there are no guarantees. As Smith and Smith also point out, parents of children with Down syndrome can also reinforce harmful ideas and misunderstandings of DS.[10]

The scholars open their article by describing a routine eye exam for their daughter, which somehow led to the following comment by an orthoptist: "Did you know before she was born that she would have Down syndrome? I always thought that if I found out I was having a baby with Down syndrome I would terminate the pregnancy." Smith and Smith hear this "casual throwaway comment" voiced "in front of our child" in its larger social context for the violent threat to people with Down syndrome that it is. They cite this as proof that the image of DS triumphs over the reality, an image that serves as the violent flip side to what Estreich described as the image of DS as "huggable ghost." They write, "It appears that as soon as someone sees 'Down syndrome,' it becomes possible to think and talk about other human beings in a way that would not be seen as permissible in any other circumstances."[11] In this context, the social image of disability is ableist in formation and significance. This image is "powerful and all-encompassing" and has become what the authors call "a pure idea." Offered up as "an almost incontestable truth," its errors are entrenched and highly resistant to change.[12]

To theorize the intransigence that characterizes the ableist adherence to this DS image, Smith and Smith turn to Jean Baudrillard's notion of the simulacrum. They cite from Baudrillard's model the four stages he suggests are involved in "the replacement of the real with an image": at first, the image "is the reflection of a basic reality"; then "it masks and perverts a basic reality"; next "it masks the absence of a basic reality"; and, finally, "it bears no relation to any reality whatsoever: it is its own pure simulacrum."[13] This latter phrasing is emphasized in various ways explicitly and implicitly through the article, manifest also in the metaphor of a hall of mirrors.[14] As it is inside a hall of mirrors, the social image of DS becomes a surface only, one that is multiplied so many times that an observer is unable to locate the real person from which the image originally emanated.

Employing Baudrillard is quite important for Smith and Smith's argument. First, the mere association with his theory links their disability studies method to critiques of contemporary capitalism, not just Baudrillard's but also—in my reading, at least—related accounts such as Guy Debord's *Society of the Spectacle* and Henri Lefebvre's three-volume *Critique of Everyday Life*, including also the way in which such twentieth-century thinking has impacted twenty-first-century critiques of neoliberalism.[15] This move reaffirms the validity of approaching people with Down syndrome as a defined disability community within neoliberal modernity, as discussed in the introduction. Just as important, however, are the consequences of this theoretical alignment, which shifts the focus of any discussion of the image of Down syndrome back on the specific viewer and implicates the social construction of disability in general. In this arrangement, the lived reality of Down syndrome loses none of its material force, while at the same time, the constructed nature of disability is emphasized. This may be a delicate balance, but it is crucial to distinguish between these two notions if we are to understand Smith and Smith's achievement.

Readers may think back to the interrogation scene of Marcelo Galvão's *Colegas* (chapter 3), which may invite two different sorts of reactions among viewers. In that scene, the presence of some twenty different actors with Down syndrome displays such a diversity of physical facial features and personalities, such a spectrum of speaking registers and styles, that it is possible some viewers may not piece together that they are all people with trisomy 21. On the other hand, those viewers familiar with the physical and functional diversity brought together in any given Down syndrome community will have no trouble at all recognizing their common bond. To be part of a community is to be at once the same and also different. What distinguishes the contemporary ableist DS image is not merely that it stakes claim to a variable set of recognizable, physical traits associated with trisomy 21, a discourse of resemblance that gains currency through the racist typology of John Langdon Down, but moreover that it also applies a deficit model of thinking to produce the idea of "something *less than* a complete person."[16] The DS image erases differences and lived materiality and offers in its place the false idea of a "homogenous group" who are "all the same."[17]

In exploring the reductive nature of this DS image, Smith and Smith thus offer five specific points to consider. "The principal tropes which constitute the image of Down syndrome include"

> 1) that the difference is a deficit; 2) that having Down syndrome somehow means that you lose your own personal identity and are part of a homogenous other; 3) people with Down syndrome "suffer" from the

condition in some way; 4) that they are always happy; and 5) that it represents a form of "eternal childhood" an existence in a permanent state of dependency.[18]

Having also analyzed Maite Alberdi's documentary film at length in the previous chapter, I note that these points are addressed and dispensed with by that director. Point number 5 is ostentatiously embedded in the title *Los niños / The Grown-Ups* itself, 4 is contradicted by Ricardo's salary woes and by Rita's frustrations with the culinary program, 3 by the representation of the mutual joy and amorous feelings shared between Anita and Andrés, 2 by the way that the ensemble approach showcases the different drives, goals, and life circumstances of the various protagonists, and 1 by Ricardo's eldercare position, for example. If Alberdi's film is successful, is it because the director confronts each of these tropes head-on; she achieves that "renewed focus on the real, the material experiences of people with Down syndrome" touted as indispensable by Smith and Smith. Reaching this focus on the real in film presumes both a perspective and an effort for modern disability filmmakers who as a matter of course must push against the grain of normative social thinking, thus against the ableist DS image.

In the realm of aesthetics, Alberdi and Galvão, in film (chapter 3) and Trias Trueta and Espinás, in prose (chapter 2), are all correcting for the errors associated with the social impact of violent ideologies and practices that have hidden people with Down syndrome from public view and categorized them as "something *less than* a complete person."[19] The particular history of Down syndrome is not unrelated to those factors shaping the long history of disability in general, as explored by Henri-Jacques Stiker in *The History of Disability* (1999). The last chapter of Stiker's book, which covers the twentieth century, makes clear that the modern social project of rehabilitation sought assimilation via "the negation of disability through adjustment, integration."[20] Depending on one's perspective, this notion of "the image of the disabled as beings to be rehabilitated,"[21] might be considered an early stage of Baudrillard's four-part progression. The very "negation of disability" (Stiker) is itself implied in the intention to "mask" (Baudrillard) a reality, to substitute for a given reality an abstracted social norm. Stiker captures well the impossibility of this situation when he writes of this negation that "it entails fusing abnormality with the normality that is established and recognized by social consensus. We are obliged to note that this constitutes a new confinement. Specificity and aberrancy are therefore forbidden and condemned. The different must be folded into the commonplace, into the accepted, into the recognized. This is aimed at resolving two problems: fear and sequestration."[22] For disability to become integrated into a normative, ableist social imaginary—so the argument goes, so the social history goes—it must disappear. This is nothing other than the accommodation of difference through annulment.[23] Negation and annulment entail no small amount of both conceptual and historical violence.

It is no surprise, then, that fear and sequestration remain the two ways through which ableist society continues to engage with disability. Fear leads to eugenics, and thus to the quotidian violence of prenatal testing, on one hand, and to episodes of mass murder, on the other.[24] Sequestration also does major social harm. It arrives ready-made to our so-called modernity, clothed in what Harlan Lane called the "mask of benevolence"[25] and smuggled in along with the religious discourses of charity and pity whose genealogy and consequences Stiker also traces throughout his book. Of course, it is possible to note certain changes that have taken place in society over the years. For instance, Smith and Smith write that "people with Down syndrome are no longer hidden away in institutions," yet also insist that "their inclusion in culture and society remains limited."[26] But even this comment suggesting that progress be regarded as self-evident is worth interrogating further. After all, it was not very long ago that sequestration was the norm. Consider the implications of the decade-spanning confinement of Judith Scott, for example, who was mentioned in the introduction: Scott died only in 2005 and spent the majority of her life hidden away in an institution before her sister went to look for her.[27] The issue of the visibility of Down syndrome is much more complex than the history of institutional sequestration. Correcting for the errors of that institutional history potentially still leaves many other isolating and alienating social practices unexamined. Even with deinstitutionalization, a large portion of adults with IDD still live in congregate housing and are thus sequestered anyway.

In particular, the proliferation of the free-floating DS image analyzed by Smith and Smith remains tied to modern forms of alienation. Alienation is central to Baudrillard's four-stage model of the simulacrum. The idea is that there exists some image of Down syndrome that is "the reflection of a basic reality," in theory and in principle. This image is closer to the reality of DS, but is then progressively substituted for another image that is further away from reality. The social mechanism through which this substitution is carried out involves the concept of alienation, now adapted by Baudrillard, Debord, Lefebvre, and others, to forms of thinking that Marx did not originally imagine in the nineteenth century. As a matter of course, Marx wrote, we are triply alienated: from the product of our work, from each other, and from ourselves.[28] Since the century of Marx and Down, trisomy 21 has become socially visible in the form of a circulating social image. This DS image hides not a single, uniform Down syndrome reality, but a number of such realities—there are as many ways to be a person with DS are as there are people with trisomy 21. The distance between the image and the reality of Down syndrome thrives on the fact that ableist modernity has continued to isolate people with Down syndrome even beyond institutional sequestration. "The image of Down syndrome is more commonly encountered in society and culture than interaction with real people who have the condition," write Smith and Smith.[29] It is, in part, because people without Down syndrome do not know people with Down syndrome—they do not come into contact with people with trisomy 21, go through schooling with them, work with them, purchase consumer goods from them, see them in popular media, see them on the ballot, and so on—that the DS image has floated free of its moorings. "The effective exclusion of those with Down syndrome from work and from education, for example, allows the victory of the image; it allows it to live on unencumbered by reality."[30] Allowed to drift far and wide—this is what I understand by Smith and Smith's assertion—the ableist DS image has in time become so divorced from its referent that it bears absolutely no relation to it.

In light of these discussions, Mateo Cabeza's documentary should be viewed in two ways at once. It asserts the material, lived reality of Down syndrome while simultaneously calling into question the social image of DS. In its centering of Jaime García and José Manuel Muñoz, the film carries out the "renewed focus on the real, the material experiences of people with Down syndrome" called for in the article by Smith and Smith.[31] Yet at the same time, the formal aesthetics of the documentary suggest a challenge to the DS image. As director, Cabeza plays with the Baudrillardian idea that has captured Smith and Smith's attention: by multiplying the image of Down syndrome in the film, but keeping his camera in the margins, and frustrating the viewer's desire to know and to learn more about the context of what they are seeing. In this there is a provocation. It is through this aesthetics of withholding, thus by emphasizing the surface and the appearance of events through simple observation and without commentary, that Cabeza's film refuses to play into ready-made ideas about people with Down syndrome. Before exploring this documentary in more detail, I first provide some context regarding the theater company Danza Mobile and the specific work titled *En vano*, since Cabeza's directorial decisions at once seem to follow logically from the social commitments of each.

Performing the Down Syndrome Reality: Danza Mobile and *En vano* (2016)

Those viewers of the fiction film *Yo, también* (2010), which featured a protagonist with Down syndrome, in addition to other secondary actors with DS,[32] will have already heard the words "Danza Mobile," but the organization itself is no work of fiction. Begun in 1995, Danza Mobile of Seville, Spain, has evolved over the years to encompass an *escuela de danza* (school of dance), a *centro de creación* (art center), and a *compañía de danza* (dance company), as well as festivals and collaborations of many types—"una larga etcétera" (a long et cetera) as the organization's website puts it.[33] Its mission has been to bring the worlds of dance and disability together though creative process: "Danza Mobile es una entidad que trabaja para el desarrollo integral de las personas con discapacidad a través de las distintas vertientes del arte" (Danza Mobile is an entity dedicated to the comprehensive development of people with disabilities through the varieties of artistic expression). Among other awards, it has been recognized by the Ayuntamiento de Sevilla (Municipal Government of Seville), the Unión de Actores e Intérpretes de Andalucía (Union of Actors and Performers of Andalucia), and the Comunidad de Madrid (Autonomous Community of Madrid). In 2017, the performance *En vano* was specifically nominated for five Lorca Awards—two of these nominations were for Jaime García and José Manuel Muñoz—and it went on to win three of these five awards from the Asociación de las Artes Escénicas de Andalucía (Association of the Scenic Arts of Andalucia), celebrated with support from the Fundación SGAE. It is unfortunate, and thus also of note, that the only two nominations it did not win were for the two performers with Down syndrome. In a sense, the fact that (only) García and Muñoz did not win for their performances reaffirms the need for what Danza Mobile is trying to achieve by pairing artistic creation and disability.

The brief publication "¿Qué es Danza Mobile?" (What is Danza Mobile?) (2020), penned by Esmeralda Valderrama Vega, who is a dancer, choreographer, and founder of Danza Mobile, delves into the activities of the organization as well as its core philosophy. The scope of its work involves "Diversidad. Arte. Participación Social, inserción laboral" (Diversity. Art. Social participation, labor inclusion), and its central premise is that "el arte dignifica a la persona" (art dignifies the person) and brings out the best in each of us.[34] As Valderrama Vega also writes, artistic development is tied to personal development: "Pensamos que el desarrollo de la creatividad es una base fundamental para crecer como personas. El ser humano tiene necesidad de dejar su impronta en todo lo que hace. Nosotros favorecemos que cada persona encuentre su identidad y pensamos que el arte es el mejor vehículo para ello" (We believe that the development of creativity is a fundamental basis for growing as people. Human beings need to leave their imprint on everything they do. We favor the idea that all people must find their identity, and we believe that art is the best vehicle for accomplishing this). In the realm of dance, this vision and mission can be understood as a direct and also creative response to the larger social situation described by Smith and Smith, that is, "the effective exclusion of those with Down syndrome from work and from education, for example."[35] Esmeralda Valderrama Vega can also be seen in certain scenes of *Que nadie duerma*, and her name can be heard spoken aloud. Before each performance of the Danza Mobile dance titled *En vano*—for example, in Germany, and in Spain[36]—she takes part in a preshow group hug and dissipation of nervous energy with the cast. These appearances document her ongoing and close connection to the day-to-day affairs of the organization.

Because *En vano* is screened somewhat indirectly through Mateo Cabeza's documentary, we may benefit from consulting two scholarly book chapters that can help us understand the nature of the inclusive theater the film takes as its subject. Julio Enrique Checa Puerta's "*En vano*: Explorar los límites de la danza inclusiva" (*En vano*: Exploring the limits of inclusive dance) (2021) investigates *En vano* itself and provides a rich context for subsequent analysis of how the production is depicted in Cabeza's film. Susanne Hartwig's "*Undoing disability* en el teatro inclusivo" (Undoing disability in inclusive theater) (2021), while it does not mention *En vano* explicitly, nonetheless identifies an artistic method that one might argue lies at the heart of the best inclusive theater. Both of these contributions make comments that will help viewers to understand Danza Mobile's commitment to inclusion as it appears indirectly through the scenes of *Que nadie duerma*.

Inclusivity in dance can be considered in two ways, as Julio Enrique Checa Puerta explains. While more conventional dance companies might invite artists with disabilities to take a small part in a performance, a truly inclusive company like Danza Mobile puts together a cast balanced between artists with and artists without functional diversity.[37] This ensures

> que aquellos artistas menos atléticos, rápidos o ágiles no se queden en la periferia de la acción performativa, y que formen parte de un auténtico proceso creativo que no eluda ni atenúa la diferenciación, sino que acepta los problemas reales de cualquier forma de integración, al tiempo que amplia notablemente la visión acerca de la normalidad.[38]

that those artists who are less athletic, quick, or agile do not remain on the periphery of the performative action, and that they form part of an authentic creative process that neither avoids nor attenuates this differentiation, but rather accepts the real problems of any manner of integration, while notably expanding understandings of what is normal.

In this conceit there is a valuable commitment to recognizing the material reality of difference, whether we understand this in terms of the need for early social access to dance for populations with DS, of the experience of cognitive/physical impairment that can be a consequence of having trisomy 21, or some combination of the two.

Checa Puerta comments on the conception of *En vano*, its implementation in various urban spaces, and aspects of the performance that may not necessarily be clear for viewers of Cabeza's film. His discussion emphasizes how the large wooden frame at the center of the piece was used as a prompt for playful improvisation during the creation of *En vano*, but he also stresses the play's reflexive character, noting that its performers work through the very concept of representation, or what he calls "los límites de la ficción" (the borders of fiction).[39] *En vano* was performed in a range of locations in Seville, Spain, such as a public square, the stage of a theater, and the patio of a penitentiary.[40] This decision itself has implications for the visibility of disability in public spaces. Of such performances, Checa Puerta writes that there is an interactive quality that is dependent on the energy of those in attendance; the four performers are paying attention to, and plausibly also responding to, the crowd's reactions.[41] At the end of the piece, we learn, the actors mix in with the crowd, before coming back to the performance space for final applause. With the exception of the end of *Que nadie duerma*, which shows how a performance of the play in a park begins—that is, with the four actors walking up to the performance area as if strangers happening upon the assembled crowd—these interactive aspects of the performances in *En vano* are somewhat harder to discern in the documentary.[42] Yet while viewers of the film may not have access to these performative aspects of the work, *Que nadie duerma* nonetheless stays true to another, equally important aspect of the performance. This is the way in which it calls attention to the manner of its construction as a performance, as a representation.

The composition of the cast for *En vano*—two actors with DS (Jaime García and José Manuel Muñoz), as well as two people without (Arturo Parrilla and Manuel Cañadas), might be thought of as a particular kind of disability ensemble.⁴³ This sort of equal pairing crafts a new social image for viewers, one that models a correction to the alienations by which people with Down syndrome are kept at a distance in society, excluded from work and education contexts, for example. The performer Arturo Parrilla, who is also the director of *En vano*, uses an interesting metaphor in suggesting how the work should be understood. Comparing the resulting theater piece to a sculpture—that is, to a work that hides the process of its own construction, showing only the result of repeated actions to shape it—"Arturo Parrilla insiste en que lo más interesante se encuentra en los huecos de la pieza . . . 'la sugerencia reside precisamente en lo que no vemos de la escultura'" (Arturo Parrilla insists that the most interesting thing is to be found in the gaps of the piece . . . 'the provocation resides precisely in what we do not see of the sculpture').⁴⁴ What we do not see in the case of *En vano*, then, interestingly enough, is precisely what we do in fact see in *Que nadie duerma*, and what will shortly receive attention in the final section of this chapter, namely: how an ensemble works together behind the scenes, before it reaches the stage, how the work looks from multiple vantage points and at different points in time, how it evolves through preparation as it acquires shape, and—as Valderrama Vega's publication also stressed—how personal development and artistic development are entwined in collaborative practice.⁴⁵

Because his focus is on the play itself, Checa Puerta offers only a few passing observations regarding Cabeza's documentary at the end of his chapter. Of these, however, his comments on the "Where Is Down?" T-shirt mentioned at the top of this chapter are among the most illuminating. He informs us that the shirt refers to another production sponsored by Danza Mobile (2016), one that coincides relatively closely with the production of *En vano*, "pero seguramente constituye un dato desconocido para el espectador del documental" (but certainly this will be something not known to the viewer of the documentary).⁴⁶ Given our previous discussion of the T-shirt's semiotic potential, Checa Puerta's comments are intriguing. He notes that the spectator's lack of a context that would render the T-shirt's message intelligible allows it to become "un signo de significado ambiguo, que introduce un nuevo elemento sujeto a la interpretación de los espectadores, cuestión que en ningún momento se hace explícita desde los elementos de la representación escénica" (a sign of ambiguous meaning, which introduces a new element subject to the interpretation of the spectators, a matter that in no moment is made explicit by the scenic representation).⁴⁷ The fact that the question "Where is Down?" might be left as a sign of ambiguous meaning in the film is, in my view, a matter that plays into the documentary director's own focus on questioning knowledge, on an aesthetics of withholding that foregrounds the interplay between presence and absence. As the group of *En vano* performers does a warm-up exercise toward the end of the film, holding hands with each other, and with Esmeralda, and swinging their arms rhythmically, someone even shouts, "Where is Down?"[48] As a consequence, the question posed by the T-shirt hovers over the documentary as a whole.

Susanne Hartwig's approach to inclusive theater in general can help us to understand how Mateo Cabeza's own vision as a filmmaker avoids normative depictions of disability. His documentary relies on a sophisticated understanding of disability (in)visibility, one that in the end has much in common with that of both Arturo Parrilla, in *En vano*, and even Danza Mobile, as an organization. Hartwig's central innovative concept is that of "undoing disability," as expressed in her chapter's title.[49] Through this phrase, she means to evoke the subtle dance by which inclusive theater both "shows and does not show disability." Such theater "escapes from the social practice of constructing a discriminatory concept of disability" by simultaneously making possible "two interpretations of a performance."[50] These two interpretations correspond to what the scholar refers to as two different levels of seeing, and what she also describes as two types of images. The opportunity is for those who view such an inclusive theater performance to begin to reconcile one level with the other, one image with the other.

What are these two interpretations, these two images? Hartwig differentiates the "persona (real)" ([real] person) from the "personaje (ficcional)" ([fictional] character), a dichotomy that one could also explain, as she herself does, as relating to mimetic and mental representations.[51] For our purposes, one might say that seeing the real person with a disability is to engage with the embodied level of disability and its meaning in the social imaginary, and that seeing the fictional character with a disability is to engage with the artistic or cultural representation of that performative role. Hartwig notes that inclusive theater has only relatively recently found the potential of playing with such a superimposition of terms. To see disability as pertaining at once to multiple "levels" of a performance—as simultaneously both a social picture and an artistic image—reveals the gaps in normative understanding. "La discapacidad que el espectador ve representada en la escena y sus conceptos de ella empiezan a discrepar" (The disability that spectators see represented in the scene and their concepts of it begin to diverge), which can then create "efectos estéticos sorprendentes y desconcertantes" (surprising and disconcerting aesthetic effects).[52]

Hartwig's bipartite model of "undoing disability" can be used to shed light on the provocations of both *En vano* and its representation in *Que nadie duerma*. Since we have spoken in this chapter of simulacra, and are now integrating a sophisticated approach to aesthetic theory, it is useful also to employ everyday language. Among Hartwig's most powerful statements in this regard are those contained in her chapter's notes. In one note, she clothes a superb theoretical intervention in plain language: "En el escenario, la discapacidad constituye una irrupción muy fuerte de la realidad, más fuerte que las demás características de los actores" (Disability constitutes a quite forceful irruption of reality onto the stage; it is a much stronger characteristic than others possessed by the actors).[53] The implication is that, in the realm of theater—which is a temporal art form, as opposed to the photograph—the visual appearance of disability can interrupt and, potentially at the very least, change normative thinking. In another note, she elaborates on what she means regarding the aforementioned surprising and disconcerting aesthetic effects, pointing out that, "por ejemplo, puede ser sumamente difícil—por contradecir a los estereotipos sociales—ver a una persona con discapacidad cognitiva e imaginarla como un artista con alto potencial" (for example, it can be extremely difficult—because it contradicts social stereotypes—to see people with a cognitive disability and imagine them as artists with high potential).[54] Forcing an encounter with this sort of difficulty is something to which Arturo Parrilla's stage direction and Mateo Cabeza's film direction both aspire, as will be discussed below. While the aesthetics of both performance and documentary are complex, their point is straightforward, if not always presented simply.

Interrupting the Down Syndrome Image: Mateo Cabeza's *Que nadie duerma* (2017)

Almost as an echo of Danza Mobile's overall vision, director Mateo Cabeza foregrounds disability but refrains from excessive commentary and even contextualization regarding what appears on the screen. He is not interested in defining, explaining, or interpreting what we see, just as he is uninterested in stereotypical or discriminatory representations of Down syndrome. His film is ostensibly an observational documentary. There is no voice-over that would promise to explain to viewers what they are seeing. Those subjects observed are captured in seemingly routine moments. They are not asked questions, nor do they speak toward the camera, as if speaking directly to an audience. Contrasting with the expository variant of documentary film, which is the idea of documentary most people may associate with educational contexts,

Figure 4.1: Jaime García and José Manuel Muñoz eat breakfast together; Jaime tries to get José Manuel to see things in a positive light. Used with generous permission of Mateo Cabeza, from the documentary *Que nadie duerma* (2017).

Figure 4.2: The four performers in the Danza Mobile production *En vano* begin the representation for an audience outdoors. Left to right: Manuel Cañadas, José Manuel Muñoz, Jaime García and Arturo Parrilla. Used with generous permission of Mateo Cabeza, from the documentary *Que nadie duerma* (2017).

Figure 4.3: Wearing his "Where Is Down?" t-shirt, and filmed indirectly through the mirrors of the practice space, José Manuel Muñoz weaves through and stands upright in the wooden frame at the center of the *En vano* performance. Used with generous permission of Mateo Cabeza, from the documentary *Que nadie duerma* (2017).

the emergence of "an observational mode of representation allowed the filmmaker to record unobtrusively what people did when they were not explicitly addressing the camera."[55] The documentary director stays true to this idea and remains unobtrusive.

Cabeza stays behind the camera and concentrates on everyday moments and conversations shared among the four-performer ensemble cast of *En vano*, as they prepare, practice, rest, relax, and perform together. But then, he also pieces *Que nadie duerma* together in a way that brings Jaime García and José Manuel Muñoz to the foreground. We do indeed see and hear from Arturo Parrilla and Manuel Cañadas, but, in a way, they have become the sidekicks. Many of the film's sequences capturing moments of extended downtime prioritize the two protagonists with Down syndrome, either alone or sharing the frame.

In one such moment early in the film, they eat breakfast together.[56] Jaime is on our left, José Manuel on our right. The two are spaced out from one another, pushed toward the edges of the frame (see Figure 4.1). A previous scene has shown José Manuel angry about something, but what exactly this is remains unclear.[57] Here he eats while occasionally shaking his head from side to side in apparent disagreement. The editing decision to follow one scene with the next suggests a certain emotional continuity. Yet it remains unclear whether José Manuel is still angry about what has happened, or whether he is in disbelief at the situation he is in. Perhaps he is even angry about the tack Jaime takes in his breakfast conversation, which is intent on getting José Manuel to focus on the positive. Jaime: "Pero la cosa es José Manuel que tienes muchos amigos que te quieren y una amiga que te quiere" (José Manuel, you have lot of friends who love you and a girlfriend who loves you). José Manuel shakes his head as if to say, "No." Jaime again, later: "Mira, José Manuel. Tus amigos, te quieren" (Look, José Manuel, your friends, they love you). José Manuel: "Sí" (Yes). Jaime: "Tu amiga que te quiere" (Your girlfriend loves you), "Y no pasa nada" (And everything is okay!). José Manuel, questioning whether Jaime is seeing the situation in the right way: "¿No pasa nada?" (Everything is okay?). Jaime, insisting now: "Venga José, queremos llevar bien" (Come on, José, we'll get along). Viewers observe a relatable, if tense, everyday moment shared among friends who are also artistic collaborators.

This breakfast scene illustrates Cabeza's observational documentary aesthetic. The simplicity of the moment, which is filmed in a single take without cuts, is matched by the director's signature, stable camera. The pacing of the conversation is natural. Jaime is trepidatious and approaches the conversation with both caution and tenderness. Yet, together with the one that precedes it, this scene also epitomizes the director's commitment to disability representation. As it was in Hartwig's description of how disability functions in inclusive theater, here, too, the presence of two actors with Down syndrome "constituye una irrupción muy fuerte de la realidad" (constitutes a quite forceful irruption of reality).[58] It is important—for both the film's subdued critique of ableist representations, and for the social stereotypes of potential spectators—that Jaime and José Manuel are having an interaction unaccompanied, unmediated, by their collaborators without Down syndrome. Their positions toward the edges the frame, as well as the dialogue of the scene—in which Jaime offers support to José Manuel, who in the end is not fully convinced—counteracts the idea of the DS image critiqued by Smith and Smith, wherein people with Down syndrome are seen as a "homogenous group" who are "all the same."[59] Cabeza's disability commitment can be seen in the everyday way that he centers the two protagonists with Down syndrome, whose on-screen presence and different subject positions may interrupt ableist understandings. But it can also be seen in the way his film leaves gaps in the viewer's understanding unexplained. Because the source of José Manuel's frustration remains unknown, the breakfast scene also works as a way of nurturing the viewer's curiosity about his state of mind.

It is perhaps a low bar, but this curiosity may itself function as an affront to the way in which the social image of cognitive difference has been shaped by normative understandings.[60]

Here a brief digression can provide a point of comparison to what Cabeza's film accomplishes. The US-based director Reid Davenport's recent documentary film *I Didn't See You There* (2022) provides a point of comparison that also fuses documentary genres and advances cinematic metaphor in service of commenting on disability themes.[61] Davenport is a person with cerebral palsy who, in many memorable sequences of his own documentary, films his everyday movements by mounting the camera on his wheelchair. Viewers catch numerous glimpses of the urban neighborhood surrounding his apartment in Oakland, California, but also of his travels to family in Bethel, Connecticut, including a pointed visit to the town's statue of P. T. Barnum—a charged figure in disability studies for his popularization of the so-called freak show.[62] From the beginning, we hear Davenport's voice-over narration, a characteristic of expository documentary. But the content of this narration tends more toward a reflexive critique than exposition.

Overall, Davenport is concerned more with the social image of disability than with his own story. His film's title plainly calls to mind the way in which drivers and pedestrians frequently stand in his way as he navigates Oakland's sidewalks and crossings. These all-too-frequent occurrences punctuate the film's narrative and interrupt its pulsating urban rhythms. But the title also works on another level. Apart from brief moments—his hand in close-up pouring a whiskey, his image captured from afar by giving the camera to his niece, his reflection in a series of business windows as he zooms by on an Oakland sidewalk—viewers themselves do not see Davenport in the film. He controls the point of view and is implicit in the film's wheelchair-mounted angle, but as a documentary subject he is mostly absent. He is present in voice and embodied experience, but his image is seldom seen. Instead of revealing himself, his camera seeks out those poetic qualities of urban life. Davenport often turns it directly upward, searching for patterns of light, textures of clouds, the visual musicality and the speed of the city sights. His voice-over drifts from frustrating everyday experiences to contemplate his own directorial practice and his photographic aesthetics and preferences. He also offers up a historical and representational lesson in the form of a critical interrogation of the legacy of the "freak show." In Oakland, a colorful circus tent has been set up in an area outside of his apartment, and Davenport returns to it again and again, screening it both directly and indirectly. Indirectly, its colorful reflection hovers imposingly over the dark shadow of his own as he turns the camera to film the windows he passes on the sidewalk. This sequence—its repetition and the film's several variations on it—is perhaps the most striking and enduring visual and mental image of the film. But what readers should most take away from this short introduction of Davenport's film is how documentaries can blend genres. *I Didn't See You There* is not merely an expository and an observational disability documentary, but also a performative or a poetic, and even a reflexive one. The way the film engages disability representation through an indirect aesthetics is something generally shared by *Que nadie duerma*.

In the case of *Que nadie duerma*, there are also ties to multiple documentary genres, not merely observational, which is clearly primary, but also some performative and interactive elements. For instance, Cabeza screens a Danza Mobile performance in a public space, alternating between the dancers and also the audience. For a moment the film seems akin to a concert video (the performative documentary mode). In another moment of the film, Jaime voices thanks to Cabeza directly ("Ah gracias, Mateo" [Oh thank you, Mateo]), for helping him find his shoes.[63] While the director does not fully break into the film from his fly-on-the-wall observational post, this subtle moment nevertheless creates doubt in the viewer's mind about whether other interactions might have been edited out (the interactive documentary mode). Most of all, however, and as Davenport will in his own film, Cabeza moves beyond the limits of mere observation to engage the reflexive documentary tradition.

Bill Nichols describes the reflexive mode of documentary as one that concerns itself with the nature of representation; thus, what matters is not what we are talking about, but rather how we are talking.[64] "Reflexive texts are self-conscious not only about form and style, as poetic ones are, but also about strategy, structure, conventions, expectations, and effects."[65] A reflexive approach can disrupt expectations about how disability should be viewed.[66] Rather than making an ethical point directly, reflexive documentaries use organization, structure, juxtaposition, and presented situations to make this point indirectly.[67] Often these films emphasize "the encounter between filmmaker and viewer rather than between filmmaker and subject."[68] Reid Davenport's film becomes reflexive when he subverts the expectation of the audience that they will be introduced to his disability, and when he shifts the center of the film away from his person toward the social image of disability itself. In this respect, what is most interesting about *I Didn't See You There* is the absence indicated in the film's title and the way in which Davenport screens himself only at a remove. By absenting himself in certain ways, he forces viewers to rework the way in which they imagine disability. Cabeza accomplishes something similar, even though he does not remove the bodies of García and Muñoz from the film. He cannot do so. Their material embodied experience is fundamental to the mission of Danza Mobile, to the inclusive choreography of *En vano*, and also to what the director wants to convey regarding the material experience and social image of disability in *Que nadie duerma*. Yet the reflexive elements of the documentary frustrate the viewer's expectation to receive ready-made stereotypes of Down syndrome in a number of ways, nonetheless.

Though viewers see bodies with trisomy 21 in Cabeza's documentary, the film is quite self-consciously concerned with what we see them do and what we do not see them do. In prioritizing this reflexive conceit, *Que nadie duerma* is in a way merely following the lead of the intercalated Danza Mobile performance, which might also be described as reflexive theater. The director blends tropes of presence and absence throughout the film. We might start with the ending of the documentary, which concludes abruptly with a hint of the beginning of a performance of *En vano*. *Que nadie duerma* ends just as a performance of the play seems about to start, with a long buildup, as the four cast members each approach the outdoor stage from a different direction. Music from stringed instruments swells as the camera shoots the cast's slow arrival from the perspective of the crowd; the figures, arms, or heads of some seven audience members are visible in the foreground of the static camera image. The four-person ensemble cast lines up, reaching down to pick up the large wooden frame at the center of *En vano*. As they push it almost vertically into place (see Figure 4.2), the editing cuts to black for the credits. A clear or full presentation of the theater performance proves elusive. The final image of the film points to what we have not seen, what we will not see.[69]

That Cabeza withholds a view of the performance at the end of the documentary is part of a more systemic aesthetics of withholding visual access. His observational style is of a particular kind. The camera is frequently set in locations where his subjects will pass into and out of the frame. Rather than track a verbal or bodily interaction visually, the camera is usually immobile. For example, as Arturo and Jaime wait in the dressing room, a conversation with the theater staff takes places off-screen. Even Jaime soon leaves the frame and we become listeners, rather than spectators. The camera never budges an inch. Even the decision to linger on a semiclosed bathroom door while someone takes a shower takes on the quality of a symbolic withholding. The editing, too, is complicit with this aesthetics. For instance, at one moment, we see José Manuel watching something off-screen to the left, but we know not what. Such decisions compound each other over the course of the film.[70] At the beginning of *Que nadie duerma* we are introduced to a workroom with large windows and a table where one or more subjects tend to gather, talk, and have fun. Toward the end of the film Cabeza shows it first being used, infused with a lively workroom atmosphere, but then empty, backlit and in shadows, as he directs the listener's attention to ambient noise and distant reverberations.[71] This interplay between presence and absence is also applied directly to the way that Cabeza films many of the documentary's performances. For instance, Jaime has a solo dance routine he performs without Arturo. We first see him practicing onstage alone, with the auditorium empty, his graceful dance choreographed to a piece of music with melodic whistling. Soon after, that same whistled melody plays as Jaime performs in front of a live audience in the auditorium—or so viewers will gather, as we do not see Jaime or the audience at all.[72] The camera shoots straight across the back of the stage from one side to the other, with only the music, the colored stage lighting, and a glimpse of Arturo's seated figure staring off-screen to cue us in as to what is happening.

By indulging in the indirect mode of representation made possible by mirrored reflection, Cabeza frequently sparks a certain curiosity in the viewer at an immediate and visual level. Many scenes are filmed in the interior practice space, as the cast members of *En vano* create and practice their dance movements together. As it is with many dance spaces, this one is lined with mirrors to facilitate choreography and keep dancers aware of their own movements, the movements of others, and the physical proximity of each dancer to the next. Here Cabeza insists on filming physical reflections as a way of getting the spectator to think about social images. Many times, he films the mirror reflection, and not the corporeal dancer. Because of where he tends to place the camera, a decision that maximizes the mirrored wall and not the floorspace, a certain confusion emerges. Some viewers may only be able to tell the difference between a body and its reflection once they have visually located the division between one paneled mirror and the next. Some viewers may find themselves visually scanning the frame to locate the real person. In this preference for indirect images, Cabeza's film resonates with the idea expressed by Hartwig, that there are "two interpretations of a performance"[73] that includes disability. Here Cabeza routinely uses mirrored reflection to bifurcate the direct material image and the indirect reflected image of the performer. This practice of filming bodies indirectly, that is, mediated by the mirrored walls, suggests something about how and what we can know about disability. That is, the material reality of Down syndrome proves elusive, unknowable, or multiple. At the very least, it exists at a remove.

This multiplication of images accomplished through mirrored reflection is also paralleled in the film's interest in other forms of mediation that place one image inside another. This begins early in the film, as we watch José Manuel watch his own performance on a laptop, for example. This pattern continues throughout the documentary. Later, for instance, when a large party is held, we witness people with and without disabilities playing music, dancing, and enjoying themselves. In front of Cabeza's camera lens we then also see the image of the party multiplied by a cell phone screen someone is using to film the same event. Screens within screens are a trope that the director uses to suggest a metacommentary on the nature of representation itself. The most interesting of these scenes are when we see the cast members with Down syndrome reviewing their practice sessions or performances on video, but we do not see the video they are watching. One of these lasts over two full minutes, as the dancers with disabilities watch and listen to a video we can only hear.[74] Part of what can be heard is an interview with Jaime. Prompted by a discussion of social labels ("etiquetas")—that is, how having the label of Down syndrome would affect someone—Jaime (in the video) then tells the story of his decision to become a part of Danza Mobile, how attached he feels to the place and the people there, to "mi familia" (my family), as he calls them. Given that the director uses an observational style rather than an expository or explanatory approach, this self-focused statement from Jaime is a true rarity. Yet the fact that it is included only at a remove, mediated by a screen within a screen, is significant. Rather than focus on Jaime's self-narration, viewers are watching Jaime watch himself. It is thus the process of narration, rather than the content of the narration, that takes center stage. This reflexive element calls attention to the constructed nature of Cabeza's documentary, and his decisions to withhold certain expected information, but it also showcases Jaime as a person possessing the discursive power of self-identification.

The indirect filming practice of foregrounding mirrored images, together with the documentary's reflexive focus on screens within screens, piques viewers' curiosity and induces a contemplative approach to what we see. In truth, these aspects of the documentary are a logical extension of what is already achieved by the large wood-paneled frame at the center of *En vano*, which also appears in these scenes and produces a similar effect. The set and the prop, the mirrors and the wooden frame, are quite often copresent: Cabeza films the practice space through its expansive mirrors, thus indirectly, and at once shoots through the wooden frame. The way in which both of these elements work together in the shots the director has included in the film can be complex. One scene, for example, begins with Manuel at left and Arturo at right. They are both outside of the wooden frame, while Jaime's figure is fully inside it.[75] One way to see such scenes—both in *En vano* and in *Que nadie duerma*—is this: visually and also symbolically, the performer is constrained by the limitations of frames of reference, by the stereotypes that make up the cultural location of disability and the DS image.[76] But the play and the film are also both interested in the agency that people with Down syndrome have, which is an idea that plays out through movements and dance as a matter of course. On-screen, the wooden frame becomes an enclosure for their figures, a metaphor for the constraints of ableist understandings of disability, but it also can be played with, subverted. In the scene just mentioned, it is Jaime who then walks through the frame and back, interacting with Manuel on both sides. In another such scene, José Manuel is shot indirectly through the room's mirrors: first he hugs the frame, then he steps through it and into it. He intentionally aligns his body with it and, standing on its supports, makes the structure his own as if it were serving his body rather than constraining it (see Figure 4.3).[77]

Que nadie duerma is an avant-garde film made up of contrasts and contradictions, and of complex visual images that nevertheless arrive on-screen ready-made from reality. In this sense, it serves as an unconventional affirmation of disability identity. This affirmation is the direct result of the active and performative bodily movements of people with DS, which carry with them implicit moral/ethical condemnations of ableist views of trisomy 21. But even the more mundane parts of the film also offer critiques of the normative view of cognitive and bodily difference.

A case in point is the film's centering of Jaime. Cabeza shows him getting excited about a hamburger, or playfully pretending to be asleep because he is not ready to start the day. Jaime does not respond at all when Arturo pats his cheek and shakes his arm. Some of this everydayness focuses on tasks that require fine motor control, like clothes folding and toothbrushing.[78] When Jaime folds his clothes, his whole body is positioned between the camera and the bed where he has laid out his shirt. This positioning is in some ways determined by an observational perspective, but it has the additional advantage of deliberately requiring viewers to stare at the material trisomy 21 body at work. We are visually distanced from the activity of folding, but we hear the sounds of a breath taken in concentration, of feet shuffling on the floor. His face is not visible.[79] When Jaime exits the frame of the shot, the take continues to focus on the folded shirt for a noticeable amount of time.[80] Cabeza's camera lingers at moments where we are being prompted to actively interpret what we see. Just as Danza Mobile does, he wants us to see people with Down syndrome as active subjects with agency and autonomy, and as producers of culture, rather than just passive consumers. This latter idea is embedded in a scene that takes place on the shore of a river and serves as a cinematic metaphor.[81] We recognize Jaime and José Manuel, who sit on a bench and draw in notebooks. Cabeza first shows viewers the close-up of a colorful hand-drawn page, and only then the buildings that have inspired it. The order of the scene's editing seems carefully chosen as a way of highlighting the relationship between reality and representation. It also frames people with Down syndrome as the producers of culture, mirroring the reality of their performative roles in the production *En vano*.

Cabeza's documentary also emphasizes certain incongruities between sound and sight. The film's use of these incongruities is evident from the outset and takes both mundane and more marked forms.[82] One mundane example is a scene where José Manuel writes dialogue in his notebook. As he puts pen to graph paper, we hear an overlayed track of his voice delivering the text, but it is not in synch with the mouth movements he makes as he thinks out what he wants to write. This is an interesting creative disjunction, as viewers might associate its somewhat formulaic use here with mainstream movies in which it appears almost as a stock image of the process of artistic creation. Yet what is significant is that here it frames José Manuel, a person with Down syndrome, as the creator in question. He is intensely at work, productive, authorial. Here is the very image of a Down Syndrome Culture, one that contrasts with the social DS image as nonproductive.[83] José Manuel is shown not merely as the subject of creative work—the social actor in a documentary—but moreover as a producer of artistic work.

Other moments where the images and the sound are not aligned are also intriguing. In one such moment toward the end of the film, we look squarely at Jaime, who is seated on the floor wearing headphones and facing the camera directly. It is as if we are watching him from inside a laptop at whose screen he is staring. Only his eyes move, he seems focused, but we are not sure whether he is hearing the same audio that we are. What we hear is a recording of his voice speaking, but in the documentary image, his mouth does not move. In a tender but strong, emotionally resonant voice, he says this:

> Vuélveme conmigo. Yo estoy contigo para, para siempre. Te juro, es que yo, la verdad, por que yo te amo a ti. Eso es la verdad. Y por favor que tú, que te sepas, que yo lloro por la noche pensando de ti. Y yo voy a luchando, oiga a luchar por ti, de tu fondo, me quiere, y yo también.[84]

> Come back with me. I am with you forever. Because I, to be honest . . . because I love you. That's the truth. And, please, you must know that

I cry at night thinking about you. And I'll fight . . . I'll fight for you. Deep down, you love me. And I love you.

Is this part of a dialogue for one of his roles in a play? Is it a sincere, nonperformed message for a loved one? Perhaps for his girlfriend, whom we see earlier in the film?[85] Once again viewers are not sure. Cabeza has constructed the film in a way that questions what we do know and what we can know, rather than offering an introduction to Down syndrome. His aesthetics of withholding, his indirect presentation, filmic metacommentary, the way he plays with presences and absences, with incongruities between sound and image, all of this preserves the unknowability and thus the autonomy of the subjects he films, just as it reserves for the viewer a space of critical reflection. In the above scene, viewers do not know precisely what Jaime is thinking, but they do see his body and mind actively engaged in thought. One is reminded of a line included at the beginning of the documentary that voices an epistemological question: "Cada uno tiene una habitación secreta que nadie conoce" (Everybody has a secret room that nobody knows).[86]

In the end, Cabeza's *Que nadie duerma* is both a somewhat perplexing disability film, shot in a reflexive style to problematize normative understandings, and also a document that fulfills the promise of the observational mode of documentary to become "an ethnographic tool."[87] Nichols writes, "Observational cinema affords the viewer an opportunity to look in on and overhear something of the lived experience of others, to gain some sense of the distinct rhythms of everyday life, to see the colors, shapes, and spatial relationships among people and their possessions, to hear the intonation, inflection, and accents that give a spoken language its 'grain.'"[88] It is important that this observational approach, mixed with reflexive elements, in a sense allows Jaime and José Manuel to appear for themselves, rather than have their creative voices mediated by some process of resignification.[89] If disability film is to function as what Mitchell and Snyder call "an alternative ethical map of living interdependently with each other,"[90] then it is at its best when, as Cabeza's documentary does, it prompts an ethical encounter and induces contemplation and critique rather than offer premade solutions. For Jaime and José Manuel to be seen as interdependent and even autonomous subjects, this encounter must take place in a location beyond the constraints of the ableist DS image. *Que nadie duerma* captures well the way in which this place already exists, and that in order to access it viewers must be willing to see differently.

Five

Interdependence and Individualism

Disability films can self-consciously engage with two levels of representation. This was the case with Marcelo Galvão's fictional narrative film, *Colegas* (chapter 3), as well as Mateo Cabeza's documentary, *Que nadie duerma* (chapter 4). In both of those films, the use of disability ensembles, along with complex documentary strategies, complicated and even multiplied the image of Down syndrome with which viewers must grapple. This chapter complements that point by analyzing two films whose disability representations are by comparison arguably much simpler. Yet, in truth, this apparent simplicity obscures a nuanced and thought-provoking representation of trisomy 21. Both Marcos Carnevale's *Anita* (2009) and Jesús Magaña Vázquez's *El alien y yo* (The alien and me) (2016) foreground themes of interdependence and individualism by establishing and then transforming stereotypical disability representations—like that of the lone figure with a disability or the discourse that frames a person with a disability as unique and special. These films discourage viewers from seeing the material experience of disability in isolation from larger social patterns. To recognize interdependence in this way is to avoid traditional binaries that associate only disability, and disability alone, with vulnerability, juxtaposed with the constructed idea of able-bodied normality, a subject position imagined to be sturdy and not vulnerable. In truth, both disabled people and nondisabled people are vulnerable and dependent—in theory, just as in practice. We are all "inevitably dependent," we are a "species being" for whom interdependence is the rule and not the exception.[1]

At first glance, both films discussed here fall squarely into the category of those that center on the "lone figure" with disability. Martin Norden discussed this trope extensively in *Cinema of Isolation*, where simultaneously he made a larger point about disability representations on the silver screen and in society.

In both realms, then, on- and off-screen, "The strategy of isolating disabled people reflects a political agenda of sizeable proportions."[2] Though Norden focused on physical disabilities, the point is just as applicable to the history of intellectual and developmental disability representations. The decision to film people with disabilities alone—that is, as loners, and quite frequently physically separated from others through cinematic convention[3]—carries a heavy symbolic weight. Historically speaking, lone figures with a disability were quite often symbols for flawed morality, not individuals possessing their own agency. Nevertheless, with the rise of independent filmmaking as a viable path in the 1960s and 1970s, and with the progressive impact of civil rights, the disability movement, and selected legislation in the anglophone contexts that Norden explores, disability on-screen began to acquire an "incidental treatment." What he means is that filmmakers "made disability very much a part of the characters' lives but spent little if any time having them 'overcome' physical and psychological difficulties. They were starting to treat the characters like people who simply happened to have disabilities."[4]

The protagonists at the center of Marcos Carnevale's *Anita* and Jesús Magaña Vázquez's *El alien y yo* are lone figures, to be sure, but their trisomy 21 nevertheless receives a somewhat "incidental treatment." Each director, in his own way, departs from the way disability has been deployed in mainstream cinema. Their protagonists are neither stand-ins for flawed morality nor prosthetic figures intended to push other able-bodied characters toward self-revelation or self-actualization. They are protagonists in the full sense, acting in and for themselves. Their disability is "incidental" in the way Norden suggests because it is presented as a matter of fact, and because the narrative arc of the film avoids a narrow focus. Because the directors are interested in exploring broader social themes, their characters speak both to the material experience of disability and also, in the humanistic mode, to the universalized idea of the interdependent subject. They are not symbols but rather metonyms, as discussed below.

Arguably contributing to the splendid way each director manages this "incidental" treatment of disability is the coherence of a film performance that comes from unity between the actor's on-screen and off-screen disability identity. That is, one can easily identify movies where disability is performed on-screen by nondisabled actors adopting a fictional role—Tobin Siebers refers to the generalized idea as "disability drag" in *Disability Theory* (2008). Sally Chivers and Nicole Markotić write that "one of the quickest paths to critical acclaim for an able-bodied actor is to play a physically disabled character in a manner that a largely uninformed audience finds convincing."[5]

Disability drag can also be seen in performances of cognitive difference and even intellectual and developmental disabilities such as autism—one notable example being Claire Danes playing the title role of *Temple Grandin* (2010) in Mick Jackson's biopic for HBO. Still, thinking specifically of filmmaking for mainstream audiences, rather than more avant-garde cinema, there are some definite limits. The genetic basis of trisomy 21 and the physical traits associated with it have made this move somewhat implausible for directors to contemplate in relation to the screening of Down syndrome. Recalling and adapting comments by Lennard J. Davis quoted in the introduction, it might be said that it is patently not possible to be a person without Down syndrome and play a person with Down syndrome in a mainstream film.[6] The reverse also holds. This is a commonsensical point, but when Down syndrome appears on the cinematic screen in a fictional film it is because the actor is a person with Down syndrome. It is the deep knowledge of twentieth-century cinema that renders this commonsensical point a matter of historical importance.

Both films under study here emphasize the hero's journey, which is admittedly a traditional plot of both literature and fiction film. Yet they also diversify this canonical narrative idea by centering both an actor and a character with Down syndrome, thus questioning who may star in this mainstream form of storytelling. The protagonist of *Anita* is a Jewish adult with Down syndrome, played by Alejandra Manzo, living with her mother in Buenos Aires. Over the course of the film, she must respond to a large-scale tragedy and a great personal loss through perseverance, by adapting to new and shifting circumstances. *El alien y yo* tells the story of a young musician with Down syndrome, played by Paco de la Fuente, living in Mexico City. As he is catapulted to ever-greater social recognition and musical fame, he must grapple with the interpersonal conflicts that arise with commercial success. It is possible to see each film as a conventional story whose innovation is nonetheless to center a person with Down syndrome. This in itself is not an unworthy premise, particularly given the sometimes paradoxical (in)visibility of trisomy 21 in today's international media landscape. Still, as a matter of course it must be said that both *Anita* and *El alien y yo* may still be seen by viewers through simple tropes of disability representation. Their lack of disability ensembles perhaps is one aspect that leaves each film open to disability studies critique. Whether or not they seek to expand expectations about what people with trisomy 21 can achieve or not achieve, they are nonetheless in dialogue with stereotypical notions of the "sadcrip" or the "supercrip." Perhaps they are even paradigmatic exercises in turning the one into the other. But another perspective on each film is simultaneously possible due to their incidental treatment of disability and focus on larger social relationships.

The subtle and not-so-subtle ways with which *Anita* and *El alien y yo* respectively dialogue with disability stereotypes will not be lost on viewers familiar with disability representations. Such viewers may appreciate, first and foremost, what it is that each film chooses to do or not do. That is, while the protagonists of Carnevale's and Magaña Vázquez's films are, in a sense, lone disabled figures—unconnected with larger disability communities—at the same time they are not isolated, but instead are even intimately connected with others. Anita has strong connections to her family and, by extension, with the Jewish community, not to mention connections established in the film with a range of individuals meant to evoke other marginalized populations living in Buenos Aires. The titular "Alien" of *El alien y yo* has strong, if unexpectedly volatile, connections with his bandmates, not to mention bonds with his mother, a love interest, and later with promotors, fans, and by implication the general public. It is notable that the urban communities with which each protagonist is connected are not Down syndrome communities. Each film in its own way inhabits that paradoxical middle ground wherein people with Down syndrome are at once highly visible, as possible exceptions to the presumed able-bodied norm of an urban environment, at the same time that they are frequently ignored or rendered invisible in that environment.

While at the beginning of *Anita* it is possible for some viewers to understand Alejandra Manzo's central character as dependent on her family, this understanding is directly and increasingly challenged as the narrative develops. Family dependence is soon displaced by a focus on Anita's place in her wider community. Perhaps for some viewers, this very idea of dependence and its juxtaposition with a quotidian fantasy of able-bodied independence is itself revealed as a fiction. The film emphasizes that we are all interdependent on others—even though the ideology of ableism may discourage many people from acknowledging this fact. For its part, *El alien y yo* begins by engaging the idea of social inclusion at a small scale, as the repercussions of bringing Paco de la Fuente's character into the band center on his being unique or special due to his disability. But because musical performance and consumption are realms of social life where uniqueness is prized, the movie soon turns his disability into an asset for the band. In the musical marketplace of the film's created world, the visual draw of Down syndrome reinforces the idea that the band's music is also aurally and aesthetically special. A tension arises in the film, such that the notion of selling out musically is inseparable from the idea that Down syndrome is a unique part of the band's brand. On one hand, the film links trisomy 21 with extreme cultural popularity—thus screening, with a wink, the wish fulfillment of a Down Syndrome Culture. On the other, this very trajectory takes for granted the notion of interdependence. That is, while the film grows increasingly hyperbolic over its duration, it is precisely due to this hyperbolic mode that the film escapes from the able-bodied/disabled dichotomy. The result is that, somewhat paradoxically, it is able to present the mundane reality of interdependence. Merely by integrating Down syndrome into the day-to-day interactions and decisions of the bandmates, this reality of interdependence is suggested for populations with and without trisomy 21 alike, who must both grapple with economic and social forces that are larger than themselves.

At least initially, each film thus offers up a disability stereotype that is presumedly familiar to viewers: the lone figure, the coded discourse of disability as unique or special, evoking sentimentality. But by leaning into these stereotypes, by developing them in a quite unconventional way, they achieve a somewhat curious effect. The subtlety of these deployments of disability representation allows viewers to decide for themselves how to make sense of what they have seen. In order to make sense of how disability is portrayed, viewers must think beyond the disabled person as an individual and consider other aspects of social life. In this discursive move, the films nudge viewers toward recognizing interdependence as the ground of social life. This is a social realm in which everything is related to everything else; no person is ever fully separated or cordoned off from any other person. Isolation is denaturalized as a set of specific social circumstances, and these are always open to change and shift. The view of people with disabilities as isolated, as having a completely distinct social existence from the those making up the imagined idea of an able-bodied majority, may be convenient, but it is not accurate.

In neither of these two films does the lone disabled protagonist serve a prosthetic function for able-bodied characters.[7] Instead, their individual journeys are intertwined with social issues that go far and beyond the idea of disability. The journey of each central character with DS has meaning in itself. At the same time, it also carries a metonymic weight, standing in for that time-honored novelistic and filmic contrivance of the "everyman," whose journey expresses something about the wider human condition. In the case of *Anita*, the film acquires complexity by pairing the notion of Down syndrome with the exploration of Argentina's Jewish community. This centering of both a disability identity and a Jewish community, along with substantial attention given to marginalized immigrant residents and unhoused populations, creates a fusion whose effect is to reinforce a minoritized culture framework for viewing Down syndrome, offsetting the extremes suggested by the lone-figure trope. This fusion acquires legitimacy from the fact that the film is a fictionalization of the real-world anti-Semitic bombing carried out in the Argentine capital in the 1990s. As a consequence, Anita's individual vulnerability is attributed to a social cause and presented as a synecdoche for a more widespread experience of social marginality that overflows the trope of disability alone. In this sense, she can be appropriately described as "one lost soul among the city's outcasts"[8]; the film thus employs the lone-figure trope to in fact suggest interdependence, not dependence, as the ground for understanding the lives of both disabled and nondisabled people.

For its part, *El alien y yo* leans into the lone-figure trope of disability to such an extreme that it delivers a lesson about the fickle nature of social attention. While not as self-consciously playful as *Colegas* or as directly obtuse as *Que nadie duerma*, the film's aesthetic composition winks at its own construction. This wink becomes literal in a moment at the end of the film when one of the main characters stares directly into the camera. *El alien y yo* is a (melo)dramatic, even sleek, portrayal of wish fulfillment, one whose very improbability directs viewers to reexamine narratives of social achievement that limit people with disabilities. The theme of disability as special is progressively displaced by a focus on the flawed interpersonal relationships of able-bodied characters, and on the crass reductionism at work in the culture of fandom. Rather than remain focused on the specific social relations involving Down syndrome, the film also functions as a meditation on and a critique of the superficiality of mainstream popular culture as a whole. By succeeding on his own terms, Pepe, the protagonist keyboard player, who is a person with Down syndrome, claims for himself access to the individualistic promise of popular, neoliberal culture.

Both *Anita* and *El alien y yo*, then, accomplish something that Mitchell and Snyder attribute to independent disability films in general: "These visual works provide opportunities for not only raising public awareness about inclusion (i.e., the sharing of public space) but, even more importantly, global disability cinema now provides viewers with an alternative ethical map of living interdependently with each other."[9] Though perhaps subtle, the lessons they offer are not instrumentalized or packaged in an easily digestible form as narratives "about disability." Although it is—always, in my classroom experience teaching disability films, at least—possible for viewers to think reductively when seeing disabled lives on-screen, these are not disabled bodies screened voyeuristically for able-bodied catharsis. Instead, each film gives us what Mitchell, Antebi, and Snyder call "nonnormative and nonhuman embodiments as a source of insight."[10] In each case there is an "ethical frame" that "disability alternatives make available."[11] In *Anita* this frame is immediately visible, while in *El alien y yo* it is implied, but given a prioritized secondary emphasis. This more expansive humanistic insight is subtle enough to be ignored, perhaps; but then again, it is also nimble enough to possibly impact how a viewer sees disability. Although these two conventional films are perhaps aiming for mainstream audiences—which is to say that they are not avant-garde epistemological critiques, as was Cabeza's film—they nevertheless, for that very reason, open up a space for contemplation that few other films about disability have been able to achieve.

Moving Beyond Dependence: Marcos Carnevale's *Anita* (2009)

Because Marcos Carnevale fashions his film as a fictionalization of history, any synopsis of *Anita* must first begin with a synopsis of the event that inspires it and that becomes a frame for understanding its narrative action. On July 18, 1994, an anti-Semitic bombing was perpetrated on the Jewish Community Center in Buenos Aires. In describing this event and its casualties, Ilan Stavans writes that the car-bomb attack on the AMIA (Asociación Mutual Israelita Argentina [Israeli-Argentine Mutual Association]) was a "nightmare" that "left almost a hundred people dead and many more injured."[12] Moreover, this death and destruction came on the heels of an attack on the city's Israeli Embassy two years prior, in which "twenty-nine people died and more than two hundred were injured."[13] Since his interest lies elsewhere, Ilan Stavans offers only a brief description of Carnevale's film as being "about a young woman with Down Syndrome who wanders Buenos Aires after her mother is killed in the AMIA bombing."[14] This history anchors the film in a Jewish point of view on the attack, and as Naomi Lindstrom writes, explains why "*Anita* has often been screened in specifically Jewish spaces."[15]

The bombing took place in "the historic Jewish neighborhood of Once, Buenos Aires, (and) was the deadliest bombing that has ever occurred on Argentine soil."[16] Because the film unfolds against this backdrop of historical trauma, it acquires certain connotations. Because its perpetrators have never been identified, the attack itself represents, as Mirna Vohnsen writes, an "unhealed wound."[17] As a Jewish woman with Down syndrome living in Buenos Aires, the character played by Alejandra Manzo does not fail to call to mind the historic vulnerability of both Jewish and disabled people to the murderous and ableist ideology of the Nazis during World War II.[18] But to see this event as only affecting Jewish people is of course a mistake, as it is an attack on the very idea of a pluralistic, humanistic society that embraces human diversity in all its forms.[19] At one point in the film, viewers see banners being brought out into one of the city's plazas that read "Hoy somos todos judíos" (Today we are all Jews) (54:24). To experience the aftermath of the attack on-screen is to consider the long history of anti-Semitism, specifically, but also to think in general of urban vulnerability and the hatred deployed against numerous targeted communities.

One of the film's greatest successes is to be found in the characterization of Anita and the performances delivered by Alejandra Manzo. As Lindstrom has written, Carnevale's film is "particularly memorable for the performance of the lead actress, a nonprofessional with Down syndrome."[20] The role itself is an intriguing one that considerably diversifies the representation of trisomy 21 on the silver screen. The historical lack of people with DS in major film roles has already been commented on in this book and elsewhere.[21] But just as crucial is what Manzo brings to the role. It is important to remember that one of the popular and thus disabling views of trisomy 21, as Sharon Smith and Kieron Smith wrote in "Down Syndrome as Pure Simulacrum," is that it is "a condition without talent."[22] Talent can of course be rendered visible in a variety of ways and captured by both documentary film (e.g., see discussions in chapter 3 and chapter 4) as well as fictional narrative. It is useful to take a close look at the first minutes of the film as a way of seeing how the script characterizes Anita carefully and how Manzo's performance already showcases her acting range, which will continue to broaden from scene to scene.

In the opening scene, when her mother, played by Norma Aleandro, draws open the shades of her room bright and early, saying in Yiddish, "Mein feigele" (My little bird), Manzo's Anita is quiet and still, not yet ready to leave the comfort of her bed. Mother and daughter share a morning routine together, staring into the same bathroom mirror as one brushes her teeth and the other arranges her hair. They sit down to eat in front of the television, and then walk down the stairs together to stand outside of their family store, whose sign reads "David Feldman e Hijos" (David Feldman and Sons). Next, while visiting her father David's gravesite, Anita wanders away. Brushing through grass she finds something that she holds aloft in triumph, her face glowing as she shouts "Una piedra" (A stone) back at her mother. Walking back home in their neighborhood, Anita tires of eating a snack and her mother reminds her that she was the one who wanted to buy it. Back in the kitchen, the pair prepares food at the stove together, and it is Anita who peppers her mom with questions: "¿Puedo revolver?" (Can I stir it?), "¿Qué hago?" (What can I do?), "¿Hoy viene Ariel?" (Is Ariel coming today?).[23]

These first minutes of the film convey some very important things about the family, about Manzo's acting range, and about her character. The death of the father has perhaps brought mother and daughter closer in a way; they are patient with each other, and inhabit each other's lives comfortably. The silences left in these beginning scenes—silences that are at once part of their relationship and their communication—convey a feeling of loss that each wears differently. By finding the stone, Anita's character demonstrates her own understanding of her father's death, of Jewish practice. Her exuberance in the moment—her shouting in the cemetery, which prompts her mother's brief admonition—conveys at once the character Anita's uneven understanding of social expectations, but also Manzo's range. These silences also have the effect of deverbalizing the film, that is, putting more attention on the fact rather than the flourish of human relationships. The idea is that it is what people do that matters more than what they say. There is in this conceit both an anticipation of *Anita*'s gradual development of the ideas of social compassion and neighborliness, and also an awareness surrounding the need to have Manzo's own expressions, movements, and dialogue convey her character's inner state. Viewers learn that the character Anita is quiet but curious, that she is quite driven to help, and that she loves Ariel, her brother. When he and his wife Nati ring the doorbell, Anita steps carefully down from the stool that she uses to access the kitchen countertop and then runs to greet them, shifting gears from acting the welcoming host to Nati to then engage in a prolonged and playful greeting ritual with Ariel.

Throughout the film, Manzo's range increasingly broadens. When Anita finds out Ariel is not taking her to the zoo but instead watching the final game of the World Cup, she responds with a mixture of disappointment and anger (09:50). When her mother comes to console her at the bedroom to Anita's room, she whispers in restrained excitement (12:04). Viewers know what she is thinking by her gaze and her movements, as when she turns and looks up to the top of the store bookcase, signaling her intention to place pencil cases high atop the shelves while her mother is out (16:10). She conveys well the anxiety of being lost (0:25:20, 1:04:09), and she snores loudly while sleeping (1:09:43). When Nori gets upset at Anita for following her instructions too literally, she cries softly in a dark corner of the room (1:16:28). When Nori trips and hurts herself, Anita is able to serve as her caretaker—dressing her wounds and responding with compassionate words, kisses, and a song (1:18:20). It is to the film's credit that Manzo is featured so consistently, and it is to her credit that the film succeeds.[24]

Still, Anita is not merely telling her own story, but also standing in for the universal or intersectional subject.[25] She is presented as a character who does not symbolize but rather metonymically represents others who suffer the direct violence and indirect injustice of her society.[26] As one reviewer of the film wrote, "It would be simplistic to read Anita as a stand-in for the victims of violence; she's more representative of all vulnerable and trusting people adrift in a confusing and unjust world. The strangers she encounters are just as lost, just as vulnerable."[27] As Hartwig has noted, Carnevale uses biblical imagery to emphasize Anita's metonymic relationship with all of humanity. In her words, "La película no denuncia la impunidad de los responsables del atentado, sino al verdadero enemigo de la sociedad: no un acontecimiento histórico singular sino la indiferencia hacia el prójimo" (The film does not denounce the impunity of those responsible for the attack, but rather the true enemy of society: not a singular historical event but rather indifference toward one's neighbor).[28] At the end of the film a quotation attributed only to "Anónimo" (Anonymous) appears in white lettering on a black screen: "A veces me gustaría preguntarle a Dios por qué habiendo tanta violencia y tanta injusticia en el mundo no hace nada al respecto; pero sé que Él me preguntaría lo mismo" (Sometimes I would like to ask God why he does nothing about all the violence and injustice that exists in the world; but I know that He would ask me the same thing), a line that Hartwig interprets in a broader interpersonal key ("Esta frase marca claramente la lectura de la película como parábola social sobre la responsabilidad y la solidaridad de cada individuo y no como una denuncia histórica" [This phrase indicates clearly the reading of the film as a social parable about the responsibility and solidarity of each individual and not as a historical denouncement]).[29]

It is important that these others, these "strangers" whom Anita metonymically represents, are not left to the viewer's imagination but instead written into the script's episodic structure. After the bombing, Anita leaves the destroyed shop floor and her home, and has to find a way to live outside of the "burbuja protegida" (protective bubble) of her mother's care.[30] She lives as a displaced person for the remainder of the film, until being happily reunited with her brother at its conclusion. As she drifts from one urban locale to the next, she bears the strain of having to face an unpredictable life, but also shows no small degree of perseverance and ingenuity.

First, she meets a divorced alcoholic Félix, after dark at a public pay phone. She gets his attention by pointing to the phone and saying, "Mami." Félix's phone conversation with his ex-wife Claudia immediately reveals his inability to earn a steady paycheck and his reputation as an irresponsible father. Anita puts him in service to her merely by holding out her hand for him to take, and he responds as she had hoped. Their time together dissolves the question of disability and able-bodiedness into the realm of human interdependence, as when Félix makes this comparison explicit: "Vos sos más inteligente que yo.... Yo también estoy perdido" (You're smarter than me... I am lost, too).[31] Later, having been intentionally left on a bus by Félix, Anita finds food and drink in a small store run by an Asian family for some of whom Spanish is a second language.[32] At first sent away by the store owners for having no money, she ingeniously copies an indigenous street musician she sees and receives some money for dancing and singing from passersby.[33] When she returns to the store, it is the oldest matriarch of the family that pushes her daughter to treat Anita with compassion. Anita is invited to eat dinner with the family and sleep over. Subsequent scenes show her settling into a routine—she is at work stocking the shelves (59:40) and even dancing in the aisle with a young male member of the family (1:02:12). This dancing is interrupted by a robbery, which broadens the range of urban hardship and tragedy with which the film grapples. Anita herself is held at gunpoint as the robbers empty the cash register. She flees from the store and runs across the urban landscape to the city's periphery. Finally, spending a rainy night on the street, under a bridge, and among discarded items, she is found by some salvagers (1:05:46). They find she has a fever and decide to take Anita to Nori, a sister of one of the men, Sixto. Nori is a nurse and gives Anita an injection to help her weather the fever, and then lets her eat, drink, and relax in the house. It is here where she is eventually reunited with her brother, Ariel.[34] Overall, Anita's geographic journey mirrors the film's broad focus on the urban social margins by moving from the privilege of the central Once neighborhood to the rural periphery of Buenos Aires.

The episodic structure of Carnevale's film brings with it the textures and feel of allegory. Through cinematic lighting and costuming, he establishes a rhythmic forward advance. "Cada etapa está marcada por otra comida, otro vestido y otro lecho, la transición entre las etapas se caracteriza cada vez por una escena nocturna" (Each stage is marked by another meal, another dress, and another bed; the transition between the stages is characterized each time by a night scene).[35] The rhythmic propulsion between and through episodes means that the viewer is only ever momentarily worried for Anita. The dangers of the city are presented on-screen only insofar as they reinforce the primary theme of neighborly compassion. The filmmaker's decision to place Anita within this allegorical structure in truth obviates some of the criticisms that are elsewhere so easily launched at problematic forms of disability representation. This is no narrative prosthesis, but a struggle for survival. Her struggle to survive, to find food and shelter, to reconnect with her family, parallels the struggles of other marginalized urban dwellers, but is not primarily intended to enrich their lives. This very aspect of the film can be at once tied to the way in which meaning-making is halted historically through anti-Semitic violence and the experience of trauma. Some viewers will undoubtedly place this film in the category of what Martin Norden called stories of "individuals whose lonely struggles against incredible odds make for . . . heart-warming stories of courage and triumph."[36] Yet there if there is a moral lesson offered up to viewers through her struggle, it is one that goes far beyond the topic of Down syndrome. For most of the film's duration, Anita is profoundly alone and dependent on others for a kind of everyday neighborly charity—for human connection, and to find food and shelter. Rather than essentialize these experiences as the consequence of an individual's disability, the allegorical structure of the film suggests they represent a tear in the collective social fabric. They are an indication that the humanistic project of creating an inclusive and universally supportive social structure has never fully succeeded, that is, that we are all dependent on others.

The most important scene in the film captures the moment that the bomb at the AMIA explodes. This is a critical historical intertext, just as it is also a prompt for the development of Anita's journey. But it is the way in which this moment unfolds on-screen that gives us insight into how successfully the film blends the story of an adult with Down syndrome, the historical specificity of the AMIA bombing, and the wider allegory of human compassion. It is a strength of *Anita* that these elements are interlinked but each is given its own importance and autonomy. Through Carnevale's use of cinematic deep focus, the scene of the bomb explosion creates three interlinked zones of the image, a tripartite division that suggests the filmmaker's approach to weaving these disparate scales of experience together: the individual, the family/community, and the wider society.

Viewers witness the moment of the bombing from inside the confines of the family store.[37] Anita's mother has left her there for only a moment, because she has to walk to the AMIA to take care of some business. Although her mother has instructed her to wait for her return to move some pencil cases to the top of a bookcase at the very back of the store, Anita is determined to do this on her own. She moves the stepladder, grabs the pencil cases, and then climbs up. We observe Anita at eye level as she goes about her task. The camera seems to be embedded high in the back wall of David Feldman e Hijos. From this point of view, one sees Anita in the immediate foreground, the shop floor in the midground, and—through the large glass windows and

Figure 5.1: Anita in the bookstore at the moment that the bomb explodes in the AMIA building, just down the street. Deep focus is used to clearly represent her in the foreground, the shop floor in the midground, and the Buenos Aires city street in the background. From Marcos Carnevale's fiction film *Anita* (2009).

glass-paned door at the front of the shop—the city street in the background. All is crisp and clearly visible. Just then she is knocked off the ladder by the force of the loud blast, whose epicenter is just down the street.

The use of deep focus here blends three distinguishable zones of the image. These three zones evoke at once distinguishable perspectives on the AMIA attack. As the film shifts our vision from the foreground to the midground and the background of the image, we at once turn our attention from the personal to the collective. In succession, we move from private space to public space, and from the individual to the more broadly social sphere. In the foreground, we see Anita atop the ladder, calmly and carefully accomplishing a task with confidence that her mother asked her not to do on her own. This is a characterization of her autonomy. The force of the explosion knocks her off the ladder onto the floor. In the midground, the shop space is clearly visible, a symbolic order blending the public and private realms. As an extension of the domestic space, the apartment atop the store, this interior has for Anita and her mom the comfort of the private home while also serving as a semipublic marketplace. Its lines of bookshelves and carefully placed stock items—whose aesthetic distribution around the store and in the window have already been the subject of the film's mother-daughter dialogue—serve as a metaphor for social order and stability. The bookcases fall like dominoes; the ceiling fan is ripped from its moorings and sways in the gust of wind and sediment. In the background, a significant stretch of the city street is clearly visible. The blast sends even cars flying atop one another. A dark wind blows through the street (background), into the store (midground), and over Anita (foreground), explosive residue perhaps bearing trace remainders, the ash of bodies and concrete. The screen blacks out.

With the camera tilted downward into the debris, a slow zoom into the destroyed store interior leads us toward Anita, who is regaining consciousness. She is captured in slow motion, crawling over the debris from the back of the store toward the street. She has a bloody nose, and uses a store counter to raise herself up.[38] The cinematic reset offered by the black screen, and the use of fore-, mid- and background in the previous shot similarly encourage viewers to see this act of resilience at once from three distinguishable and overlapping viewpoints. It is simultaneously the act of a confused—and, due to dramatic irony, we know now motherless—individual Anita, and by extension both the metonymic resilience of the Jewish community in Buenos Aires and the wider social fabric of a diverse Argentine society. As she steps through the now glass-less door frame of the store into the public space, a disorienting, then tragic, soundtrack serves to unite the personal tragedy of her expulsion from the comforts of home and family and the social rupture wrought by anti-Semitic violence. The camera cranes upward to capture her from above, a further reconciliation of the small- and large-scale stories fused in the attack. With steady bravery she moves toward the explosion to find her mother, but two passing women embrace her and carry her along with them away from the destruction of the blast. They enter and take seats on a bus that takes them all to a hospital.

Anita receives attention for what are only minor wounds, and the nurse soon leaves her to attend to more urgently injured. We see a close-up of her face as she stares at those who are less fortunate than she is. The close-up lasts a full thirty seconds: her fixed stare eventually shifts to head and eye movements that suggest her thoughts regarding what has happened, and what she will do next.[39] The marked length of this shot encourages viewers to inhabit her material experience and point of view. She decides to leave the hospital and soon becomes lost in the city. The camera oscillates back and forth between extreme high-angle views of her walking or sitting, shot from tall urban buildings, and eye-level street views. Her hand movements convey at once the deliberateness of her actions and her increasing anxiety. She holds them aloft in the air, in front of her body as guides when leaving the hospital, to protect her from the flurry of activity all around. Out on the street she pauses, pushes them up toward her face and wiggles her thumbs and forefingers rhythmically in a familiar exercise of self-calming. As the sequence concludes, viewers see her gently turning to and fro at a street corner, the music suggesting she is enjoying the air even as she remains confused about where to go. The scene is a superb example of Manzo's talent to convey so much merely through facial expression and bodily movements.

As should already be clear, *Anita* moves viewers beyond a number of interconnected and reductive ideas that tend to accompany films featuring disabled protagonist characters: perceptions of childishness, the primacy of the question of institutionalization, and degrees of verbalization. Given that the association of disability—and of Down syndrome specifically—with childishness haunts the ableist social imagination, it is no surprise to see this association deployed in some accounts of *Anita*, whose protagonist is clearly an adult. Using the pejorative term with which Maite Alberdi's *Los niños* took umbrage (see chapter 3), a review on the Argentine blog Radio María states that the film "retrata la historia de una niña con síndrome de Down" (tells the story of a girl/child with Down syndrome).[40] This prejudicial language also appears in academic scholarship; for instance, when Vohnsen refers to Anita as "a childlike protagonist," insists that the bomb disrupts a "happy childhood," and characterizes the film as a "child-centered narrative."[41] As a counterexample, Hartwig is consistent in referring to Anita as "una adulta" (an adult).[42]

Socially speaking, the idea that people with DS are childlike is one of the justifications used to legitimize their institutionalization. What Erving Goffman called the total institution appeared on-screen in Galvão's *Colegas*, where escape and total freedom become the most reasonable response to such incarceration. Aspects of the institutional approach are still observable in the reality captured in Alberdi's *Los niños*, where the presence of structured social programs, coupled with the promises of discourse on integration and autonomy, would make such a totalizing critique less convincing. The complete lack of a discourse on institutionalization in Carnevale's *Anita* can be explained in two ways. In the historical sense, the lack of an institution for Anita is consistent with the generalized lack of coordinated support for populations with disabilities. This situation is evident even in the United States, despite its being home to a disability movement that has inspired shifts in the global discourse on disability rights, and it is arguably more acute across the uneven geographies of Latin America. Interestingly, in the independent assessments of two characters in Carnevale's film, Félix and Nori, bringing Anita to the police would only have led to her being placed in a mental institution.[43] In the cinematic sense, the film's pursuit of allegory is more effective precisely because the institution, which would have the effect of deuniversalizing the protagonist, is absent. In a practical sense, both historically and cinematically, the reality is that adults with Down syndrome who are fortunate to have stable families many times live with their parents. It is in this practical sense that *Anita* shines, offering viewers a contextualized and detailed—and quite realistic—cinematic portrait of the life of an adult with trisomy 21.

Carnevale's treatment of Anita's Down syndrome remains "incidental" against the allegorical background of the film, which indeed pushes far beyond her own story. Still, it must be emphasized, this allegorical context does not dispense with a certain realism regarding the material experience of disability. That the treatment of Down syndrome is "incidental" does not mean that it cannot also be believable, accurate, and even empowering. The range of Monzo's acting, as suggested above, is a key strength of the film in this respect. So is the script. At the large scale of film narrative, Anita's urban wanderings make sense only and precisely because she is an adult with an intellectual disability. Whereas a cognitively abled person would presumably be able to reconnect with her brother somewhat quickly—finding a way to his house, place of work, most frequented spaces, by or making a phone call, or working indirectly through the emergency response contacts to locate him, just to mention a handful of strategies that would fit with the film's narrative diegesis—Anita's character is not comfortable navigating that complex social world. In one scene in particular, she is unable to tell Félix the name of her family's store or details that would help him reunite her with family. In this sense, the reason she is lost for so long is not unconnected to her intellectual disability, but it is also the reason she is reunited with her brother. It is the unique visible stamp of trisomy 21 that sparks the climactic reunion between Anita and Ariel. In the context of his ad hoc photography work, Félix recognizes a person with Down syndrome on a database and asks to enlarge the image, at which point he recognizes Anita mistakenly registered as one of those killed in the AMIA attack. He reports this information (off-screen), and Ariel is able to inform Nati that Anita is alive. Later, Nori's brother Sixto recognizes Anita's photo on the televised news as one of those missing in the attack, and Ariel is reunited with Anita at Nori's house.[44] At the level of the script, IDD is a defining aspect of Anita's experience, of all that happens to her in the film. It is a rare thing for a film to be able to balance the specificity of disability experience and more universalizing aspirations. Carnevale's *Anita* balances well the film's disparate aims and—perhaps even because of these—manages to craft a realistic and sympathetic portrait of an adult with trisomy 21 while also addressing larger-scale human conflict and suffering through the frame of the AMIA bombing.

Winking at the Mainstream: Jesús Magaña Vázquez's *El alien y yo* (2016)

There are some general structural and thematic similarities shared by both *Anita* and *El alien y yo*. Each film centers a single protagonist with Down syndrome, focusing on a set of new relationships forged between this protagonist and their able-bodied peers, and leveraging their story to make a pointed comment on a broader social issue. In fact, both showcase the talent of their central actors and imbue their fictitious characters also with talent (there, Anita's perseverance, ingenuity, and resourcefulness; here, Pepe's musical talents and marketable charisma). Yet there are also profound differences. If *Anita* is an immersive film built on silences, subtlety, and a foundation of disability realism, then *El alien y yo* is the opposite: loud, unsubtle, and intentionally hyperbolic. The film can be seen as a critique of the aesthetic superficiality of the entertainment business, thus making the point that this can potentially be reclaimed in the interests of celebrating disability inclusion. Where *Anita* draws strength from combining disability with a larger theme of social interdependence, *El alien y yo* is increasingly individualistic. While Carnevale's film fashions a nuanced and positive disability representation and balances this emphasis with a broader understanding of vulnerable urban communities, Magaña Vázquez's film leans into a two-dimensional representation of its protagonist as a performer with Down syndrome who claims a place for himself and his loved ones in the cutthroat music business. This two-dimensionality perhaps leads to some problematic aspects, and in the end viewers may be right to wonder whether *El alien y yo* is a story of disability inclusion or merely an argument for neoliberal individualism.

The overall plot development can be read as a celebration of difference. The film begins with a trio of able-bodied youngsters who play in a stagnating band called Da Feels. Lead guitar player Lauro, drummer Agus, and bassist Rita are seeking inspiration and success, but they need something that will make them stand out. As Rita says, speaking directly to the camera, they want to be "más originales, o más diversos" (more original, or more diverse)

(3:59). Enter Pepe, a keyboardist with Down syndrome. During auditions, Pepe stands out—specifically impressing Lauro (7:00)—and he subsequently joins the band. The main tension of the film, musically speaking at least, is ostensibly one of aesthetics. Lauro aims to be the poster boy for punk—or at least a certain commercialized image of punk whose day, in truth, has come and gone several times in North American markets since the 1980s. When we first see him, he dresses in black, wears a chain around his neck, has several piercings (ear, nose, eyebrows, lip), and sports a mohawk (2:37).[45] Pepe's look is understated, and he has more of a pop sensibility. This primary tension sustains the rest of the narrative arc of the film: punk against pop, guitar versus synthesizer, the copycat against the original, the poseur juxtaposed with the image of authenticity. In parallel, a romantic tension evolves between Pepe and Rita. Questions of attraction and sexuality, and even parenthood, receive greater attention as Pepe gradually displaces Lauro as the face of the band. They have been catapulted to success with the help of a new manager, Don Gramófono, have been given a new name, Los Puercos Pastel (The Pastel Pigs), and have a new pop style, branded as *tecnoanarcumbia* (techno-anarchocumbia). In fact, questions of romance bookend the entire film, which begins with Pepe and Rita's implied sexual encounter, and ends with Pepe kissing Rita's pregnant belly. Rita then hugs him, stares straight at the camera, and gives the audience a wink.

The film's final and literal wink is merely the final indication that *El alien y yo* is attempting to inhabit two different narrative spaces. Start to finish, Rita is the vehicle for uniting these two spaces, and she routinely breaks character to address the camera directly—either to explain her state of mind or comment on certain situations important to the plot. There are also other points where attention is called to this fourth wall of the art form, for example, when Lauro half-notices Rita talking to the camera and asks what she is doing, or when their manager looks directly at the camera and shushes Rita's voice-over so he can have a conversation with Pepe's mother.[46] This dual narrative strategy parallels the film's two interlinked perspectives on disability.

On the one hand, its treatment of trisomy 21 is incidental, insofar as the theme of functional diversity is presented as a "condición de vida y nada más; es un hecho que hay que enfrentar e incluir en la sociedad" (condition of living and nothing more; it is a fact that must be faced and included in society).[47] Down syndrome is framed in a very matter-of-fact way, and filmed from a quite circumscribed point of view. It is incidental to Pepe's musical abilities. The barriers to Pepe's success in love and work are here purely social—thus the result of ableist ideology that the various able-bodied characters express or confront to various degrees—and not at all material in any way. He can achieve whatever he wishes. To a certain degree, one can imagine the film evolving just the same way with a central, able-bodied, nerd character instead of a disabled protagonist. Pepe lacks confidence and life experience, but even these circumstances are not overtly tied to his being a person with Down syndrome. In the end, the film suggests that Pepe can indeed have it all, which he does precisely by inhabiting the prefabricated social role of the self-obsessed, individualistic musician. It is by hewing closely to a somewhat problematic ideal of musical success that the arc of the narrative demonstrates Pepe's complete independence from social limitations. In lieu of screening the reality of human interdependence and its importance for both disabled and nondisabled communities, the film celebrates a parable of neoliberal individualism. Increasingly with the help of his manager, he manages to craft a persona in which Down syndrome has become a pure image, a spectacle to be sold for its novelty, and upon which he is able to capitalize.

It is to Magaña Vázquez's credit that this theme of disability inclusion is imagined broadly enough so as to comment on many of the same issues that were featured in Maite Alberdi's documentary *Los niños*—issues that are crucial for advancing the human rights of people with disabilities in general and with trisomy 21 in particular. From this perspective a powerful social message is communicated to viewers regarding work and economic independence, love and sex, and also parenthood. Pepe battles ableist prejudice on-screen, and, moreover, he succeeds in garnering greater social prestige. He earns a spot in the band, attracts a musical following, has sex for the first time, and impregnates his love interest. At the film's close, the implication is that he will become a father and that his intimate relationship with Rita will continue to evolve. This point of connection with the theme of disability inclusion is also mirrored to some degree in the treatment of aesthetic questions at the center of the film. As the band members adopt new ways of working together musically, their evolving sound is presented as a fusion of disparate punk and pop influences. The resulting style, which Pepe himself creates and baptizes as "techno-anarchocumbia,"[48] suggests that any and all differences can be assimilated into new musical products. Simultaneously, this musical mash-up plays as a playful jab directed at the fickle nature of commercial music branding and the listening publics that the market has produced as consumers. Implicitly it recalls Theodor W. Adorno's critique of the regressive listener who craves popular music that is "just like" what came before, but with an aroma of originality: "again and again and with stubborn malice, they demand the one dish they have once been served."[49] Pepe is the first member of the band to see how they can have fun creating music while also giving the audiences what they want. But this thematic coupling of disability inclusion with matters of aesthetics and style is not wholly convincing. This is because the film remains ambivalent about the relationship between substantive matters of inclusion and the relative superficiality of aesthetics.

One problem is that *El alien y yo* wants viewers to believe that to be open-minded about musical aesthetics and style is at once to be open-minded about disability inclusion. On one hand, the superficiality of an aesthetics divorced from substance is presented as the driving factor of the musical economy. While not entirely incorrect in the realm of musical consumption, this idea is then replicated problematically in the notion that Pepe is someone who just happens to look different. As the film progresses it leans further and further into this notion, it sends the message that inclusion and success for populations with Down syndrome are possible only to the degree that they function by able-bodied expectations. The consumer market yearns to assimilate every form of difference. While the image of DS is marketable to an image-obsessed society, the genetic basis of trisomy 21 and the material experience of Down syndrome are themselves conceived of as limitations. Freed from corporeality and cognitive difference, disability becomes a free-floating image. It becomes merely a matter of cultural style. One thinks of Bérubé's comment—"The point is not to try to pretend that all disabilities are purely a matter of social stigma; the point, rather, is to insist that 'function' can never be a meaningful measure of human worth."[50] By telling this particular success story in the way that it does, *El alien y yo* erases the material experience and cognitive difference of Down syndrome. Functional diversity is replaced by cultural diversity, and strong constructivism is placed in service to an able-bodied individualist ethos that in truth continues to threaten unborn generations of people with trisomy 21.[51]

Another problem is that the film itself continues to demean and "other" the protagonist with Down syndrome even as it welcomes him into the world of able-bodied privilege. This contradiction is evident in the fictional world of the film, thus at the level of diegesis, but is also evident in certain decisions made in the script and plot. The title of the film itself—which is carried over from "El alien agropecuario" (The agricultural alien), the original short story from which it was adapted[52]—expresses an anxiety about disability that is never fully settled. The idea that Pepe is an "alien" is incontrovertibly infused with able-bodied stigma. The character is repeatedly "othered" in the film as this idea carries over into the dialogue. In an early scene, the bandmates start drinking without offering Pepe a beer, at which point he says, "Yo también quiero" (I want one, too). He soon falls down from drunkenness and cuts his head, at which point Lauro declares that he looks more like an alien than anything else and that from now on they will call him "el alien." His bandmates talk about him in the third person as the Alien, both when speaking to each other in front of him, and also when directly addressing him. Once Lauro has made Pepe the fourth member of the band, Rita cautions Lauro and Agus that "no sabemos su edad mental" (we don't know his mental age), but Lauro insists that he stay, saying, "Somos tres locos y medio" (We are three and a half crazy people). During the first sixteen minutes of the film Agus the drummer refers to Pepe repeatedly using the R-word. The frequency of this talk decreases as the film moves on, and as he and Rita grow closer together, but the stigmatization continues. Relatively late in the film, Rita herself calls him a "niño" ("Ándale pués niño" [Go ahead in, kid]). At the end of the film, Lauro uses the R-word in an expression of his jealously that Pepe and Rita are together.[53] The film seems to overemphasize social stigma as a way of eliciting the viewer's sympathy for Pepe, but also as an excuse for eliding more subtle reflections on the material experience of Down syndrome. There is no "ethical map" or "disability alternative" presented here.[54] Being a person with a disability can be a way of being in the world that challenges explicit and implicit assumptions about able-bodiedness in society, shifting how one sees temporality and social value. But Pepe does not want to live differently; he wants the able-bodied successful life that we all see screened in the mainstream media. And in the film, at least, his character gets to have it.

One gets the sense that a certain parallel is intended by the filmmaker between the claiming of the word "alien" and the reclaiming of words like "punk" and "queer" that historically turned social marginalization into an identarian position pushing back against hegemonic normative culture. Yet the problem is that Pepe does not himself claim this word until it is already thrust upon him by other characters.[55] Just before their first gig together, Pepe rejects being called a "Down" and says he prefers the stigmatized term "Alien."[56] The voice-over narration of the film, which uses this word, is spoken not by Pepe but instead by Rita. Having Pepe do the voice-over for his own tale would surely have resulted in quite a different film. Yet the decision to have Rita narrate feels purposeful—it helps to create some distance between us and Pepe, such that audience members are enticed into seeing him as the famous and unreachable rock star, in much the same way that Rita does. At one moment half an hour into the film, Rita looks directly into the camera and, says: "Nos gustaba pensar que el alien en realidad había llegado en una nave espacial. Que le había gustado tanto este planeta que

Figure 5.2: Pepe is reaching the peak of his success and now has the manager's support for being in the center of the stage. Also pictured: Rita on bass, Agus on drums. Lauro is absent. From Jesús Magaña Vázquez's fiction film *El alien y yo* (2016).

renunció a su hogar, y se quedó a vivir entre los seres humanos. Pero no. Lamentablemente mamá alien existía" (We liked thinking that the alien in reality had arrived in a spaceship. That he had liked this planet so much that he gave up on his home, and he stayed to live among human beings. But no. Unfortunately, mama Alien existed).[57] Viewers see the bottom of a spaceship improbably descending into the shared courtyard of an apartment complex. Its circular shadow grows larger and larger as it approaches. The scene is perhaps meant to be humorous, but the humor is ableist, a way of dehumanizing the character with trisomy 21.

Such elements of the film are presumably intended to recreate the way in which fan culture creates a mythos around the image of the successful artist, in the process both exoticizing and eroticizing him. When Pepe's journey to stardom is still just beginning, his male bandmates make fun of him for being a virgin and hire a sex worker to have sex with him. By the end of the film, a female fan is asking Lauro whether the Alien is "superdotado" (well endowed) and Rita is affirming his sexual prowess as she talks directly to the viewers. Musical success is portrayed as synonymous with participation in a constructed idea of mainstream, hegemonic, and ableist masculinity. Throughout the film, Lauro and Agus call Rita a Yoko Ono, both anticipating that she and Pepe will end up together and replicating the toxic masculinity of the rock music world. Pepe reaches the pinnacle of musical success, but he does so by leaving his disability community behind and by fully embracing a mainstream, image-obsessed, individualistic music culture.[58]

In the course of Pepe's musical journey, he displaces Lauro as the leader of the band. However, in a way he remains trapped in a position of dependence. Near the beginning of the film Lauro says, "El alien es de todos" (The Alien belongs to everyone) and Rita replies, "Hablas de él como si fuera una mascota" (You talk about him as if he were a pet).[59] Pepe passes from being seen as the possession of Lauro, and a vehicle for the band's success, to being the possession of the music industry, a vehicle for the success of his manager. The reality is that Lauro, Agus, and Rita—and later Don Gramófono—are all using him for their own success. Pepe himself is not passive in this relationship, and it is clear from the earliest segments of the film that he wants exactly what his bandmates want—to be loved by the crowd and to be seen as successful. In the band's first performance, Pepe moves his keyboard back toward center stage three times after Lauro puts him out of the spotlight, finally stating loudly, "No, aquí" (No, here) (15:47–16:17). Later, he pumps his arms to get the crowd fired up both before and after his keyboard solo on the song "Puta ciudad" (Damn city) (17:40). He wants the attention as much as they do. Not only was the band's "techno-anarcocumbia" style his idea, but his playful donning of a pig mask during a meeting with their manager (27:30) is what arguably prompts the new band name of Los Puercos Pastel.[60] Moreover, one of the early successful music videos they make is for a song whose lyrics focus on a Martian who has success with earthly women, not to mention the fact that ten of the twelve tracks on their debut album are from the Alien, and only two are from Lauro.[61] The members of the band are looking to sell out, and the image of who they all are is more important to them than the reality. Pepe's contributions to their success are definitive, and in due course he claims ownership of this success for himself. The manager tells Lauro once and for all that Pepe will be in the center of the stage (see Figure 5.2). At the end of the film, as Rita tells us, Pepe truly has it all: "Y entonces así, sin quererlo, el Alien obtuvo todo lo que otros desean, el dinero, la fama, la chica, y muy pronto hasta un mini-alien" (And just like that, without wanting it, the Alien got what everybody wants, money, fame, the girl, and very soon even a mini alien).[62]

The main strength of *El alien y yo* as a musical fiction is that it sets out to combat one of the traps of disability representation—that people with Down syndrome cannot have talent or be successful through their own efforts or on their own terms. Smith and Smith write:

> In a society where the individual is king, the worst possible position to be in is that of someone whose very existence appears to negate indi-

vidualism, someone who is forever consigned to a role of "a Downs" or an "other" in society. Whilst some disabilities could be celebrated such as neurodiversity, which is often positioned as a desirable quality, as it is more closely aligned with perceptions of "talent" . . . people with Down syndrome continue to be positioned as "less than" and are often seen as "all the same."[63]

The strength of Magaña Vázquez's film lies in its creative reclaiming of individualism for Pepe's character. In the moment that he definitively kicks Lauro out of the band, he delivers a final message with compelling confidence "No soy niño, no soy idiota, no soy retardado, soy el Alien, y soy bien chingón" (I am not a child, I am not an idiot, I am not retarded, I am the Alien and I am goddamn awesome).[64] *El alien y yo* leans so far against the "negation of individualism" for people with Down syndrome that it comes out the other side. Pepe's journey emphasizes that people with Down syndrome have the equal right to pursue success in all its forms, and even to be individualists and image-obsessed social climbers.

The problem is that the telling of this particular story rests on a faulty foundation. Don Gramófono tells the band early on that what sells is pop. You must give the people what they want to hear, and then they will love you. This message of *El alien y yo* is a paradigmatic example of how inclusion in practice risks assimilation, how short-term or small-scale changes preserve the ills of the existing system. In truth, only a certain amount of difference will be tolerated, as suggested by the film's own musical metaphor for disability, the latter understood as just another difference in style. It is a tale of assimilation so individualist as to deny participation and possibility to the vast majority of people with Down syndrome. In this sense, the film sells the fiction that the image of disability can be completely severed from its material ground, that developmental and cognitive difference are merely a matter of appearance. Moreover, *El alien y yo* wants us to believe that the musical market absorbs all differences, that the realm of consumption is a free space where performers with trisomy 21 are on equal footing with nondisabled performers. Perhaps this is one of the unstated messages contained in Rita's final wink to the audience.[65]

The real question is how much viewers are willing to invest in the film's winking aesthetic. In his intentionally hyperbolic presentation of trisomy 21, Magaña Vázquez delivers a meteoric rise from exclusion to high visibility. This cinematic wish fulfillment relies heavily on Pepe's individual creativity and individualistic drive for success as a way of combating an entrenched social image of Down syndrome. To use Smith and Smith's words, *El alien y yo* shows viewers who might expect people with Down syndrome to be "less than" that they can be so much more; it demonstrates that people with Down syndrome are not "all the same" but instead creative individuals with unique attributes. Perhaps the character Pepe's extreme independence on-screen is the necessary foil for the limiting social image of someone with trisomy 21 as extremely dependent.

Conclusion

Amplification and Interpretive Power

By way of conclusion, I return to the central idea that animates this book. People with Down syndrome possess a culture. They are producers of culture. Through their speech, writing, dancing, acting, and other creative endeavors, through their everyday lives, people with DS are already crafting an idea of trisomy 21 that differs from the ableist social image described and analyzed so well by Kieron Smith and Sharon Smith (2021). Down Syndrome Culture is an organizing principle for attending to the ways in which the achievements of people with trisomy 21 are having an impact across the globe. The chapters of this book have explored that premise by looking at cultural production in selected Iberian and Latin American spaces. Overall, this study has attempted to amplify the work of several people with Down syndrome who are also producers of culture. These are Andy Trias Trueta (chapter 2); Ana Rodríguez, Ricardo Urzúa, Andrés Martínez, Rita Guzmán, Ariel Goldenberg, Rita Pokk, and Breno Viola (chapter 3); Jaime García and José Manuel Muñoz (chapter 4); and Alejandra Manzo and Paco de la Fuente (chapter 5). These examples come from writing, from acting, and from dance. At the same time, we can return to selected examples brought up in the introduction to this book as a way of broadening this notion of Down Syndrome Culture even further.

In the area of fashion, Isabell Springmühl's designs have traveled far from her native Guatemala, even gracing the runways of London Fashion Week 2016. Her work, which honors folkloric traditions, has also been displayed in the Museo Ixchel del Traje Indígena (Ixchel Museum of Indigenous Textiles and Clothing) in Guatemala City. The designer's creation of "Down to Xjabelle" seeks to correct for the lack of diversity in clothing lines. As she has pointed out, "Debido a nuestras características físicas, a veces resulta difícil encontrar ropa bonita que nos quede bien" (Due to our physical characteristics, sometimes it can be difficult to find good-looking clothing that fits us well). Springmühl's line weaves this DS disability identity into larger understandings of Guatemalan folk traditions and international high fashion / haute couture. The designer's acknowledgment of the specificity of the material, embodied experience of Down syndrome need not present any departure from the goals of disability theory. Instead, it squares with the neomaterialist insistence—by Siebers, by Mitchell, Antebi, and Snyder—that emphasizing the body is a crucial part of reformulations of the social model of disability. Springmühl's fashion line is itself part of producing Down Syndrome Culture. To appropriate words from the editor's introduction to *The Matter of Disability*, one can think of her designs—either on the runway, or in her customer's daily lives—as producing disability as "matter in motion."[1]

Second, in the realm of politics there is Bryan Russell Mujica, who ran for a Senate seat in Peru in 2019 and who continues to advocate for human/disability rights after graduating from the Universidad San Ignacio de Loyola with a degree in journalism. Mujica's story is paralleled in a film made for Galician television and filmed in Gallego also with the support of the Instituto Catalán de las Empresas Culturales. In director Breogán Rivero's Galician-Catalan coproduction *A síndrome Carareco* (The Cacareco syndrome) (2011), Iago, played by Tonet Ramírez, wants to run for the political office of mayor. The actor Tonet Ramírez works in the municipal government of Lleida, but has said that there is little overlap between his off-screen role and his on-screen portrayal. The Catalan-speaking actor had to speak his lines in Gallego and has underscored that he also had to learn to act for the film. Challenging the ableist assumptions regarding the social and professional roles that people with trisomy 21 can exercise, the film dramatizes the political process with a focus on Iago's family members (brother and mother). The theme of political representation acquires a greater resonance in consideration of the nonfictional intersections of Down syndrome and politics.

For these three people with Down syndrome who are highly visible in society—Springmühl, Mujica, and Ramírez—representation matters. Representation—by which I mean cultural, social, and directly political representation—is fundamental to understanding people with Down syndrome as active subjects.[2] The way their stories are told, where they are told, to whom, and how their stories are received, are all important for their continued success in business, politics, and visual culture. Looking at what people with Down syndrome do through a cultural lens is a call to reconceive the emancipatory potential of identitarian politics. Down Syndrome Culture itself is a corrective to the reality that in many conversations and social spaces across the globe, "Down syndrome remains more illness than identity."[3]

The notion of Down Syndrome Culture does not seek to sidestep the complicated issues of embodiment and cognitive difference that have been theorized to date, nor to disentangle the copresence of material and social factors, and certainly not to forge a purely cultural understanding of trisomy 21 that discards genetics and lived material experience. Instead, it supposes that a cultural understanding is crucial to ensuring the rights of people with DS. This cultural understanding might be seen as folding together the social and medical realms, as allowing for the material experience of impairment while acknowledging the social constructions of ableism. Although brief, this conclusion is also important in its insistence that DS Culture is a method of amplification. The idea of amplifying presumes that people with Down syndrome already possess a culture, an idea introduced at the start of this this book, and adapted from the work of Joseph Straus. People with Down syndrome also already have a voice in society. As Andy Trias Trueta wrote, "L'arma més poderosa que tenim és la nostra veu" (The most powerful weapon that we have is our voice).[4] Importantly, this DS voice is multimodal. Following the insights from the neomaterialist work of Mitchell, Antebi, and Snyder discussed in the introduction, we can look to people with trisomy 21 and see bodies that are inscribing the world in terms at once material, practical, and theoretical.

The amplification of Down Syndrome Culture is a necessity in a world where ableist culture is king. What Stuart Murray writes in *Disability and the Posthuman* (2020) about disability in general is perhaps particularly true as regards intellectual and developmental disabilities such as trisomy 21: he writes that "Disability does not always shout out."[5] His interest lies in the specifically posthuman, and thus in what might also be called enhancement tech: "Indeed, part of the interaction between disabled presence and contemporary assistive technologies concerns the *amplification* of the vocal."[6] But we can think of amplification also in squarely humanist terms. Narrative—both in prose and on the cinema screen—is itself an amplification. If it is true that disability "does not always shout out," then cultural narratives are important vehicles for carrying the voices of people with Down syndrome far and wide.

Another form of amplification exists, and it is the particular idiom in which the present book has been composed. If existing disability studies scholarship is any guide, there is a particular role to be played by those with familial connections to people with Down syndrome in promoting Down

Syndrome Culture within the academic project of disability studies. Scholars who have family relationships with people with Down syndrome have made some of the strongest condemnations of ableism that are specifically relevant to the experience of trisomy 21. I am thinking here of Michael Bérubé in the United States, but also of Jhonatthan Maldonado Ramírez in Mexico, of Kieron Smith and Sharon Smith in the United Kingdom, and of Susanne Hartwig in Germany. (Remember, too, that director Maite Alberdi herself has a family connection to a person with Down syndrome—her aunt.) As Jay Timothy Dolmage writes in *Academic Ableism* (2017), the barriers to increasing the number of disabled faculty members in higher education, and specifically in research-intensive positions, are considerable: among them discrimination, harassment, and also expectations for "hyper-productivity and individual flexibility."[7] Thus, those people who do enjoy such positions have the responsibility to amplify the cultural narratives being forged by people with Down syndrome. This is not a substitute for the political project of disability rights, nor should it be offered as a way of "speaking for" (as Maldonado Ramírez emphasizes), but it is certainly an allied project.

This book has been a specific kind of amplification. By looking at life writing as well as both documentary and fictional narrative films, this amplification of Down Syndrome Culture is intended to fill a gap in the existing disability studies scholarship on intellectual and developmental disabilities in general and on trisomy 21 in particular. This project's methodological approach has mixed documentary and fiction films together, sometimes in the same chapter. This has been purposeful. Mitchell and Snyder have written that "one cannot fully understand the form of disability documentary alone without a necessary juxtaposition alongside disability fiction films."[8] Their point was that "the stakes are very high in . . . in(ter)dependent disability film": "These works understand serious social dangers and attempt to imagine more habitable worlds for members of multiple marginalized communities (racial, queer, female, cognitive, sensory, psychiatrically and physically disabled people)."[9] The films under study in the later chapters of the present book—while they have been made in Iberian and Latin American spaces, and while many have been released after 2014—serve equally well as illustration of their point that

> disability film tries to ease audiences into a comfort with non-normative functionality and the appearance of non-normative bodies. Each film brings audiences into the lives of their disabled characters and helps us negotiate these difficult social questions brought on by

the historical exclusion of disabled people from social participation in a fairly gentle way. This is what independent disability film offers us at this historical moment of which we write (i.e. largely films made between 2000 and 2014). Expressing the desperate circumstances of many disabled peoples' lives is not the terrain that disability film inhabits. But, perhaps paradoxically, this desperation forms the complete background of the film narrative they generate.[10]

The messages that are sent regarding the social image of Down syndrome in documentary and fiction films are often related. Perhaps it is even appropriate to say that, in the best of cases, they should be related.

The films under study here—whether documentary (*Los niños*, chapter 3), avant-garde documentary (*Que nadie duerma*, chapter 4), fictionalized history (*Anita*, chapter 5), or more wildly inventive fictions (*Colegas*, chapter 3; *El alien y yo*, chapter 5)—all do exactly what Mitchell and Snyder assert. They broach questions about the exclusion of people with Down syndrome from social participation in an ableist society. These questions are geared toward issues of institutionalization, autonomy, creativity, work, family, love, sexuality, and parenthood—in a word, the rights of people with trisomy 21. Even when the critique of these films is relatively trenchant, their tone is still "fairly gentle," but the critique is there nonetheless. What the films selected do well is portray a full spectrum of approaches to the same set of questions. One might say that *Los niños* is embedded realism, that *Que nadie duerma* is purposely obtuse or cerebral, that *Colegas* and *El alien y yo* are raucous and celebratory, that *Anita* is understated and melodramatic. But they all draw force from the material experiences of many people with Down syndrome who do not appear on-screen. All of those actors with Down syndrome viewers see on-screen carry the weight of an entire community in the process of forming a cultural identity. It is important that this identity is a diasporic one—forged in relation to film representations, and perhaps also prose cultures (think Trias Trueta and Èxit21, chapter 2). DS Culture will be strengthened the more that common ground can be found across national and linguistic borders.

In his book *Fables and Futures*, George Estreich underscores a matter of great importance for communities who share a position of cognitive difference with respect to the ableist norm. "For those who are skilled with language, at ease with abstraction, and able to process, retain, and manipulate large quantities of information, a key question is how to imagine the people who either lack those abilities or have them to a lesser degree: those who, in a competitive economy, find it more difficult to perform their value."[11] Those who have what Estreich calls "interpretive power" thus share a responsibility for the "ethical act" of describing, of imagining socially, people who live with intellectual disabilities. Given the circumstances surrounding Estreich's book—that is, that he writes as the cognitively abled father of a daughter with Down syndrome—his statement necessarily reads first as a call for scholars and allies of people with IDD to help change the conversation. But his statement applies equally, as this book has also shown, to people with Down syndrome themselves. What is Andy Trias Trueta's *Ignorant la SD* (chapter 2), if not a book with interpretive power, an ethical act by way of which the author reveals himself in words and attempts to forge a call to action for a diasporic community? The present book also showcases another set of people with Down syndrome who have interpretive power. Those cinematic and social actors who act in these incredible films from Argentina, Brazil, Chile, Mexico, and Spain are performing if not also interpreting a role. But at once they are reconfiguring the social image of Down syndrome. In appearing on-screen, they are tracing their material experiences, social aspirations, and everyday disability practice into the wider world.

What Down Syndrome Culture does—what the people, actors, social actors, and representations discussed in this book do—is combat the image of Down syndrome as "a pure idea."[12] They bring this "pure idea" into a realm of visibility where it can be contemplated. They embed this social image in the material ground of everyday life. I share with Sharon and Kieron Smith the idea that what DS Culture does—what the (auto)biographies, documentaries, and fiction films analyzed in each chapter of this book do—is "create spaces where the real can begin to supplant the image of Down syndrome."[13] This is far from nothing. In my view, it is a valuable tool toward realizing the full, sturdy citizenship that is so important for DS communities in the twenty-first century.

Notes

Introduction

1. I devoted individual chapters of each to the intersection of Down syndrome and culture. Down syndrome, autism, and cognitive disability were also the subjects of individual chapters of the collection I edited titled *Disability in World Film Contexts* (Wallflower Press / Columbia University Press, 2016).
2. Siebers 2010: 15.
3. Siebers 2010: 4. Judith Scott is not mentioned in the book outside of the introduction. My own article on Judith Scott and this documentary was published in the journal *Cultural Studies* (2010), revisited in chapter 4 of *Disability Studies and Spanish Culture*, and here I have continued thinking through her legacy.
4. Siebers 2008: 15.
5. In *The Biopolitics of Disability* (2015), for example, Mitchell and Snyder look back to feminist disability scholarship from the 1990s and wonder whether it is time for a return to the subject of impairment. I previously discussed this idea in *Cognitive Disability Aesthetics* (2018), and I return to it in the first chapter of the present book in relation to a different set of sources, including Siebers's posthumously published and unfinished essay as included in *The Matter of Disability* (2019).
6. As I acknowledge in chapter 1, this does not mean that different or more radical theoretical approaches or praxis should be excluded from consideration. Instead, my aim in this book is to think in practical terms about people for whom, many times, the most tangible everyday gains still prove elusive.
7. See *Journal of Literary and Cultural Disability Studies* issues 4.2, "Disability and Postcolonialism," edited by Clare Barker and Stuart Murray; and 4.3, "The Geo-politics of Disability," edited by David T. Mitchell and Sharon L. Snyder.
8. In my previous books *Disability Studies and Spanish Culture* (2013) and *Cognitive Disability Aesthetics* (2018) I reviewed this literature in greater depth. One might add to my comments therein the names of Emily Difilippo, Susanne Hartwig, and Eduardo Ledesma, in particular, among many others in a growing list.

9. See Garrido-Cumbrera et al. 2016: 121.
10. See my discussion of this campaign in Fraser 2013: xx–xxi.
11. Cardenas 2010: 135. On the UN Convention in Latin America see also Antebi and Jörgensen 2016a: 1.
12. As I discussed in *Disability Studies and Spanish Culture*, LISMI originally stood for Ley de Integración Social de los Minusválidos. See Fraser 2013: xxv, as well as the present book's chapter 2.
13. Antebi and Jörgensen 2016a: 3–4; drawing on writings by Federico Fleischmann (Mexico) and James Charlton (Nicaragua).
14. Antebi and Jörgensen 2016a: 2.
15. Note, too, that in this book, I also hesitate to frame Latin America and Spain as "Catholic" nations, or to speculate on whether this descriptor can explain the state of Down Syndrome Culture in these geographic areas. Such speculation remains outside the scope of the book.
16. Antebi and Jörgensen 2016a: 5, drawing from Brogna 2009. This statement carries within it several meanings. The editors are specifically determined to "juxtapose individual and collective models of disability studies" that, to some degree, can be associated with US-based and Latin American approaches, respectively (2016a: 5). They are also wary of the way in which colonial power persists in a form of extractive cultural analysis that envisions Latin America as productive of raw materials that are analyzed in North America: "The South too often serves as raw material for imported theoretical processing and export" (2016a: 5–6).
17. Antebi and Jörgensen 2016a: 6. I will say that my own earlier experiences seeking evidence of disability studies as an academic project in Spain square with these comments. I reflected on this in *Deaf Culture in Spain* (2009), with the caveat that there is still, in anglophone circles, a distance if not also a friction between Deaf studies and disability studies (see also Burch and Kafer 2010; Fraser 2013).
18. Moscoso 2020: 5–6.
19. See Moscoso and Platero 2017, 2020. Moscoso is also interested in disability themes prior to the nineteenth century.
20. Maldonado Ramírez 2018: 62. To speak about Down syndrome and sexuality is to acknowledge two problems: "El primero se refiere a los discursos médicos y morales que envuelven al sujeto con síndrome de Down como una persona 'dependiente,' 'discapacitada,' 'minusválida,' 'inocente' e 'infantil,' la cual 'nunca' podrá desarrollar y comprender como persona 'normal' los diferentes procesos de su vida cotidiana—y extracotidiana—a nivel físico y social. . . . La segunda es la concepción esencialista que aún se tiene de la sexualidad, ya que muchas personas e instituciones jurídicas, médicas y religiosas la siguen llevando al plano monógamo-heterosexual-reproductiva" (The first refers to the medical and moral discourses that envelop the subject with Down syndrome as a person who is "dependent," "disabled," "handicapped," "innocent," and "a child," who will "never" be able to develop and understand as a "normal" person does the different processes of their daily—and extra-daily—life on a physical and social level. . . . The second is the essentialist conception that is still held regarding sexuality, given that many people and legal,

medical, and religious institutions continue to situate it within the monogamous-heterosexual-reproductive context). On sexuality and disability see Robert McRuer and Anna Mollow's *Sex and Disability* (2012) as well as Michael Gill's *Already Doing It: Intellectual Disability and Sexual Agency* (2015).

21. Maldonado Ramírez 2017: 145. On his research, in Puebla, Mexico, on the experiences of caregivers of people with Down syndrome and diagnoses of children with Down syndrome, both in Puebla, see Maldonado Ramírez 2015 and 2016, respectively.

22. This company had already been seen in the fiction film *Yo, también* (see Fraser 2013; it is discussed further in chapter 4 of the present book).

23. Kafer 2013: 11.

24. See the quotation from Siebers, drawing on Castells, that appears earlier in this introduction.

25. Norden 1994: 1.

26. This idea is also present in discussion of prose literary representation; see Mitchell and Snyder 2000: 52; Quayson 2007, and the discussions in Fraser 2018.

27. Chivers and Markotić 2010a: 1; Mogk 2013b: 1.

28. See the discussion of "disability drag" in Siebers 2008: 114–19.

Chapter 1

1. Siebers 2008: 4. While many scholars have pointed out drawbacks of neoliberal inclusion strategies and the minoritized identity model, I continue here with the positive framing of DS Culture, as one tool among many more within the twenty-first-century toolbox—see my previous discussion of Mitchell and Snyder 2015; Mollow and McRuer 2012; Titchkosky 2011; McRuer 2010; and others in Fraser 2018.

2. This is cited and adapted from the very title of Straus's essay (2013: 460).

3. Davis 2013: 14, 11.

4. Garland-Thomson 2009: 83.

5. Garland-Thomson 2009: 81.

6. Bérubé 2016a: 57.

7. Davis 1997: 1.

8. Smith and Smith 2021: 289.

9. As Mitchell and Snyder write in *Narrative Prosthesis*, disability is a problem in need of a solution in "nearly every culture" (the quotation is from Murray 2020: 48).

10. Mitchell and Snyder 2015: 160.

11. Mitchell and Snyder 2015: 158.

12. Mitchell and Snyder 2015: 1.

13. Mitchell and Snyder 2015: 158.

14. Thomas 1999: 125, qtd. in Mitchell and Snyder 2015: 2.

15. Fraser 2018.

16. The quotation is from Simpson (2018: 200; see also mention of "Down's

racial system," Estreich 2019: 32; Smith and Smith 2021: 290.). Simpson makes a contrast with "William Ireland, who, unlike Down, for example, based his classification on pathological anatomy, rather than racial atavism" (2018: 200).

17. I am thinking here of the broad theorizations advances in Michel Foucault's *The Birth of the Clinic* or the *History of Madness*.

18. I discussed this film in *Disability Studies and Spanish Culture* (2013), and must recommend the compelling analysis put forward by Michael Gill in his chapter "Refusing Chromosomal Pairing: Inclusion, Masculinity, Sexuality and Intimacy in *Yo, tambièn* (2009)" (2016; see also Gill 2015).

19. Estreich 2019: xi.

20. Estreich 2019: xiii, 9; see also his book *The Shape of the Eye: A Memoir*, published in 2013.

21. Estreich 2019: xiii.

22. Estreich 2019: 53.

23. Estreich 2019: 63.

24. "Our understanding of Down syndrome is endlessly complex, but it is always wedded to the technology of the day" (Estreich 2019: 62). See also McDonagh, Goodey, and Stanton 2018b: "This is not to suggest that the trisomy 21 associated with Down's Syndrome, for instance, did not exist prior to the actual discovery of the chromosomal variation. We merely warn against jumping to the conclusion that it would have placed you in any of the categories suggested by the above historical labels at any given point in time, or that having the physical appearance of such a chromosomal variation would have meant the same thing as it does today in terms of social position, recognition or responses" (4).

25. Fanon 1965: 47.

26. Mitchell, Antebi, and Snyder 2019a: 2.

27. Mitchell, Antebi, and Snyder 2019a: 9.

28. Mitchell, Antebi, and Snyder 2019a: 7.

29. Mitchell, Antebi, and Snyder 2019a: 9, citing from Huffer 2009: 28.

30. Mitchell, Antebi, and Snyder 2019a: 1.

31. Mitchell, Antebi, and Snyder 2019a: 7.

32. Mitchell, Antebi, and Snyder 2019a: 8.

33. Mitchell, Antebi, and Snyder 2019a: 8, 9.

34. Matter and consciousness are distinguishable only by an analytical view. While there are many different ways to connect today's posthumanism with its philosophical precursors, I am thinking in particular of Henri Bergson's nondualistic critique of the categories through which matter and consciousness are routinely separated in the Western imagination, a tradition that has in no small part influenced poststructuralism, especially through Gilles Deleuze, and that has been carried forward by a range of other thinkers—a list in which I would privilege Elizabeth Grosz (see Bergson 2001, 1998, 1912; Grosz 2005, 2004; also the mention of Grosz by Mitchell and Snyder 2019: 249). The quoted material in this sentence is from Mitchell, Antebi, and Snyder 2019a: 2.

35. Siebers 2019: 39.

36. Siebers 2019: 43; see also 39–40.
37. Antebi 2019: 230, 231.
38. Mitchell and Snyder 2015: 10–11; 2019: 252.
39. Mitchell and Snyder 2019: 253. See a similar question by McRuer 2010: 174, invoked in the present book as well as in Fraser 2018.
40. As George Estreich (2019: 136) notes, DS is not solely fixed by genetics, of course. There are both genetic variations and social variations to take into account.
41. This and above quotations from Murray 2020: 5.
42. This phrase, taken from McRuer's *Crip Theory* (2006), is used as an epigraph for Murray's book *Disability and the Posthuman* (2020) and is commented on in the body text (e.g., 6).
43. Murray 2020: 5.
44. Murray 2020: 6.
45. Davis 2013: 11.
46. E.g., see Murray 2020: 55–57; Estreich 2019: 17.
47. Mitchell and Snyder 2019: 250.
48. Murray 2020: 13.
49. Murray 2020: 20.
50. Siebers 2008: 14, cited in Murray 2020: 53.
51. Murray 2020: 26.
52. See Murray 2020: 40, drawing from Kafer 2013.
53. See Mitchell and Snyder 2015: 205, 211, discussed also in Fraser 2021: 87–88; and Murray 2020: 185.
54. McRuer 2018: 4.
55. McRuer 2006: 11.
56. McRuer 2006: 19.
57. McRuer 2018: 13.
58. Fundamental for this understanding of nationalism are my own reflections on Richard Handler's *Nationalism and the Politics of Cultures in Quebec* (1988) and David Lloyd's "Nationalisms against the State" (1997).
59. McRuer 2018: 116, 11.
60. Mitchell, Antebi, and Snyder 2019a: 7.
61. McRuer 2018: 46.
62. Mitchell and Snyder 2019: 250, citing "politically sturdy citizens" from Abbas 40.
63. Wolfe 2010: xv; see discussion in Murray 2020: 44.
64. Murray 2020: 9.
65. See Siebers 2008: 15.
66. Mitchell, Antebi, and Snyder 2019a: 7.
67. McRuer 2018: 46, cited from Douzinas 2010: 93.
68. Mitchell, Antebi, and Snyder 2019a: 7.
69. Mitchell and Snyder 2019: 249.
70. Estreich 2019: 133.
71. Murray 2020: 24.

72. Nussbaum 2009: 2; cited in Murray 2020: 25.
73. Siebers 2008: 15.

Chapter 2

1. See Straus 2013 and the discussion in this book's introduction.
2. Straus 2013: 466.
3. Charlton 1998: 16.
4. Charlton 1998: 17.
5. Charlton 1998: 6–7.
6. As discussed in *Cognitive Disability Aesthetics*, "One need only look at the essays published in two of the field's top-tier journals: *Disability Studies Quarterly* (DSQ) and *Journal of Literary and Cultural Disability Studies* (JLCDS), for example. The special sections appearing therein—e.g.: on cognitive impairment, edited by Lucy Burke (JLCDS 2.1 [2008]); on emotion and disability, edited by Elizabeth Donaldson and Catherine Prendergast (JLCDS 5.2 [2011]); on disability and madness, edited by Noam Ostrander and Bruce Henderson (DSQ 33.1 [2013]); on autism and neurodiversity, edited by Emily Thornton Savarese and Ralph James Savarese (DSQ 30.1 [2010]); and on learning disabilities, edited by David J. Connor and Beth A. Ferri (DSQ 30.2 [2010])—are significant contributions that precede the present book in the attention they place on intellectual, developmental and psychiatric disabilities."
7. Mitchell and Snyder 2015: 36, 38, 62. They go even further, insisting that "something within the social/minority models of disability is also amiss, and perhaps unwittingly fueling neoliberal strategies of inclusion on a more superficial level than has been acknowledged to date" (2015: 63). Mitchell and Snyder write that "the social model is itself a creature of late liberalism's strategic embrace of devalued identities and its corrective efforts to include rather than exclude what Nicole Markotić and Sally Chivers refer to as 'the problem body'" (2015: 37).
8. Here one must attend to the speculative, thus temporal/cyclical, tendencies of capitalism: "Neoliberalism continues to oversee greater and more pressing exclusions with respect to the terms undergirding opportunities for integration that then go unfunded or receive drastic cuts at a later point in time" (Mitchell and Snyder 2015: 37).
9. McRuer 2010: 173.
10. McRuer and Mollow 2012: 7.
11. McRuer 2010: 174; see also Straus 2013.
12. Kittay, Jennings, and Wasunna 2005: 443. The scholar's critique stems from the Marxian dictum that we are, in Kittay's words, "a species being," and she asks, "Who is in any complex society is not dependent on others, for the production of our food, for our mobility, for a multitude of tasks that make it possible for each of us to function in our work and daily living?" (Kittay, Jennings, and Wasunna 2005: 445; Kittay 2001: 570; see also Kittay 1999). Though we might pretend otherwise, all human beings are "inevitably dependent" in certain ways throughout the course of our lives (Kittay, Jennings, and Wasunna 2005: 443).

13. See also Titchkosky, who writes: "A further issue with individualizing disability is that this perception can act as a barrier to reflection on who and what is considered disabled" (2011: 5).

14. Mitchell and Snyder 2015: 7.

15. My work has also dealt with this population due to a family connection with Down syndrome (see Fraser 2010). The introduction of my book *Cognitive Disability Aesthetics* (2018) established the relative invisibility of intellectual disability in the interrelated historical, social, and theoretical fields, and placed an emphasis on Down syndrome where possible. Trisomy 21, as a disability that has both biological and physiological aspects, just as a cognitive component, can sometimes take on the role of a borderline classification or a limit case. In fact, Garland-Thomson (2005: 83) and Davis (2013: 11) refer to these unique aspects of Down syndrome from time to time in their writings. But in spite of what trisomy 21 may contribute to the study of ableism in general, it is necessary to assert that Down syndrome merits its own place within the developing discipline.

16. See for example, *Life as We Know It* (1996), "Disability and Narrative" (2005) and *The Secret Life of Stories* (2016a).

17. Bérubé 2016a: 116.

18. Bérubé 2016a: 116.

19. Bérubé 2016a: 1.

20. Bérubé 2016a: 2, 19.

21. Bérubé 2016a: 25.

22. On inspirations, Bérubé 2016a: 20. Bérubé writes: "It may be objected here that Siebers's and Straus's work, in extending disability studies beyond the readings of individual bodies and minds, depends more on ideas about physical disability than on ideas about intellectual disability" (2016a: 26). See my attempt at broadening this conversation in *Obsession, Aesthetics and the Iberian City* (Fraser 2021) where I also draw from the work of Siebers and Straus to comment on urban, rather than strictly literary, aesthetics.

23. "As for my emphasis on the 'fictional' nature of the intellectual disabilities I examine here: I am relying on the ancient—and yet always critical—insight that literary characters are not real people" (Bérubé 2016a: 29). Also, "One of the tasks undertaken by disability studies so far has been to point out these tropes and these characters, and to critique them for their failure to do justice to the actual lived experiences of people with disabilities. That project is long overdue and still needed; yet it sometimes proceeds as if characters in literary texts could be read simply as representations of real people" (Bérubé 2005: 570).

24. Bérubé 2005: 572. Another example, already mentioned in the introduction to this book, appears in *The Secret Life* (2016a: 57).

25. See Mitchell and Snyder 2015: 1, 160; 2010: 199. See also Bérubé 2016a: 56–57, who writes of "the general reluctance, in disability studies as in the disability rights movement, to talk about disability in terms of function" (56); and also previous discussion in my *Cognitive Disability Aesthetics*.

26. Bérubé 2005: 576.

27. Couser 2002: 109.

28. Goldstein 2016; Jörgensen 2016; Juárez-Almendros 2017: chapter 4; Meruane 2016.

29. Antebi and Jörgensen 2016a: 15.

30. Resina 2019: 3.

31. Couser 2002: 109, 110. "One important issue in disability autobiography, then, is the way in which and the extent to which the narrative depicts the protagonist as involved in a distinctive disability-based culture or a community of people with disabilities" (Couser 2002: 116).

32. Couser 2011: 233. See further comments regarding what he designates as "the new disability memoir": "These narratives are distinguished by their emphasis on disability as the term is understood in Disability Studies, to refer to social cultural, legal and architectural obstacles to those with impairments—the added penalty that societies impose on those whose bodies are significantly atypical. For these writers impairment is not the same as disability" (Couser 2013: 232).

33. Smith 2019: 76; see also Deleuze 2001; Smith and Watson 2018.

34. This quotation comes from the FCSD site itself; see https://fcsd.org/ca/qui-som/historia/. LISMI also appears in my discussions in Fraser 2013a, 2013b. See also "Derechos humanos y discapacidad" 2009 for more information about the state level.

35. The organization ONCE also deserves mention, and has a complex history that Roberto Garvía recounts and analyzes in his book *Organizing the Blind: The Case of ONCE in Spain* (2017). In my *Beyond Sketches of Spain: Tete Montoliu and the Construction of Iberian Jazz* (2022), I briefly explore the construction of blindness in Spain with reference to Garvía's book.

36. CERMI 2012: 3. One reads in LISMI the use of the now antiquated word *minusvàlid/minusválido*, which also is used in CERMI, which has kept its original letters in the abbreviated form despite its long form having been updated to replace *minusválido* (handicapped) with *personas con discapacidad* (people with disability).

37. Trias Trueta 2018: 67, also 73–74, 83.

38. See Novell 2009: 138; also Bou 2009; Gregori 2000; Villa 1990. It is interesting that Trias Trueta includes and explains a verse by Joan Manuel Serrat (46 and 146).

39. Dalmau and Bataller 2015: 46.

40. See Schejbal and Utrera 2004.

41. "Ja queden clars els objectius de l'associació: sensibilitzar la societat, fer costat a les famílies, millorar la qualitat de vida dels fills fins a la seva integració a la vida educativa i social, crear serveis. El nom de l'associació és ASTRID 21, format així: AS, per associació; TRI, per trisomia (tres cromosomes en el parell 21); la D és inicial de Down, el científic de la descoberta." Dalmau and Bataller 2015: 44.

42. The original Catalan is "Es considera que a Espanya—no hi ha dades exactes—, hi ha unes 34.000 persones amb Síndrome de Down. Partint d'aquesta xifra es calcula que a Catalunya hi ha uns 5.400" (Galdon and Ruiz 2021: 68).

43. Dalmau and Bataller 2015: 46.

44. The original Catalan is "Èxit 21 és el primer mitjà digital que serveix

d'altaveu a les persones amb discapacitat intel·lectual i té per objectiu donar un canal a aquells a qui la societat nega la paraula i, sobretot, incidir directament en la manera en què els mitjans generalistes representen la discapacitat i la síndrome de Down" (Galdon and Ruiz 2021: 67; see also Trias Trueta 2018: 19, 116, 122).

45. See fcsd.org/product-category/llibreria/. For instance: *La Barcelona que et falta* (a selection of articles published in Èxit21 by Jordi Rius), *Mallkó i Papá* (written and illustrated by the father of a child with trisomy 21), and also versions of Trias Trueta's *Ignorant la SD* in Catalan, Spanish, and English.

46. Mitchell and Snyder 2019: 253; see this book's introduction.

47. Smith 2019: 81–82.

48. Another book about DS, though not studied in this chapter, that might interest readers is *Joana* (2002) by Joan Margarit. See also the third chapter of my book *Disability Studies* (Fraser 2013) for an analysis of *Quieto* (2008) by Màrius Serra, which does not deal with DS but does explore disability in the context of a father-son relationship.

49. Mitchell 2000: 311–12.

50. Mitchell 2000: 312.

51. Espinàs 2016: 5, 86.

52. Further relevant information can be found in Fraser 2018.

53. See El Refaie 2012.

54. See Fraser 2013 and 2018, respectively.

55. Espinàs 2016: 38, 52, 79, 119, 128.

56. Espinàs 2016: 127, 43.

57. On staring see Espinàs 2016: 47–48; Garland-Thomson 2009; the pages of Gallardo and Gallardo are unnumbered, but those interested should consult Fraser 2013a, 2018.

58. See https://www.elperiodico.com/es/sociedad/20190207/muere-hija-josep-maria-espinas-protagonista-el-teu-nom-es-olga-7291114

59. Espinàs 2016: 6.

60. Espinàs 2016: 20–21; also 127–28.

61. Espinàs 2016: 42.

62. Espinàs 2016: 33.

63. Espinàs 2016: 64.

64. Espinàs 2016: 98, 97.

65. Espinàs 2016: 48.

66. Espinàs 2016: 27.

67. Espinàs 2016: 59.

68. On "subnormal," see, e.g., Espinàs 2016: 87, 93, though he critiques it; on the M-word (*mongólico*) see Espinàs 2016: 40; also Ferrusola 1989: 8.

69. Espinàs 2016: 69, 97–98, 130.

70. Couser 2013: 456. Couser does not mention Down syndrome here though he does so later. "With particularly severe or debilitating conditions, particularly those affecting the mind or the ability to communicate, the very existence of first-person narratives makes its own point: that people with condition 'X' are capa-

ble of self-representation. The autobiographical act models the agency and self-determination that the disability rights movement has fought for, even or especially when the text is collaboratively produced. One notable example is *Count Us In: Growing Up with Down Syndrome*, a collaborative narrative by two young men with the syndrome in question. Not only is the title cast in the imperative mood—'count us in'—the subtitle puns on 'up' and 'down,' a bit of verbal play that challenges conventional ideas about mental retardation, such as that those with it never really mature. Autobiography, then, can be an especially powerful medium in which disabled people can demonstrate that they have lives, in defiance of others' common sense perceptions of them. Indeed, disability autobiography is often in effect a post-colonial, indeed an anti-colonial, phenomenon, a form of autoethnography, as Mary Louise Pratt has defined it" (Couser 2013: 458).

71. Couser 2013: 458.

72. See Espinàs 2016: 95; Trias Trueta 2018: 39–48. Espinàs notes that sexuality "és un tema que durant molts anys s'ha suprimit en l'anàlisi de la situació dels subnormals, i del qual ara es parla una mica" (is a topic that for many years has been suppressed in the analysis of the situation of the disabled, and that is now being discussed a bit) (118; on the topic see Gill 2016, 2015).

73. Trias Trueta 2018: 15, 17, 18, 18, 139, chapter 14, "El somni de la meva vida" (My life's dream).

74. Trias Trueta 2018: 82.

75. Trias Trueta 2018: 19–20, 20.

76. Trias Trueta 2018: 24.

77. Trias Trueta 2018: 156.

78. Trias Trueta 2018: 21. This M-word is used by Espinàs and also by Trias Trueta (23, 32, 104, 113, 134), who seems to want readers to confront the mundanely dark history of the term and the ableist ideology it encapsulates and expresses. As Smith and Smith also note about the anglophone context, "We are still not entirely free of this definition of those with Down syndrome as 'mongolism' even if the descriptor is declining in use" (2021: 290).

79. Trias Trueta 2018: 27, 130.

80. Trias Trueta 2018: 17.

81. Trias Trueta 2018: 22.

82. Couser 2013: 457.

83. Trias Trueta 2018: 23.

84. Trias Trueta 2018: 10–11; Cohen, Nadel, and Madnick 2002.

85. Trias Trueta 2018: 13; and 115–19, where Andy also writes about the trip and Katy's efforts in Barcelona.

86. Trias Trueta 2018: 16.

87. See his comments about the Centre Mèdic Barcelona Down in particular Trias Trueta 2018: 34, 114).

88. Trias Trueta 2018: 18, 37. He also mentions the Associació Síndrome de Down d'Andorra (2018: 98–100). Espinàs mentions "una entitat que s'havia fundat feia poc, Aspanias, Associació de Pares de Nens i Adolescents Subnormals. S'adreçaven a mi, van dir-me, perquè jo escrivia a la premsa i podia ajudar-los a

difondre l'existència de l'associació i a sensibilitzar la societat sobre un tema que pràcticament era tabú" (an organization that had recently been founded, Aspanias, Association of Parents of Subnormal Children and Adolescents. They were talking to me, they said, because I was writing in the press and could help them to spread the word about the association's existence and raise awareness about a topic that was practically taboo) (2016: 24).

89. Trias Trueta 2018: 73–74, 83–85; the quotation is from 94, while the chapter runs from 113 to 122.
90. See also Trias Trueta 2018: 70, 136–37.
91. Trias Trueta 2018: 19; see also chapter 10, "La meva experiència brasilera" (My Brazilian experience).
92. Trias Trueta 2018: 19.
93. Couser 2011: 233.
94. Mentioned by Espinàs 2016: 24.
95. Trias Trueta 2018: 23; also 53.
96. Straus 2013: 466.
97. Couser 2013: 458.
98. Couser 2002: 116; see also Finger 2004.

Chapter 3

1. E.g., Antebi 2009; Antebi and Jörgensen 2016b; Juárez-Almendros 2002, 2017; Minich 2014.
2. Some of the most poignant disability studies research related to Chile has focused on the prose writings of Lina Meruane (see Ávalos 2018; Antebi and Jörgensen 2016b).
3. See also Bérubé 2002, 2005, 2016.
4. The tensions surrounding these issues and their historical motivation have been addressed at greater length in Fraser 2018, from which this chapter cites where relevant.
5. Bérubé 2016: 56; Mitchell and Snyder 2015: 160; McRuer 2010: 172; see also Fraser 2018.
6. Mouesca 2005: 11.
7. Arenillas and Lazzara 2016: 5.
8. Garland-Thomson 1996, 1997, 2005; Davis 2013.
9. Leuzinger 2020: 293.
10. Bohrer Gilbert 2017: 112, partially cited also in Leuzinger 2020: 294.
11. Bohrer Gilbert 2017: 112; see also Nascimento and Menegasso 2017.
12. These are *Do Luto à Luta* (2005, dir. Evaldo Mocarzel); *De arteiro a artista: A saga de um menino com síndrome de Down* (2012, dir. Rodrigo Paglieri); *Meu olhar diferente sobre as coisas* (2013, dir. Gilca Maria Motta de Silveira), which has people with DS behind the camera as well as in front of it; and *Outro olhar* (2014, dir. Renata Sette) and *Outro olhar: Convivendo com a diferença* (2015, dir. Renata Sette). See Leuzinger 2020: 294; who considers short films from 2015 as well.
13. Bohrer Gilbert 2017: 113.

14. Herrero 2014: 7.
15. Introduced in Norden 1994; see also Chivers 2011; Chivers and Markotić 2010b; Enns and Smit 2001; Fraser 2016; Mogk 2013a.
16. On the latter two films see Fraser 2010, 2011, 2013; Gill 2016.
17. See Mitchell and Snyder 2015, 2016.
18. Snyder and Mitchell 2010: 198.
19. Snyder and Mitchell 2010: 198.
20. Snyder and Mitchell 2010: 198; see Norden 1994 for a comprehensive approach to this trope.
21. See also Morris 2002.
22. Zuin, Denari, and Vicente 2021: 222–23.
23. Kittay, Jennings, and Wasunna 2005: 445; Kittay 2001: 570; see also Kittay 1999; Kittay and Carlson 2010.
24. "Who is in any complex society is not dependent on others, for the production of our food, for our mobility, for a multitude of tasks that make it possible for each of us to function in our work and daily living?" (Kittay 2001: 570).
25. See Contardi 2002; Francis 2009.
26. See Lane 1993; Shapiro 1994; Stiker 1997.
27. Alberdi, qtd. in Matheou 2017.
28. In line with Corbett O'Toole (2013), the present author also discloses a familial relationship with a person with Down syndrome from which an academic interest in filmic representations has developed.
29. Herr, Gostin, and Koh 2003; Carey 2009.
30. See Wehman 1995; Migliori et al. 2007.
31. See also Corro Penjean 2016.
32. Corro et al. 2007: 9.
33. "Los temas y los personajes remontaron la pantalla desde las periferias del orden social, desde la oscuridad de la historia, desde los patios traseros de la cultura y de la nación. Los nuevos realismos latinoamericano y chileno, exasperaron los conflictos de clase, de raza, de género, de la propiedad de la tierra, las estructuras de poder, el monopolio occidental de la representación, aun el predominio de la razón sobre otras facultades" (Corro et al. 2007: 52 ; see also 30, 34; Mouesca 2005).
34. Corro et al. 2007: 10.
35. Corro et al. 2007: 74 n. 4.
36. In Chile in the 1990s, Iván Pinto has written, "Conflictos como la afectividad, el reconocimiento, la sexualidad, la aceptación del otro, fueron los ejes de guiones cinematográficos" (2009: 14).
37. See Corbin 2012.
38. Arenillas and Lazzara 2016: 14–15.
39. Mitchell and Snyder 2010: 181–82; see also 2000: 52.
40. Balza 2011: 58.
41. Mitchell and Snyder 2010: 202.
42. Corro et al. 2007: 97.
43. On embodiment and culture in the disability studies context, see Siebers

2013; Snyder, Brueggeman, and Garland-Thomson 2002; Snyder and Mitchell 2006.

44. Alberdi 2016: 0:07:16; also at 0:42:22 and 1:15:27.

45. While the film as a whole might be considered a mixture of the observational and expressive modes, in the senses outlined by Bill Nichols (2013), *Los niños* tends toward the latter in the sense that "se avoca a demostrar cómo el conocimiento encarnado da entrada a un entendimiento de los procesos más generales que están en funcionamiento en la sociedad" (229).

46. Similar segments that capture multiple people dancing also occur periodically throughout the film, 0:07:04, 0:33:47; Anita practices a wedding dance at 0:43:48 after watching the Peru video, and reenacts dialogue from the wedding ceremony in her chef's uniform outside wile Rita watches on; later Anita and Andrés practice the wedding dance at 0:44:46.

47. Davis 2013: 11; Garland-Thomson 2009: 83. "It is patently not possible to be born a person with Down syndrome and become someone who does not have Down syndrome (although some cosmetic surgeries to normalize the faces of people with Down syndrome are available, and now drug therapies are being researched to improve cognitive skills) . . . why is it that disability is often the identity that is left out—not choosable?" (Davis 2013: 11). On the productive tension between recognizing impairment and affirming the social construction of disability see also Mitchell and Snyder 2015; Fraser 2018.

48. Balázs 1970: 56, 62.

49. Antebi and Jörgensen 2016a: 3. On the larger processes and historical shifts related to the public visibility and invisibility of people with disability, see Stiker 1997; Fraser 2018. On disability in Latin American culture see also Antebi 2009; Juárez-Almendros 2013, 2017; Minich 2014.

50. On this see the discussion in Fraser 2018: 60–63.

51. Garland-Thomson 2009: 9–10. 2002, 2005; cf. Mulvey 1999.

52. Garland-Thomson 2009: 6, 49, 81.

53. Garland-Thomson 2009: 6.

54. Garland-Thomson 2009: 11, 33.

55. Alberdi 2016: 0:01:18–0:02:10.

56. In Alberdi 2016, the original Spanish is "nunca ha crecido" (0:02:44).

57. Alberdi 2016: 0:04:07; again at 0:52:59.

58. Alberdi 2016: 0:04:51, 0:05:40, and 0:06:36, respectively.

59. Alberdi 2016: 0:29:46.

60. In order, these are Alberdi 2016: 0:16:28, 0:37:08, 0:27:20, 0:41:24.

61. Alberdi 2016: 1:03:40.

62. Alberdi 2016: 1:04:21.

63. These moments occur at Alberdi 2016: 0:42:45, 0:49:19, and 0:51:35.

64. These moments occur at Alberdi 2016: 0:48:44, 0:22:46, and 1:05:48.

65. See McRuer and Mollow 2012; Gill 2015, 2016.

66. In order, the above moments come from Alberdi 2016: 0:59:56 (under covers), 1:00:48 (adopt a child), 0:19:26 (Pamela), 0:57:55 (Rita and Dani), 0:55:30 (contraception).

67. The quotation in the text comes from Alberdi 2016: 0:55:31. Keep in mind the above quotation from Corro et al. 2007: 97.
68. Alberdi 2016: 0:45:46.
69. This sequence runs from Alberdi 2016: 0:28:06 to 0:29:33.
70. Alberdi 2016: 0:25:20 and 0:26:15 (elderly woman); 0:13:26 and 0:14:00 (grandmother).
71. Zacco 2017.
72. Quoted in Zacco 2017.
73. Zacco 2017.
74. See Antebi and Jörgensen 2016a: 3–4.
75. Alberdi 2016: 0:44:29. This can be understood as a counterpart to an earlier scene when Andrés is asked by a server if he is allowed to drink alcohol, and he has to explain that, yes, he can (0:24:39). The server is left invisible and off-screen in line with the overall camera strategy of the film.
76. Alberdi 2016: 0:51:55.
77. See Alberdi 2016: 1:08:35, 1:09:36, 1:09:53.
78. Alberdi 2016: 1:11:25 (speech), 1:12:44 (ballad), 1:13:30 (singing).
79. See Leuzinger 2020: 299.
80. Cited in Leuzinger 2020: 300. See also the master's thesis by Veronezi (2018), which is devoted entirely to the film *Colegas* and includes interview scripts with the director and protagonists.
81. Collin 2020: 220.
82. Veronezi 2018: 8.
83. Galvão 2012: 00:01:35.
84. Leuzinger 2020: 303.
85. See the appendix interview in Veronezi 2018.
86. See Nascimento and Menegasso 2017: 139, which comments on these masks, linking the image of the clown with the idea of social perceptions.
87. Galvão 2012: 0:01:54.
88. Galvão 2012: 0:10:20.
89. Galvão 2012: 0:05:30.
90. Collin 2020: 217.
91. Galvão 2012: 0:15:10.
92. The former scene is discussed by Zuin, Denari, and Vicente 2021: 223; the quotations are from 222–23 and refer to a section of the LBI (Brazilian Inclusion Law) of 2015.
93. Galvão 2012: 00:16:44.
94. This scene last almost two minutes; see Galvão 2012: 0:17:23–0:19:14.
95. One might even see this as an inversion of what Mitchell and Snyder call narrative prosthesis. One persisting question regarding the film, which does not obviate the above analyses, regards how disability figures also into the characterization of the two detectives, who are portrayed as having a physical disability and an intellectual disability. One might argue that Galvão is trying to deconstruct the trope of the able-bodied detective, but if that is the case, my own opinion is

that this move is not successful, which opens this aspect of the film up to critique. Leuzinger's take on this is that Galvão is showing "la 'anormalidad' del mundo 'normal,' tal y como se manifiesta en la estupidez de los agentes Souza y Ferrari y en la discapacidad física del agente Fonseca, a quien solo le queda el dedo del corazón en la mano izquierda" (the "abnormality" of the "normal" world, just as it is manifested in the stupidity of the agents Souza and Ferrari and in the physical disability of the agent Fonseca, whose left hand only has the middle finger) (Leuzinger 2020: 303).

    96. Leuzinger 2020: 302.
    97. Nascimento and Menegasso 2017: 135.
    98. Kafer 2013: 27. See also McRuer's *Crip Theory* (2006) and *Crip Times* (2018).
    99. Collin 2020: 227.
    100. From Movimiento Down 2013, cited in Leuzinger 2020: 299.

Chapter 4

    1. As Susanne Hartwig points out, "El término *diversidad funcional* se acuña en 2005 (Romañach/Lobato 2005) para reemplazar otros términos considerados peyorativos, como *discapacidad* o *minusvalía*. En la presente contribución, se utilizarán indistintamente los términos *diversidad funcional* y *discapacidad*" (2020a: 9 n. 1).
    2. Estreich 2019: xv.
    3. See esp. Norden 1994; Chivers and Markotić 2010b; Mogk 2013a.
    4. Mitchell and Snyder 2016: 18.
    5. Email from director to author; also Nichols 2013.
    6. Mitchell and Snyder 2016: 22.
    7. Snyder and Mitchell 2006: x.
    8. All quotations this paragraph are from Smith and Smith 2021: 287.
    9. See Smith and Smith 2021: 295; drawing on Piepmeier 2012; Jarman 2013; also Fraser 2013.
    10. Smith and Smith 2021: 288–89.
    11. This and above quotations cited in Smith and Smith 2021: 287.
    12. Smith and Smith 2021: 288.
    13. Smith and Smith 2021: 291, citing Baudrillard 1983: 11.
    14. Smith and Smith 2021: 288, 289, 291, 302. The final quotation is from 288, where the authors cite from Kellner 2019.
    15. E.g., Baudrillard makes a brief appearance as a point of reference also in Mitchell and Snyder 2015: 70, 193. See also Debord 1995; Lefebvre 2002, 2005, 2008.
    16. See Smith and Smith 2021: 290–91; the quotation is from 289; a similar point was made by Bérubé.
    17. Smith and Smith 2021: 290.
    18. Smith and Smith 2021: 292, for point number one they cite "Dobzhansky 631–32."

19. Smith and Smith 2021: 289.
20. Stiker 1999: 136.
21. Stiker 1999: 136.
22. Stiker 1999: 136.
23. Stiker 1999: 137.
24. See respectively Carlson 2010; Estreich 2010; Piepmeier 2012; Mitchell and Snyder 2019.
25. Lane 1992.
26. Smith and Smith 2021: 289.
27. On Scott see Fraser 2010, 2013.
28. See Marx's "Private Property and Communism," in McLellan 1977: 91; the discussion in Merrifield 2002: 78; and also Fraser 2019: 52–54.
29. Smith and Smith 2021: 288.
30. Smith and Smith 2021: 303.
31. Smith and Smith 2021: 287.
32. See Fraser 2013: 7–8.
33. See https://danzamobile.es; also Checa Puerta 2021: 85.
34. Valderrama Vega 2020: 67.
35. Smith and Smith 2021: 303.
36. Cabeza 2017: 0:42:55 (Germany) and 1:05:26 (Spain).
37. Checa Puerta 2021: 85.
38. Checa Puerta 2021: 86, drawing on Benjamin 2002.
39. Checa Puerta 2021: 95; the quotation is from 89.
40. Checa Puerta 2021: 89; see also 93.
41. Checa Puerta 2021: 90, 92.
42. On the ending of the film *Que nadie duerma*, see Checa Puerta 2021: 90, citing Sánchez 2009.
43. Checa Puerta (2021) elaborates, drawing on the work of Tobin Siebers: "Como sostiene Siebers, la presencia de dos bailarines con diversidad funcional ensancha igualmente las nociones sobre la estética, amplía nuestra visión de la diversidad humana y sus diferencias, y pone sobre la mesa perspectivas que cuestionan las presuposiciones apreciadas por la historia de la estética, al convertir la diferencia física y mental en un valor significativo por sí misma (Siebers 2010)."
44. Checa Puerta 2021: 87, citing from Parrilla's own statement at https://www.mesdedanza.es/programacion/2016/en-vano/
45. Checa Puerta (see 2021: 87–88) explicitly distances himself from this conception of the work as absence in various moments of his chapter. While his analysis is enlightening regarding the piece as a whole, my own focus is thus somewhat different, and of course is not a direct reading of *En vano* but rather a reading of *En vano* through *Que nadie duerma*, an approach that for me has highlighted how the *huecos* (gaps) are an important part of both.
46. Checa Puerta 2021: 96.
47. Checa Puerta 2021: 96–97.
48. Cabeza 2017: 1:00:34.
49. Hartwig 2021; see also Hartwig 2019.

50. This and above quotations are from Hartwig 2021: 65. See also the explanation of what Hartwig accomplishes in Gómez, Navarro, and Velloso 2021: 14, which is "una vía alternativa a la que denomina '*undoing disability*' y que consistiría, según sus propias palabras, en 'oscilar entre una lectura estética y una lectura política.' Esta doble lectura vuelve la discapacidad visible e invisible a la vez, la tematiza y supera.'"

51. See Hartwig 2021: 65–66.
52. Hartwig 2021: 66–67.
53. Hartwig 2021: 68 n. 14. Here she is explicitly rephrasing her own statement from a previous article on theater (Hartwig 2019: 74), but also establishing ties to Ato Quayson's notion of *Aesthetic Nervousness* (2007) in prose literature (to which one can add both Bérubé 2005 and Mitchell and Snyder 2000).
54. Hartwig 2021: 67 n. 7, citing also Diehl 2012: 143.
55. Nichols 1991: 33.
56. Cabeza 2017: 0:10:06–0:11:20.
57. In one moment, José Manuel walks past the camera to a position off our left; Arturo and Manuel notice he is upset and go over to talk with him. He declares: "Odio. Odio" (I hate it. I hate it). "Yo voy a mi rollo y punto" ("I do my own thing and that's that!") (0:09:44).
58. Hartwig 2021: 68 n. 14.
59. Smith and Smith 2021: 290. This critique of the DS image is crucial in another scene from the documentary where an outdoor performance is given in Germany in front of a somewhat large audience. We see Arturo and Jaime, dressed the same, in front of microphones, moving in unison, slowly, evoking laughter from the audience, a spoken English script that insists, "We are not the same" with translation to German read aloud off a paper conflicting with the idea that they are looking and moving in exactly the same way. The choreography of "the similar" is what evokes laughter, as they scratch their behinds at the same time, and suddenly wiggle a finger in the same ear. It is a corporeal humor, a costumed similarity and a cognitive contrast (0:45:33–0:48:49), including even a small hand-sized doll with Arturo's fingers for legs, wearing the same outfit they share. The laughter continues, but we often don't see what the audience is laughing or smiling at. They take a bow when it is over (0:48:49). The camera lingers in the aftermath, as someone sweeps up the patio.
60. The film itself begins with a sequence that is also meant to induce curiosity at a visual level (0:00:19–0:00:51). Viewers see close-up shots of what initially look like two different colored expanses, dividing the screen precisely in half. It is a balanced composition. But then, shadows of people can be seen, from left to right or from right to left, even starting in the middle. Because these shadows never cross to the other half of the screen, viewers realize these are close-ups of corners where two walls meet. This beginning seems calibrated to force viewers into a curious state of mind, but at the same time it recalls the allegory of Plato's cave, and also calls attention to indirect representation, which is an aesthetic value of *Que nadie duerma* and Cabeza's interrogation of the DS image, as will be explored in the body text of this section.

61. I was able to see this film in the Loft Film Festival in October 2022 at Tucson's Independent Loft Cinema.

62. See also Fraser 2018: "Inspired by the pioneering work of Leslie Fiedler (*Freaks: Myths and Images of the Secret Self*, 1978) and Robert Bogdan (*Freak Show: Presenting Human Oddities for Amusement and Profit*, 1988)—and tying into earlier work on stigma by Erving Goffman (1963) and more recent theorizations of performativity by Judith Butler (1993)—Garland-Thomson's edited volume *Freakery* (1996) invigorated academic interest in investigating the cultural resonance of freak shows. These shows reached their peak between 1840–1940 (Garland-Thomson 1996: 23), and found a widespread resonance through the efforts of P. T. Barnum that continue to echo in today's circus shows."

63. As Jaime walks off-screen to find his shoes he says, "Ah gracias Mateo," suggesting Mateo has pointed the way (0:32:46).

64. Nichols 1991: 56, 67.

65. Nichols 1991: 57.

66. See Fraser 2019, on the film *Mones com la Becky*, by Joaquim Jordà and Núria Villazán.

67. Nichols 1991: 59.

68. Nichols 1991: 60.

69. Cabeza 2017: 1:05:59 (the approach) and 1:07:27 (the cut to black).

70. Cabeza 2017: 0:31:55 (Jaime), 1:02:34–1:02:52 (bathroom door), and 0:50:46 (José Manuel).

71. Cabeza 2017: 0:52:20 and then 1:04:25–1:05:10.

72. Cabeza 2017: 0:33:53–0:34:34 (empty auditorium) and 0:38:04–0:38:22 (live performance).

73. Hartwig 2021: 65.

74. Cabeza 2017: 0:06:00 (Manuel), 0:58:58 (party; see also the similar sequence and effect from 0:23:40 to 0:25:54), and from 0:16:06 to 0:18:25 (video).

75. Cabeza 2017, e.g., 0:05:46–0:06:00 (wooden frame), and 0:07:27 ("one scene . . .").

76. Elsewhere Jaime's body is captured between a framing bookcase and the wooden frame on each side of him (0:11:57).

77. Cabeza 2017: 0:12:59–0:13:54 (wooden frame as enclosure) and 0:12:25–0:12:59 (José Manuel; see figure 4.3).

78. Cabeza 2017: 0:35:20 (hamburger), 0:38:18 (waking up), and on folding clothes and toothbrushing see 0:27:27–0:28:26; 0:39:43–0:39:56; 1:02:52–1:03:28.

79. Smith and Smith consider in their article how the faces of people with Down syndrome are often prioritized in advertising, whereas here we have a different approach to the embodiment of trisomy 21: "People with Down syndrome are being included for their aesthetic qualities only. Their disability is clearly visible on their faces, so their presence allows the advertiser to demonstrate their inclusion, without potentially ruining the normative aesthetic of their advert" (2021: 299).

80. Cabeza 2017: 1:03:29–1:04:15; see also shirt folding from 0:31:01 to 0:31:22, where Jaime is so absorbed in his task he ignores Arturo speaking to him from the other room.

81. Cabeza 2017: 0:57:48–0:58:29.

82. Beginning in the first minute of the documentary, for example (0:00:52–0:01:29). We see the workroom, and at the worktable is a solitary figure, his back to us. But what we see is not matched with what we hear, which is a voice describing a choreography of two dancers.

83. The scene is from Cabeza 2017: 0:40:08–0:41:28. Mitchell and Snyder write that "nonproductive bodies are those inhabitants of the planet who, largely by virtue of biological (in)capacity, aesthetic nonconformity, and/or nonnormative labor patterns, have gone invisible due to the inflexibility of traditional classifications of labor (both economic and political). They represent the nonlaboring populations—not merely excluded from, but also resistant to, standardized labor demands of productivity particular to neoliberalism" (2015: 211). See also chapter 2 of Fraser 2021.

84. Cabeza 2017: 1:01:20–1:02:19.

85. Jaime relaxes with his girlfriend on a couch, she bites his chest, he protests she'll mess up his shirt, and she gives him a smile (0:06:26).

86. Cabeza 2017: 0:11:53.

87. Nichols 1991: 41.

88. Nichols 1991 42.

89. Remember the rejection, by Mitchell, Antebi, and Snyder, of the notion that "disability is *only* capable of being resignified" (2019a: 9).

90. Mitchell and Snyder 2016: 18.

Chapter 5

1. See Kittay, Jennings, and Wasunna 2005: 443, and the extended discussion in Fraser 2013: 2–4.

2. Norden 1994: 2.

3. I.e., on the other side of a banister; see Norden 1994: 1.

4. Norden 1994: 225. Hartwig provides a quite effective definition of Norden's idea of "incidental treatment": "La diversidad funcional no es el tema principal; no se perfilan detalles de la diversidad ni la explican relacionándola, por ejemplo, a la culpa o al mérito del individuo afectado o de su entorno, puesto que no se cuenta la historia que hay detrás. La diversidad funcional tampoco exterioriza un defecto moral y las personas afectadas no son ni víctimas ni héroes, y por ende, no despiertan excesivamente ni compasión ni admiración. La diversidad funcional es su condición de vida y nada más; es un hecho que hay que enfrentar e incluir en la sociedad y que, en consecuencia, indica el grado de cohesión del grupo y la disposición a la solidaridad de cada individuo" (Functional diversity is not the principal theme; details of diversity are not explained by relating it, for example, to the faults or merits of the individuals affected or their environment, given that the story behind it is not told. Neither does functional diversity externalize a moral defect and the people affected are neither victims nor heroes, and thus they do not excessively awaken either compassion or admiration. Functional diversity is a condition of living and nothing more; it is a fact that must be faced and included in society

and that, consequentially, indicates the degree of group cohesion and the attitude of each individual regarding solidarity) (Hartwig 2020b: 197–98).

5. Chivers and Markotić 2010a: 1.

6. The original quotation is from Davis 2013: 11, and is discussed in the introduction to this book.

7. Hartwig asserts this point in other words when she writes of Anita that she is not one of those disabled protagonists who "mejoran a los demás; tampoco se recuperan de su discapacidad ni desarrollan poderes extraordinarios ni fracasan trágicamente" (2020b: 198; see also the same page's reference to Mitchell and Snyder 2000 and the notion of prosthesis, specifically).

8. King 2012.

9. Mitchell and Snyder 2016: 18.

10. Mitchell, Antebi, and Snyder 2019a: 7.

11. Mitchell, Antebi, and Snyder 2019a: 9, citing also Huffer 2009: 28, as discussed in the introduction.

12. Mirna Vohnsen delves further into the history of Jewish migration to Argentina, and the circumstances that led the AMIA, in 1949, to attempt to centralize some 120 of the city's Jewish organizations (2019: 90). The film *Anita* includes a scene where the number of dead is stated as eighty-six (1:01:15).

13. Stavans 2016: 17; see also Vohnsen 2019: 91.

14. Stavans 2016: 18.

15. Lindstrom 2018: 229.

16. Vohnsen 2018: 73.

17. Vohnsen 2018: 73; see also Stavans 2016: 17–18; Vohnsen 2019: 91–92.

18. On the latter see Mitchell, Antebi, and Snyder 2019a: 31–32.

19. While some sectors of society regarded the bombing as an entirely Jewish problem, others openly expressed their solidarity with the victims and survivors. *18-J* and *Anita* manage to reverse the standard image of the AMIA bombing as a solely Jewish problem (Vohnsen 2019: 88). Vohnsen makes explicit the point that Carnevale is "non-Jewish" (2019: 87), perhaps as evidence that the film should be interpreted as a national reflection on trauma. Consider her statement that "in line with this argument, I propose that cultural memory can be prompted by traumatic events such as the AMIA bombing and, when this occurs, it raises significant issues about the concept of national identity" (2019: 88).

20. Lindstrom 2018: 229.

21. See Fraser 2013, 2018.

22. Smith and Smith 2021: 292.

23. Carnevale 2009: 0:6:22.

24. Carnevale 2009: 09:50 (disappointment and anger), 12:04 (restrained excitement), 16:10 (shelves), 0:25:20, 1:04:09 (being lost), 1:09:43 (snoring), 1:16:28 (crying in the corner), 1:18:20 (as caretaker).

25. See also Hartwig 2020b: 195, "Algunas veces, Anita gira sobre sí misma con la boca abierta, las manos entrelazadas, constituyendo la imagen emblemática de una persona perdida en un mundo incomprensible."

26. See Vohnsen 2018: 79.
27. King 2012; see also Vohnsen 2019: 88.
28. Hartwig 2020b: 196.
29. Hartwig 2020b: 196. The movie quotation is from Carnevale 2009: 1:38:00.
30. Hartwig 2020b: 195.
31. Carnevale 2009: 28:52 ("Mami"), 42:11 ("inteligente").
32. Carnevale 2009: 50:28. One finds opposing descriptors regarding the family's origins (Chinese/Korean) in Vohnsen 2018 and Hartwig 2020b.
33. Carnevale 2009: 51:42. She also encounters an indigenous busker from Humahuaca and takes up a spot singing and dancing alongside him, at which point he asks her to let him work in peace and soon leaves for a less crowded, less competitive spot. By begging there, she makes enough money to buy food from the store.
34. Carnevale 2009: 59:40 (stocking), 1:02:12 (dancing), 1:05:46 (salvagers). Also interesting is Félix's statement that if he had known she was a survivor of the AMIA, he could have taken a photograph of her and won the Pulitzer Prize (1:25:08).
35. Hartwig 2020b: 193.
36. Norden 1994: 3.
37. Carnevale 2009: 16:16–16:53.
38. Carnevale 2009: 17:21.
39. Carnevale 2009: 21:06–21:36.
40. See "Anita—La Película" 2011.
41. Vohnsen 2018: 73, 78, 85. Note further that Vohnsen calls Anita a child twice in one paragraph (2018: 74), instead of using the option of "daughter"; to be fair, both "adult" and "child" are used throughout the article, but the insistence is on the fact of her childishness, not on a critique of the director's vision. The more relevant term, "daughter"—given the plot's centering of the mother-daughter relationship's presence and absence—also appears but is used less frequently. For instance, there is a two-to-one "child" to "daughter" ratio in one paragraph on page 77.
42. Hartwig 2020b: 193.
43. See Carnevale 2009: 1:20:53 and 1:24:04.
44. Carnevale 2009: 44:06 ("one scene"), 1:17:30 (photography work), 1:22:18 ("Anita is alive"), 1:28:35 (televised news), 1:32:02 (reunited).
45. Magaña Vázquez 2016: 3:59 (diverse), 7:00 (impressing Lauro), 2:37 (mohawk).
46. See Magaña Vázquez 2016: 37:18, 31:44.
47. Hartwig 2018: 198.
48. Magaña Vázquez 2016: 21:19.
49. See my discussion of Adorno in "Note on Theodor W. Adorno and Jazz Criticism" (2022: xvii–xxvi). The quotations are from Adorno's essays "On Jazz" (2002a: 476) and "On the Fetish-Character of Music and the Regression of Listening" (2002b: 307).

50. Bérubé 2016a: 57.
51. See Estreich 2019 and the discussion in the introduction.
52. Carlos Velázquez, the author of that story, says that it was inspired by the drummer of the Argentine rock band Reynols, who is a person with Down syndrome (see Vargas 2016).
53. Magaña Vázquez 2016: 9:27 (beer), 11:34 ("el alien"), 13:25 ("mental age"), 13:37 ("three and a half"), 7:26, 14:59 ("retrasado"), 50:54 ("ándale pués niño"), 1:08:37 ("retardado").
54. Mitchell and Snyder 2016: 18; Mitchell, Antebi, and Snyder 2019a: 9.
55. Magaña Vázquez 2016: first, Lauro, 11:34, then Rita, 14:14.
56. Magaña Vázquez 2016: 15:08.
57. Magaña Vázquez 2016: 30:40–31:00.
58. Magaña Vázquez 2016: 38:14 (virgin), 52:45 (sex worker), 58:46 ("super-dotado"), 1:08:00 (sexual prowess), 4:22, 11:15, 1:00:51 (Yoko Ono).
59. Magaña Vázquez 2016: 33:33; see also Laura saying "mi pinche alien" (my damn alien) 56:44.
60. Magaña Vázquez 2016: 15:47–16:17 (keyboard location), 17:40 (solo), 27:30 (band name).
61. Magaña Vázquez 2016: 43:18; the album is titled *Sesión con el Alien*, 43:43.
62. Magaña Vázquez 2016: 1:15:56.
63. Smith and Smith 2021: 290.
64. Magaña Vázquez 2016: 1:13:00.
65. Magaña Vázquez 2016: 19:47 (pop sells), 1:16:41 (final wink).

Conclusion

1. Mitchell, Antebi, and Snyder 2019a: 8.
2. On active subjectivity, see Siebers 2019: 43; see also 39–40, mentioned in the introduction.
3. Estreich 2019: 137.
4. Trias Trueta 2018: 156.
5. Murray 2020: 52.
6. Murray 2020: 52.
7. Dolmage 2017: 177–78, drawing on Price 2011.
8. Mitchel and Snyder 2016: 18.
9. Mitchel and Snyder 2016: 19–20.
10. Mitchel and Snyder 2016: 20.
11. Estreich 2019: 66.
12. Smith and Smith 2021: 288.
13. Smith and Smith 2021: 289.

Bibliography

Adorno, Theodor W. 2002a. "On Jazz." *Essays on Music*. Edited by Richard Leppert, translated by Susan H. Gillespie. Berkeley: University of California Press. 470–95.

Adorno, Theodor W. 2002b. "On the Fetish-Character of Music and the Regression of Listening." *Essays on Music*. Edited by Richard Leppert, translated by Susan H. Gillespie. Berkeley: University of California Press. 288–317.

Alberdi Soto, Maite, dir. 2015. *La Once*. Micromundo Productions.

Alberdi Soto, Maite, dir. 2016. *Los niños*. Micromundo Productions.

Alberdi Soto, Maite, dir. 2020. *El agente topo*. Micromundo Productions.

"Anita Follows Innocent's Journey." 2012. *Boston Herald* (April 20). https://www.bostonherald.com/2012/04/20/anita-follows-innocents-journey/

"Anita—La Película." 2011. *Radio María* blog (July 29).

Antebi, Susan. 2009. *Carnal Inscriptions: Spanish American Narratives of Corporeal Difference and Disability*. New York: Palgrave Macmillan.

Antebi, Susan. 2021. *Embodied Archive: Disability in Post-revolutionary Mexican Cultural Production*. Ann Arbor: University of Michigan Press.

Antebi, Susan, and Beth E. Jörgensen. 2016a. "Introduction: A Latin American Context for Disability Studies." *Libre Acceso: Latin American Literature and Film through Disability Studies*. Edited by Antebi and Jörgensen. Albany: SUNY Press. 1–26.

Antebi, Susan, and Beth E. Jörgensen, eds. 2016b. *Libre Acceso: Latin American Literature and Film through Disability Studies*. Albany: SUNY Press.

Arenillas, María Guadalupe, and Michael J. Lazzara. 2016. "Introduction: Latin American Documentary Film in the New Millennium." *Latin American Documentary Film in the New Millennium*. Edited by Arenillas and Lazzara. New York: Palgrave. 1–19.

Ávalos, Etna. 2018. "Discapacidad, feminismo y sexualidad en *Sangre en el ojo* de Lina Meruane." *Revista de Estudios de Género y Sexualidades* 44.1: 37–48.

Balázs, Béla. 1970. *Theory of the Film: Character and Growth of a New Art*. Translated by Edith Bone. New York: Dover.

Balza, Isabel. 2011. "Crítica feminista de la discapacidad: El monstruo como figura de la vulnerabilidad y la exclusión." *Dilemata* 3.7: 57–76.
Barker, Clare, and Stuart Murray. 2010. "Disabling Postcolonialism: Global Disability Cultures and Democratic Criticism." *Journal of Literary and Cultural Disability Studies* 4.3: 219–36.
Barrera, Lola, and Iñaki Peñafiel, dirs. 2006. *¿Qué tienes debajo del sombrero?* Perf.: Judith Scott. Alicia Produce.
Baudrillard, Jean. 1983. *Simulations.* Translated by Paul Foss, Paul Patton, and Philip Beitchman. New York: Semiotext(e).
Benjamin, Adam. 2002. *Making an Entrance. Theory and Practice for Disabled and Non-disabled Dancers.* New York: Routledge.
Bergson, Henri. 1998. *Creative Evolution.* Translated by Arthur Mitchell. Mineola, NY: Dover.
Bergson, Henri. 1912. *Matter and Memory.* Translated Nancy Margaret Paul and W. Scott Palmer. London: G. Allen; New York: Macmillan.
Bergson, Henri. 2001. *Time and Free Will: An Essay on the Immediate Data of Consciousness.* Translated by R. L. Pogson. Mineola, NY: Dover.
Bérubé, Michael. 1996. *Life as We Know It: An Exceptional Child Grows Up.* Boston: Beacon Press.
Bérubé, Michael. 2005. "Disability and Narrative." *PMLA* 120.2: 568–76.
Bérubé, Michael. 2016a. *The Secret Life of Stories: From Don Quixote to Harry Potter, How Understanding Intellectual Disability Transforms the Way We Read.* New York: New York University Press.
Bérubé, Michael. 2016b. *Life as Jamie Knows It: A Father, a Family and an Exceptional Child.* New York: Vintage.
Bogdan, Robert. 1988. *Freak Show: Presenting Human Oddities for Amusement and Profit.* Chicago: University of Chicago Press.
Bohrer Gilbert, Ana Cristina. 2017. "Narrativas sobre síndrome de Down no Festival Internacional de Filmes sobre Deficiência Assim Vivemos." *Interface* 21.60: 111–21.
Bou, Enric. 2009. *Panorama crític de la literatura catalana, VI Segle XX: De la postguerra a l'actualitat.* Barcelona: Vicens Vives.
Brogna, Patricia, ed. 2009. *Visiones y revisiones de la discapacidad.* Mexico City: Fondo de Cultura Económica.
Burch, Susan, and Alison Kafer, eds. 2010. *Deaf and Disability Studies: Interdisciplinary Perspectives.* Washington, DC: Gallaudet University Press.
Cabeza, Mateo, dir. 2017. *Que nadie duerme.* Perf.: Jaime García and José Manuel Muñoz. Filmin.es.
Cardenas, Sonia. 2010. *Human Rights in Latin America: A Politics of Terror and Hope.* Philadelphia: University of Pennsylvania Press.
Carey, Alison C. 2009. *On the Margins of Citizenship: Intellectual Disability and Civil Rights in Twentieth-Century America.* Philadelphia: Temple University Press.
Carlson, Licia. 2001. "Cognitive Ableism and Disability Studies: Feminist Reflections on the History of Mental Retardation." *Hypatia* 16.4: 124–46.

Carlson, Licia. 2010. *The Faces of Intellectual Disability: Philosophical Reflections.* Bloomington: Indiana University Press.

CERMI. 2012. "30 años de la LISMI: Un recorrido de inclusión." http://riberdis.cedd.net/bitstream/handle/11181/4273/treinta_años_de_la_LISMI.pdf

Charlton, James I. 1998. *Nothing about Us without Us.* Berkeley: University of California Press.

Checa Puerta, Julio Enrique. 2020. "Festival *ÍDEM*, entre producción y creación artística." *Inclusión, integración, diferenciación: La diversidad funcional en la literatura, el cine y las artes escénicas.* Edited by Susanne Hartwig. Berlin: Peter Lang. 23–38.

Checa Puerta, Julio Enrique. 2021. "*En vano*: Explorar los límites de la danza inclusiva." *Ficciones y límtes: La diversidad funcional en las artes escéncias, la literatura, el cine y el arte sonoro.* Edited by Alba Gómez García, David Navarro, and Javier Luis Velloso Álvarez. Berlin: Peter Lang. 85–102.

Chivers, Sally. 2011. *The Silvering Screen: Old Age and Disability in Cinema.* Toronto: University of Toronto Press.

Chivers, Sally, and Nicole Markotić. 2010a. "Introduction." *The Problem Body: Projecting Disability on Film.* Edited by Chivers and Markotić. Columbus: Ohio State University Press. 1–21.

Chivers, Sally, and Nicole Markotić, eds. 2010b. *The Problem Body: Projecting Disability on Film.* Columbus: Ohio State University Press.

Cohen, William I., Lynn Nadel, and Myra E. Madnick, eds. 2002. *Down Syndrome: Visions for the 21st Century.* New York: Wiley-Liss.

Collin, Len, dir. 2016. *Sanctuary.* Perf.: Charlene Kelly and Kieran Coppinger.

Collin, Len. 2020. "Shooting Actors Who Have Intellectual Disabilities: A Reflexive Analysis on the Making of the Feature Film *Sanctuary*." *Disability and Dissensus: Strategies of Disability Representation and Inclusion in Contemporary Culture.* Edited by Katarzyna Ojrzyńska and Maciej Wieczorek. Leiden: Brill. 217–35.

Contardi, Anna. 2002. "From Autonomy to Work Placement." *Down Syndrome across the Life Span.* Edited by Monica Cuskelly, Anne Jobling, and Susan Buckley. Philadelphia: Whurr. 139–46.

Corbin, Megan. 2012. "Neutralizing Consent: The Maternal Look and the Returned Gaze in *El infarto del alma*." *Lucero* 22.1: 55–75.

Corro, Pablo, Carolina Larraín, Maite Alberdi, and Camila van Diest. 2007. *Teorías del cine documental chileno, 1957–1973.* Santiago: Pontificia Universidad Católica de Chile.

Corro Penjean, Pablo. 2016. "Experiencia, técnica y territorio en el documental chileno de fines de los cincuenta." *Literatura y lingüística* 34: 55–70.

Couser, G. Thomas. 2013. "Disability, Life Narration and Representation." *The Disability Studies Reader.* Edited by Lennard J. Davis. London: Routledge. 456–59.

Couser, G. Thomas. 2002. "Signifying Bodies: Life Writing and Disability Studies." *Disability Studies: Enabling the Humanities.* Edited by Susan L. Snyder, Brenda J. Brueggemann, and Rosemary Garland-Thomson. New York: Modern Language Association. 109–17.

Couser, G. Thomas. 2009. *Signifying Bodies: Disability in Contemporary Life Writing*. Ann Arbor: University of Michigan Press.
Couser, G. Thomas. 2011. "Introduction: Disability and Life Writing." *Journal of Literary and Cultural Disability Studies* 5.3: 229–42.
Davenport, Reid, dir. 2022. *I Didn't See You There*. Perf.: Reid Davenport. Ajna Films.
Dalmau, Jordi, and Miquel Bataller. 2015. "D'una carta a un pregó." *Revista de Girona* 291: 44–46.
Davis, Lennard J. 1997. "Introduction: The Need for Disability Studies." *The Disability Studies Reader*. Edited by Davis. New York: Routledge. 1–6.
Davis, Lennard J. 2013. *The End of Normal: Identity in a Biocultural Era*. Ann Arbor: University of Michigan Press.
Debord, Guy. 1995. *The Society of the Spectacle*. Translated by Donald Nicholson-Smith. New York: Zone Books.
Deleuze, Gilles. 2001. *Empiricism and Subjectivity: An Essay on Hume's Theory of Human Nature*. Translated by Constantin V. Boundas. New York: Columbia University Press.
De los Ríos, Valeria, and Catalina Donoso Pinto. 2016. "Apuntes sobre el documental chileno contemporáneo." *Revista Nuestra América* 10 (January–July): 207–19.
"Derechos humanos y discapacidad. Informe España 2009." 2009. La delegación del CERMI Estatal para la Convención de la ONU.
Diehl, Lis Marie. 2012. "Menschen mit Behinderung als professionelle Schauspieler: Das Modell Künstlerarbeitsplatz." *Theater und Öffentlichkeit: Theatervermittlung als Problem*. Edited by Myrna-Alice Prinz-Kiesbüye, Yvonne Schmidt, and Pia Strickler. Zurich: Chronos. 141–58.
Dobzhansky, Theodosius. 1995. "Differences Are Not Deficits." *The Bell Curve Debate: History Documents, Opinions*. Edited by Russell Jacoby and Naomi Glauberman. New York: Times Books. 630–39.
Dolmage, Jay Timothy. 2017. *Academic Ableism: Disability and Higher Education*. Ann Arbor: University of Michigan Press.
Douzinas, Costas. 2010. "*Adikia*: On Communism and Rights." *The Idea of Communism*. Edited by Costas Douzinas and Slavoj Žižek. London: Verso. 81–100.
Dowling, Chris, dir. 2014. *Where Hope Grows*. Perf.: David De Sanctis. Godspeed Pictures.
Eltit, Diamela, and Paz Errázuriz. 1994. *El infarto del alma*. Santiago de Chile: F. Zegers.
Enns, Anthony, and Christopher R. Smit. 2001. "Introduction." *Screening Disability: Essays on Cinema and Disability*. Edited by Enns and Smit. Lanham, MD: University Press of America. ix–xviii.
Espinàs, Josep. 2016. *El teu nom és Olga*. Barcelona: La Campana.
Estreich, George. 2013. *The Shape of the Eye: A Memoir*. New York: Penguin.
Estreich, George. 2019. *Fables and Futures: Biotechnology, Disability, and the Stories We Tell Ourselves*. Cambridge, MA: MIT Press.
Fanon, Frantz. 1965. *A Dying Colonialism*. Translated by Haakon Chevalier. New York: Grove.

Farelly, Bobby, dir. 2023. *Champions*. Perf.: Kevin Iannucci, Madison Tevlin, and Matthew Von Der Ahe. Focus Films.
Ferrusola, Marta. 1989. "Los diez libros de mi vida." *El Ciervo* 38.461/462 (July–August): 8.
Fesser, Javier, dir. 2018. *Campeones*. Perf.: Gloria Ramos. Morena Films.
Fiedler, Leslie. 1978. *Freaks: Myths and Images of the Secret Self*. New York: Simon and Schuster.
Finger, Anne. 2004. "Writing Disabled Lives: Beyond the Singular." *PMLA* 120.2: 610–15.
Francis, Leslie P. 2009. "Understanding Autonomy in Light of Intellectual Disability." *Disability and Disadvantage*. Edited by Kimberley Brownlee and Adam Cureton. Oxford: Oxford University Press. 200–215.
Fraser, Benjamin. 2010. "The Work of (Creating) Art: Judith Scott's Fiber Art, Lola Barrera and Iñaki Peñafiel's *¿Qué tienes debajo del sombrero?* (2006) and the Challenges Faced by People With Developmental Disabilities." *Cultural Studies* 24.4: 508–32.
Fraser, Benjamin. 2013a. *Disability Studies and Spanish Culture: Films, Novels, the Comic and the Public Exhibition*. Liverpool: Liverpool University Press.
Fraser, Benjamin. 2013b. "Salvador García Jiménez, 'autor de minorías': La novela *Angelicomio* (1981) y el modelo social de la discapacidad." *Bulletin of Spanish Studies* 90.8: 1339–56.
Fraser, Benjamin, ed. 2016. *Cultures of Representation: Disability in World Cinema Contexts*. New York: Wallflower Press / Columbia University Press.
Fraser, Benjamin. 2018. *Cognitive Disability Aesthetics: Visual Culture, Disability Representations and the (In)visibility of Cognitive Difference*. Toronto: University of Toronto Press.
Fraser, Benjamin. 2019a. *Visible Cities, Global Comics: Urban Images and Spatial Form*. Jackson: University of Mississippi Press.
Fraser, Benjamin. 2019b. "Joaquim Jordà and Núria Villazán's *Mones com la Becky* [Monkeys like Becky] (1999) and the New Global Disability Documentary Cinema." *Disability Studies Quarterly* 39.2: no pag. https://dsq-sds.org/article/view/5902
Fraser, Benjamin. 2021. *Obsession, Aesthetics and the Iberian City: The Partial Madness of Urban Planning*. Nashville: Vanderbilt University Press.
Fraser, Benjamin. 2022. *Beyond Sketches of Spain: Tete Montoliu and the Construction of Iberian Jazz*. Oxford: Oxford University Press.
Galdon, Anna, and Sergio Ruiz. 2021. "L'èxit d'un cromosoma més." *Capçalera* 187 (June): 66–71.
Gallardo, María, and Miguel Gallardo. 2007. *María y yo*. Bilbao: Astiberri.
Gallardo, María, and Miguel Gallardo. 2015. *María cumple 20 años*. Bilbao: Astiberri.
Galvão, Marcelo, dir. 2012. *Colegas*. Perf.: Ariel Goldenberg, Breno Viola, and Rita Pokk. Gatacine.
Garland-Thomson. Rosemarie, ed. 1996. *Freakery: Cultural Spectacles of the Extraordinary Body*. New York: New York University Press.

Garland-Thomson, Rosemarie. 1997. *Extraordinary Bodies: Figuring Physical Disability in American Culture and Literature.* New York: Columbia University Press.

Garland-Thomson, Rosemarie. 2002. "Integrating Disability, Transforming Feminist Theory." *Feminisms Redux: An Anthology of Literary Theory and Criticism.* Edited by Robyn Warhol-Down and Diane Price Herndl. New Brunswick, NJ: Rutgers University Press. 487–513.

Garland-Thomson, Rosemarie. 2005. "Disability and Representation." *PMLA* 120.2: 522–27.

Garland-Thomson, Rosemarie. 2009. *Staring: How We Look.* Oxford: Oxford University Press.

Garvía, Roberto. 2017. *Organizing the Blind: The Case of ONCE in Spain.* New York: Routledge.

Garrido-Cumbrera, Marco, Jorge Chacón-García, Olta Braçe, and Johannes Schädler. 2016. "The Convention on the Rights of Persons with Disabilities UN: Analysis of the Implementation in Andalucía (Spain) of Article 33." *Revista Chilena de Terapia Ocupacional* 16.2: 119–26.

Gill, Michael. 2015. *Already Doing It: Intellectual Disability and Sexual Agency.* Minneapolis: University of Minnesota Press.

Gill, Michael. 2016. "Refusing Chromosomal Pairing: Inclusion, Masculinity, Sexuality and Intimacy in *Yo, también* (2009)." *Cultures of Representation: Disability in World Cinema Contexts.* Edited by Benjamin Fraser. New York: Wallflower Press. 47–62.

Goldstein, Kevin. 2016. "La cara que me mira: Demythologizing Blindness in Borges's Disability Life Writing." *Libre Acceso: Latin American Literature and Film through Disability Studies.* Edited by Susan Antebi and Beth E. Jörgensen. Albany: SUNY Press. 47–61.

Gómez, Alba, David Navarro, and Javier Velloso. 2018. "Introducción: Sobre límites, imágenes ficcionales y realidades diversas." In *Ficciones y límites: La diversidad funcional en las artes escénicas, la literatura, el cine y el arte sonoro.* Edited by Gómez, Navarro, and Velloso. Berlin: Peter Lang. 9–21.

Gregori, Carme. 2000. "El caminant de la terra: Els primers llibres de viatges de Josep M. Espinàs." *Caplletra* 28: 121–44.

Grosz, Elizabeth. 2004. *The Nick of Time: Politics, Evolution, and the Untimely.* Durham, NC: Duke University Press.

Grosz, Elizabeth. 2005. *Time Travels: Feminism, Nature, Power.* Durham, NC: Duke University Press.

Gull, Jane, dir. 2016. *My Feral Heart.* Perf.: Steven Brandon. Studio Soho.

Handler, Richard. 1988. *Nationalism and the Politics of Cultures in Quebec.* Madison: University of Wisconsin Press.

Hartwig, Susanne. 2019. "Espacio(s) teatral(es) y diversidad funcional." *Revista de Literatura* 91.161: 57–76.

Hartwig, Susanne. 2020a. "Introducción: Representar la diversidad funcional." *¿Discapacidad? Literatura, teatro y cine hispánicos vistos desde los disability studies.* Edited by Hartwig. Berlin: Peter Lang. 7–21.

Hartwig, Susanne. 2020b. "La diversidad funcional como parábola social: *El hijo de la novia* (2001) y *Anita* (2009)." *Iberoamericana XX* 74: 185–201.
Hartwig, Susanne. 2021. "*Undoing disability* en el teatro inclusivo." *Ficciones y límtes: La diversidad funcional en las artes escéncias, la literatura, el cine y el arte sonoro.* Edited by Alba Gómez García, David Navarro, and Javier Luis Velloso Álvarez. Berlin: Peter Lang. 65–84.
Hayles, N. Katherine. 1999. *How We Became Posthuman: Virtual Bodies in Cybernetics, Literature, and Informatics*. Chicago: University of Chicago Press.
Herr, Stanley S., Lawrence O. Gostin, and Harold Hongju Koh, eds. 2003. *The Human Rights of Persons with Intellectual Disabilities: Different but Equal*. Oxford: Oxford University Press.
Herrero, Thaís. 2014. "Cinema à base de sol." *Página22* (April): 7.
Huffer, Lynn. 2009. *Mad for Foucault: Rethinking the Foundations of Queer Theory*. New York: Columbia University Press.
Jackman, Mick, dir. 2010. *Temple Grandin*. Perf.: Claire Danes. HBO Films.
Jarman, Michelle. "Entanglements of Disability, Ethnicity, and Relations: Orienting toward Belonging in George Estreichs's *The Shape of the Eye*." *Journal of American Culture* 36.3 (2013): 194–205.
Jörgensen, Beth E. 2016. "Negotiating the Geographies of Inclusion and Access: Life Writing by Gabriela Brimmer and Ekiwah Adler-Beléndez." *Libre Acceso: Latin American Literature and Film through Disability Studies*. Edited by Susan Antebi and Beth E. Jörgensen. Albany: SUNY Press. 63–79.
Jörgensen, Beth E. 2020. "La escritura autobiográfica de la discapacidad: La teoría articulada en primera persona." *Inclusión, integración, diferenciación: La diversidad funcional en la literatura, el cine y las artes escénicas*. Edited by Susanne Hartwig. Berlin: Peter Lang. 71–88.
Juárez-Almendros, Encarnación. 2013. "Disability Studies in the Hispanic World: Proposals and Methodologies." Special section of the *Arizona Journal of Hispanic Cultural Studies* 18: 151–261.
Juárez-Almendros, Encarnación. 2017. *Disabled Bodies in Early Modern Spanish Literature: Prostitutes, Aging Women and Saints*. Liverpool: Liverpool University Press.
Kafer, Alison. 2013. *Feminist Queer Crip*. Bloomington: Indiana University Press.
Kellner, Douglas. 2019. "Jean Baudrillard." *The Stanford Encyclopedia of Philosophy*. Winter 2019 edition. Edited by Edward N. Zalta. https://plato.stanford.edu/archives/win2019/entries/baudrillard/
King, Loren. 2012. "*Anita*: Lost Soul Adrift in Argentina." *Boston Globe* (April 20). http://archive.boston.com/ae/movies/articles/2012/04/20/anita_puts_a_face_on_argentinas_lost_souls/
Kittay, Eva Feder. 1999. *Love's Labor: Essays on Equality, Dependence and Care*. New York: Routledge.
Kittay, Eva Feder. 2001. "When Caring Is Just and Justice Is Caring: Justice and Mental Retardation." *Public Culture* 13.3: 557–79.
Kittay, Eva Feder, and Licia Carlson, eds. 2010. *Cognitive Disability and Its Challenge to Moral Philosophy*. Malden, MA: Wiley-Blackwell.

Kittay, Eva Feder, with Bruce Jennings and Angela A. Wasunna. 2005. "Dependency, Difference and the Global Ethic of Longterm Care." *Journey of Political Philosophy* 13.4: 443–69.

Lane, Harlan. 1993. *The Mask of Benevolence: Disabling the Deaf Community*. New York: Vintage.

Lefebvre, Henri. 2002. *Critique of Everyday Life*. Vol. 2. Translated by John Moore. New York: Verso.

Lefebvre, Henri. 2005. *Critique of Everyday Life*. Vol. 3. Translated Gregory Elliott. New York: Verso.

Lefebvre, Henri. 2008. *Critique of Everyday Life*. Vol. 1. Translated by John Moore. New York: Verso.

Lerner, Justin, dir. 2010. *Girlfriend*. Perf.: Evan Sneider. Wayne / Lauren Film Company.

Leuzinger, Mirjam. 2020. "¿Hacia un séptimo arte inclusivo? El cine brasileño a través del prisma de los *disability studies*." *Inclusión, integración, diferenciación: La diversidad funcional en la literatura, el cine y las artes escénicas*. Edited by Susanne Hartwig. Berlin: Peter Lang. 293–308.

Lindstrom, Naomi. 2018. "Afterword: Film Studies, Jewish Studies, Latin American Studies." *Evolving Images: Jewish Latin American Cinema*. Edited by Nora Glickman and Ariana Huberman. Austin: University of Texas Press. 225–34.

Lloyd, David. 1997. "Nationalisms against the State." *The Politics of Culture in the Shadow of Capital*. Edited by Lisa Lowe and David Lloyd. Durham, NC: Duke University Press. 256–81.

Luzzani, Tomás. 2009. "Anita." *A Sala Llena* blog (August 27). https://asalallena.com.ar/anita/

MacGregor, John. 1999. *Metamorphosis: The Fiber Art of Judith Scott*. Oakland: Creative Growth Art Center.

Maldonado Ramírez, Jhonatthan. 2015. "Repensar el cuidado desde la experiencia de la interdependencia: Una aproximación antropológica a cuidadores del sujeto disagnosticado con syndrome de Down en la ciudad de Puebla." *Memorias virtuales seminario internacional género y cuidado: Teorías escenarios y políticas*. Bogotá: Universidad Nacional de Colombia. 40–59.

Maldonado Ramírez, Jhonatthan. 2016. "Verificación clínica: Apuntes etnográficos sobre la experiencia progenitora del Síndrome de Down." *Tratado breve de concupiscencias y prodigios*. Edited by Mauricio List Reyes and Fabián Giménez Gatto. Mexico City: La Cifra Editiorial. 59–76.

Maldonado Ramírez, Jhonatthan. 2017. "¿Quién habla por? La semiótica de representación en la ventriloquial capacitista." *Graffylia* 15.25 (July–December): 141–51.

Maldonado Ramírez, Jhonatthan. 2018. "Sexualidad y syndrome de Down: ¿Crees que ellos no quieren tocar y ser tocados?" *Salud y sexualidad: La salud frente a las diversas sexualidades*. Edited by Andrea Avilez Ortega and Adriana Virgen Gatica. Mexico City: Fundación Arcoíris por el Respeto a la Diversidad Sexual. 61–71.

Marr, Matthew J. 2013. *The Politics of Age and Disability in Contemporary Spanish Film.* New York: Routledge.

Marx, Karl. 1977. "Private Property and Communism." *Karl Marx: Selected Writings.* Edited by David McLellan. Oxford: Oxford University Press. 87–96.

Matheou, Demetrios. 2017. "*The Grown-Ups* Interview: Moving Documentary Casts Down's Syndrome in a New Light." *British Film Institute* blog, November 9.

McDonagh, Patrick, C. F. Goodey, and Tim Stanton, eds. 2018a. *Intellectual Disability: A Conceptual History, 1200–1900.* Manchester: Manchester University Press.

McDonagh, Patrick, C. F. Goodey, and Tim Stanton. 2018b. "Introduction: The Emergent Critical History of Intellectual Disability." *Intellectual Disability: A Conceptual History, 1200–1900.* Edited by McDonagh, Goodey, and Stanton. Manchester: Manchester University Press. 1–25.

McRuer, Robert. 1997. *The Queer Renaissance: Contemporary American Literature and the Reinvention of Lesbian and Gay Identities.* New York: New York University Press.

McRuer, Robert. 2010. "Disability Nationalism in Crip Times." *Journal of Literary and Cultural Disability Studies* 4.2: 163–78.

McRuer, Robert. 2018. *Crip Times: Disability Globalization, and Resistance.* New York: New York University Press.

McRuer, Robert, and Anna Mollow, eds. 2012. *Sex and Disability.* Durham, NC: Duke University Press.

Merrifield, Andy. 2002. *Metromarxism: A Marxist Tale of the City.* New York: Routledge.

Meruane, Lena. 2016. "Blind Spot: (Notes on Reading Blindness)." *Libre Acceso: Latin American Literature and Film through Disability Studies.* Edited by Susan Antebi and Beth E. Jörgensen. Albany: SUNY Press. 29–46.

Migliori, Alberto, et al. 2007. "Integrated Employment or Sheltered Workshops: Preferences of Adults with Intellectual Disabilities, Their Families, and Staff." *Journal of Vocational Rehabilitation* 26: 5–19.

Minich, Julie A. 2014. *Accessible Citizenships: Disability, Nation and the Cultural Politics of Greater Mexico.* Philadelphia: Temple University Press.

Mitchell, David T. 2000. "Body Solitaire: The Singular Subject of Disability Autobiography." *American Quarterly* 52.2: 311–15.

Mitchell, David T., Susan Antebi, and Sharon L. Snyder. 2019a. "Introduction." *The Matter of Disability: Materiality, Biopolitics, Crip Affect.* Edited by Mitchell, Antebi, and Snyder. Ann Arbor: University of Michigan Press. 1–36.

Mitchell, David T., Susan Antebi, and Sharon L. Snyder, eds. 2019b. *The Matter of Disability: Materiality, Biopolitics, Crip Affect.* Ann Arbor: University of Michigan Press.

Mitchell, David T., and Sharon L. Snyder. 2000. *Narrative Prosthesis: Disability and the Dependencies of Discourse.* Ann Arbor: University of Michigan Press.

Mitchell, David T., and Sharon L. Snyder. 2010. "Introduction: Ablenationalism and the Geo-politics of Disability." *Journal of Literary and Cultural Disability Studies* 4.2: 113–25.

Mitchell, David T., and Sharon L. Snyder. 2015. *The Biopolitics of Disability: Neoliberalism, Ablenationalism and Peripheral Embodiment.* Ann Arbor: University of Michigan Press.

Mitchell, David T., and Sharon L. Snyder. 2016. "Global In(ter)dependent Disability Cinema: Targeting Ephemeral Domains of Belief and Cultivating Aficionados of the Body." *Cultures of Representation: Disability in World Cinema Contexts.* Edited by Benjamin Fraser. New York: Wallflower Press. 1–17.

Mocarzel, Evaldo, dir. 2005. *Do Luto à Luta.* Brasil: Casa Azul Produções Artísticas / Circuito Espaço de Cinema.

Mogk, Marja Evelyn, ed. 2013a. *Different Bodies.* Jefferson, NC: McFarland Press.

Mogk, Marja Evelyn. 2013b. "Introduction." *Different Bodies.* Jefferson, NC: McFarland Press. 1–16.

Morris, M. 2002. "Economic Independence and Inclusion." *Down Syndrome: Visions for the 21st Century.* Edited by William I. Cohen, Lynn Nadel, and Myra E. Madnick. New York: Wiley-Liss. 17–81.

Moscoso, Melania. 2020. "La discapacidad más allá del relato: La abyección física en la vida social y la cultura contemporánea." *Papeles del CEIC* 2: 1–11. http://dx.doi.org/10.1387/pceic.21839

Moscoso, Melania, and R. Lucas Platero. 2017. "Cripwashing: The Abortion Debates at the Crossroads of Gender and Disability in the Spanish Media." *Continuum: Journal of Media & Cultural Studies* 31.3: 470–81.

Moscoso, Melania, and R. Lucas Platero. 2020. "The Production of 'Dependent Individuals' within the Application of Spanish Law 39/2006 on Personal Autonomy and Dependent Care in Andalusia, Basque Country and Madrid." *The Legacies of Institutionalisation: Disability Law and Policy in the "Deinstitutionalised" Community.* Edited by Claire Spivakovsky, Linda Steele, and Penelope Weller. Oxford: Hart. 207–19.

Motta da Silveira, Gilca Maria, dir. 2013. "Meu olhar diferente sobre as coisas." http://www.meensina.org.br/site/2016/02/assista-o-documentario-meu-olhar-diferente-sobre-as-coisas/. Accessed April 30, 2019.

Mouesca, Jacqueline. 2005. *El documental chileno.* Santiago: LOM.

Movimento Down. 2013. "*Colegas* emociona o público em pré-estreia no Rio de Janeiro." http://www.movimentodown.org.br/2013/01/colegas-emociona-o-publico-em-pre-estreia-no-rio-de-janeiro/. Accessed September 23, 2018.

Mulvey, Laura. 1999. "Visual Pleasure and Narrative Cinema." *Film Theory and Criticism: Introductory Readings.* Edited by Leo Braudy and Marshall Cohen. New York: Oxford University Press. 833–44.

Murray, Stuart. 2020. *Disability and the Posthuman: Bodies, Technology, and Cultural Futures.* Liverpool: Liverpool University Press.

Naharro, Antonio, and Álvaro Pastor, dirs. 2009. *Yo, también.* Perf.: Pablo Pineda. Match Factory.

Nascimento, Liara Pires Barcelos do, and Luciana Sparsa Menegasso. 2017. "*Cole-*

gas: Analise crítica do filme frente ao preconceito da sociedade." *Direito e cinema temático*. Anais do III Simpósio Regional Direito e Cinema em Debate. Edited by Fernando de Brito Alves. Jacarezinho, PR: UENP & PROJURIS. 130–45.

Nichols, Bill. 1991. *Representing Reality*. Bloomington: Indiana University Press.

Nichols, Bill. 2013. *Introducción al documental*. Translated by Miguel Bustos García. Mexico City: Universidad Nacional Autónoma de México.

Nilson, Tyler, and Michael Schwartz. 2019. *Peanut Butter Falcon*. Perf.: Zak Gottsagen. Armory Films.

Norden, Martin F. 1994. *Cinema of Isolation: A History of Physical Disability in the Movies*. New Brunswick, NJ: Rutgers University Press.

Novell, Pepa. 2009. "Cantautoras catalanas: De la *nova cançó* a la *nova cançó d'ara*: El paso y el peso del pasado." *Journal of Spanish Cultural Studies* 10.2: 135–47.

Nussbaum, Martha C. 2009. *Frontiers of Justice: Disability, Nationality, Species Membership*. Cambridge, MA: Belknap/Harvard University Press.

O'Toole, Corbett. 2013. "Disclosing Our Relationships to Disabilities: An Invitation for Disability Studies Scholars." *Disability Studies Quarterly* 33.2: no pag.

Paglieri, Rodrigo. 2012. "De arteiro a artista: A saga de um menino com síndrome de Down." https://www.youtube.com/watch?v=E3kdnGkZNWs. Accessed April 30, 2019.

Parrilla, Arturo, dir. *En vano*. 2016. Perf.: Jaime García and José Manuel Muñoz. Danza Mobile.

Peebles, Alison, dir. 2003. *After-Life*. Perf.: Paula Sage. Gabriel Films.

Piepmeier, Alison. 2012. "Saints, Sages, and Victims: Endorsement of and Resistance to Cultural Stereotypes in Memoirs by Parents of Children with Disabilities." *Disability Studies Quarterly* 32.1: no pag.

Pinto, Iván. 2009. "Cine, política, memoria: Nuevos entramados en el documental chileno." *Cinémas d'Amérique Latine* 17: 12–25.

Price, Margaret. 2011. "It Shouldn't Be So Hard." *Inside Higher Ed* (February 6). https://www.insidehighered.com/advice/2011/02/07/it-shouldnt-be-so-hard

Quayson, Ato. 2007. *Aesthetic Nervousness: Disability and the Crisis of Representation*. New York: Columbia University Press.

Resina, Joan Ramon, ed. 2019. *Inscribed Identities: Life Writing as Self-Realization*. London: Routledge.

Sánchez, José A. 2009. "La mirada y el tiempo." *Arquitecturas de la mirada*. Edited by Ana Buitrago. Alcalá de Henares: Ediciones de la Universidad de Alcalá. 13–55.

Schejbal, Jan, and David Utrera. 2004. "Les traduccions en txec i eslovac d'obres literàries catalanes i viceversa." *Quaderns: Revista de traducció* 11: 45–57.

Sedgwick, Eve Kosofsky. 2003. *Touching Feeling: Affect, Pedagogy and Performativity*. Durham, NC: Duke University Press.

Sette, Renata, dir. 2014. *Outro olhar*. Brasil: Maria Farinha Filmes.

Sette, Renata, dir. 2015. *Outro olhar: Convivendo com a diferença*. Brasil: Maria Farinha Filmes.

Shapiro, J. P. 1994. *No Pity*. New York: Three Rivers.

Siebers, Tobin. 2008. *Disability Theory*. Ann Arbor: University of Michigan Press.
Siebers, Tobin. 2010. *Disability Aesthetics*. Ann Arbor: University of Michigan Press.
Siebers, Tobin. 2013. "Disability and the Theory of Complex Embodiment." *The Disability Studies Reader*. Edited by Lennard J. Davis. 4th ed. New York: Routledge. 275–82.
Siebers, Tobin. 2019. "Returning the Social to the Social Model." *The Matter of Disability: Materiality, Biopolitics, Crip Affect*. Edited by David T. Mitchell, Susan Antebi, and Susan L. Snyder. Ann Arbor: University of Michigan Press. 39–47.
Simpson, Murray K. 2018. "Idiocy and the Conceptual Economy of Madness." *Intellectual Disability: A Conceptual History, 1200–1900*. Edited by Patrick McDonagh, C. F. Goodey, and Tim Stanton. Manchester: Manchester University Press. 190–210.
Smith, Sharon, and Kieron Smith. 2021. "Down Syndrome as Pure Simulacrum." *Journal of Literary and Cultural Disability Studies* 15.3: 287–305.
Smith, Sidonie. 2019. "Autobiographical Inscription and the Identity Assemblage." *Inscribed Identities: Life Writing as Self-Realization*. Edited by J. R. Resina. London: Routledge. 75–90.
Smith, Sidonie, and Julia Watson. 2018. *Life Writing in the Long Run: A Smith and Watson Autobiography*. Ann Arbor: University of Michigan Press.
Snyder, Sharon L., Brenda J. Brueggemann, and Rosemarie Garland-Thomson, eds. 2002. *Disability Studies: Enabling the Humanities*. New York: Modern Language Association.
Snyder, Sharon L., and David T. Mitchell. 2006. *Cultural Locations of Disability*. Chicago: University of Chicago Press.
Snyder, Sharon L., and David T. Mitchell. 2010. "Body Genres: An Anatomy of Disability in Film." *The Problem Body: Projecting Disability on Film*. Edited by Sally Chivers and Nicole Markotić. Columbus: Ohio State University Press. 179–204.
Stavans, Ilan. 2016. *Borges, the Jew*. Albany: SUNY Press.
Stiker, Henri-Jacques. 1997. *A History of Disability*. Translated by William Sayers. Ann Arbor: University of Michigan Press.
Straus, Joseph N. 2013. "Autism as Culture." *The Disability Studies Reader*. 4th ed. Edited by Lennard J. Davis. New York: Routledge. 460–84.
Thomas, Carol. 1999. *Female Forms: Disability, Human Rights, and Society*. London: Open University Press.
Titchkosky, Tanya. 2011. *The Question of Access: Disability, Space, Meaning*. Toronto: University of Toronto Press.
Trias Trueta, Andy. 2018. *Ignorant la SD: Memòries i reflexions*. Barcelona: Fundació Catalana Síndrome de Down.
Valderrama Vega, Esmeralda. 2020. "¿Qué es Danza Mobile?" *Inclusión, integración, diferenciación: La diversidad funcional en la literatura, el cine y las artes escénicas*. Edited by Susanne Hartwig. Berlin: Peter Lang. 67.
Vallée, Jean Marc, dir. 2011. *Café de Flore*. Perf.: Marin Gerrier.
Van Dormael, Jaco. 1995. *The Kiss*. Included with *Lumière et compagnie*. Cinétévé / Fox Lorber, Belgium.

Vargas, Karina. 2016. "El ángel exterminador." *Milenio* (September 29). https://www.milenio.com/blogs/qrr/carlos-velazquez-el-alien-y-yo

Veronezi, Daniela Priscila de Oliveira. 2018. "Constuçao do sujeito com síndrome de *Down* no cinema brasileiro: Estudo do dispositivo de inclusão social a partir do filme 'Colegas.'" Thesis, Mestre em Comunicação. Universidade Federal de Goiás, Faculdade de Informação e Comunicação.

Vértiz de la Fuente, Columba. 2016. "'El alien y yo,' comedia sobre el Síndrome de Down." *Proceso* 2083 (October 2): 72–74.

Villa, Rafael. 1990. "Josep M. Espinàs, l'ofici de pensar." *Revista del Centre de Lectura de Reus*: 4–5.

Vohnsen, Mirna. 2018. "Revisiting the AMIA Bombing in Marcos Carnevale's *Anita*." *Evolving Images: Jewish Latin American Cinema*. Edited by Nora Glickman and Ariana Huberman. Austin: University of Texas Press. 73–88.

Vohnsen, Mirna. 2019. *Portrayals of Jews in Contemporary Argentine Cinema: Rethinking Argentinidad*. Woodbridge: Tamesis.

Wayne Tan, Wei Yu. 2021. *Blind in Early Japan*. Ann Arbor: University of Michigan.

Wehman, Paul. 1995. "Supported Employment for People with Disabilities: What Progress Has Been Made?" *Down Syndrome: Living and Learning in the Community*. Edited by Lynn Nadel and Donna Rosenthal. New York: Wiley-Liss. 263–75.

Wolfe, Cary. 2010. *What Is Posthumanism?* Minneapolis: University of Minnesota Press.

Zacco, María. 2017. "*Los niños*: El filme chileno que cambió una ley." *ANSA Latina* (April 15).

Zuin, Luiz Fernando, Fátima Elisabeth Denari, and Aparecido Renan Vicente. 2021. "Sexualidade e deficiência: Reflexões a partir de um curta metragem." *Ensino & Pesquisa, União da Vitória* 19.2: 216–26.

Index

Abbas, Asma, 29
ableism
   barriers to autonomy, 64, 69, 132
   construction of normality, 48–50
   disability as lack, 9, 37, 48, 93–94, 137
   eugenics, 20, 26, 38, 95
   false promise of inclusion, 36
   and individualism, 29, 44
   infantilization, 13, 42, 49, 65, 94, 128, 134
   and institutionalization, 47, 81–82, 95, 128
   mask of benevolence, 95
   misrepresentation, 11, 53
   and neoliberalism, 5, 29, 36
   parasitism in, 23–24
   and prenatal testing, 4, 20–21, 25, 52, 95
   neurotypical self-isolation, 75
   stigma, 17, 50, 52, 133–35
   in university structures, 142
Adorno, Theodor W., 132
Andorra, 54
Antebi, Susan, 5–8, 22–25, 28–31, 40, 69–70, 119–20, 140–41, 146n16
Arenillas, María Guadalupe, 58–59, 67
Argentina, 2, 10, 14, 61, 88, 116, 118–20
art. See dance; drawing; fashion; fiber art; film; literature; museums; music; photography; sculpture; theater;
art brut, 3
autism, 15, 34, 36, 46–47, 51, 116

Balázs, Béla, 69–71
Bérubé, Jaime, 37, 39–40
Bérubé, Michael, 17, 20, 37–40, 92, 133, 142
Barthes, Roland, 16
Baudrillard, Jean, 92, 94–96
Bohrer Gilbert, Ana Cristina, 59–60
Brandon, Steven, 77
Brazil, 2, 13, 54, 57–60, 77–78, 86, 88, 144
Butler, Judith, 9

Canada, 77
Cañadas, Manuel, 13, 88, 99, 103–4
Carlson, Licia, 35–36
Castells, Manuel, 4
Catalan/Catalunya, 1–2, 7, 12, 34, 41, 43, 45–46, 51, 55, 140
Checa Puerta, Julio Enrique, 13, 98–100
Charlton, James, 18, 35
Chile, 2, 8, 13, 57–59, 63–69, 73–77, 86, 88
Chivers, Sally, 11, 115–16
comics
   Cavall Fort (magazine), 42, 49
   María y yo, 46–47
   María cumple 20 años, 46–47

Coppinger, Kieran, 77
Couser, G. Thomas, 12, 40–41, 43, 51, 53, 55–56

dance, 2, 13, 68–69, 84, 97–99, 109–11. *See also* Danza Mobile.
Danza Mobile, 2, 10, 13, 88, 90, 96–111
Davis, Lennard, 16–18, 26, 29, 69, 116
deafness, 61
Deafness, xii, xv, 146n17
Debord, Guy, 93, 95
De la Fuente, Paco, 2, 14, 116–17, 131–37, 139
Deleuze, Gilles, 41
De Sanctis, David, 77
disability
  and art, 3–4, 11
  cerebral palsy, 106–7
  and colonization, 22, 52
  construction of, 5, 10, 24
  cultural location, 90, 11
  and democracy, 10, 29, 36–37, 39, 41
  as epistemological construction, 4–5, 9–10, 89–90, 113
  and ethics, 22–23, 25, 31, 67, 88, 107, 113, 119–20
  as functional diversity, 87, 131, 133, 163n4
  identity, 4–5, 7, 10, 15–17, 27–32, 36, 40
  and neoliberalism, 27–28, 36, 58–59, 93, 150n8
  and nonproductive labor, 27, 112, 163n83
  social image of, 11, 87, 106–7
  and self-advocacy/representation, 19, 25, 29, 34–36, 39–41, 44, 51–53, 153–54n70
  and technology, 25–26, 141, 148n24
  as (un)knowable, 30, 50, 88, 109, 113
  See also autism; Down syndrome; IDD;
disability organizations
  Aspanias, 12, 55, 154n88
  ASDA, 12

ASTRID21, 12, 43, 55
Catalan Down Syndrome Foundation, 7, 34, 41–43, 45, 54–55
Center for Creative Growth, 61
Chile Inclusion Network, 76
Down España, 6–7
European Down Syndrome Association, 41–42
Éxit21, 12, 43, 54–56, 143
in Mexico, 7
Organization of Disabled Revolutionaries in Nicaragua, 8
Spanish Committee of Representatives of Persons with Disability, 42
World Down Syndrome Congress, 20
disability rights, 4–5, 27, 31, 36, 86
  access to work opportunities, 6, 10, 13, 51, 74–76
  ADA, 9, 17
  Assembly of Human Rights (FCSD), 34, 54
  autonomy, 27, 30, 63–65, 68, 72
  barrier removal, 6, 18–19, 29, 39, 44, 67, 77, 131, 142
  challenges to rights-based models, 7, 31
  financial independence, 62, 74–75
  and Latin America, 7
  low-level agency, 25, 30, 36
  marriage, 13, 34, 51, 62–63, 68–69, 71–73, 80, 82
  movement in US, 8–9, 17–18, 35–37, 39, 59–60, 115, 128–29, 151n25
  movement in UK, 60
  parenthood, 63, 68, 131–32, 136, 143
  sexuality, 9, 14, 62–63, 73–74, 82, 131–32, 135, 146n20, 154n72. *See also* queer studies.
  sturdy citizenship, 25, 29, 36, 43, 45, 144
  and Spain, 7
  ubiquity of representations, 38

UN Convention on the Rights of Persons with Disabilities, 6–7, 59, 76–77
disability studies
  as academic/political project, 4, 8, 17, 28–29, 37, 69, 87, 91, 146n17
  approach to Down syndrome, 2, 91–92
  disability drag, 12, 38, 115–16
  disability ensembles, xiii–xiv, 8, 12–13, 61–63, 65–66, 77–78, 80–86, 94, 100
  feminist, 19, 36
  freak shows, 106, 162n62
  and function, 17, 20, 48–49, 87, 93, 98, 105, 131, 133, 142
  global extension, 1, 5–9, 11, 14, 27–28, 40, 57, 119
  Global South, 8
  and impairment, 5, 18–22, 26, 39, 41, 81, 87, 99, 141
  and inclusion, 11, 13, 29–31, 36–37, 41, 52, 57–59, 63–64, 77–78, 85–87, 97–99, 101, 132–33, 150n7
  interdependence, 19, 31, 36, 64, 88, 113–14, 117–19, 124
  Journal of Literary and Cultural Disability Studies, 6, 13, 90–91, 150n6
  in Latin America, 8
  medical model, 4–5, 17–21, 34, 48–49, 54, 57, 62
  narrative prosthesis, 14, 61, 124, 158n95
  neomaterialist, 23, 25, 37–38, 140–41
  postcolonialist, 24, 145n7
  sadcrip/supercrip, 48, 87, 116
  social model, 4–5, 15–19, 22–25, 34, 38, 48–49, 57, 140
  and staring, 16, 69–70
  in university structures, 6, 28
Dmitriev, Val, 54
Dolmage, Timothy, 142
Down, John Langdon, 15, 20, 43, 93, 95
Down syndrome
  access to education, 6, 43, 63–64, 96, 98, 140
  autonomy, 27, 64, 68, 71–72, 76–77
  cultural/identarian model of, 1, 4, 10, 15, 19–20, 27–28, 30, 34–35, 37, 55, 140
  and early care, 54
  embodiment, 4, 16, 18, 31
  and family members, 35, 45, 53–55, 65, 91, 117, 121–22, 129, 142
  as filmic symbol of human diversity, 59–60
  health risks, 21, 51, 64, 87
  heterogeneity, 34, 50, 81, 93, 95, 105, 137
  (mis)understandings of, 55
  pride in, 20, 22, 90
  as projected image, 87–88, 91–94
  as simulacrum, 91–96
  social image of, 13, 88–89, 91–92, 96, 100, 108–9, 138–39, 143–44
  and tensions within disability studies, 4–5, 16–20, 24–25
  and visibility, 4, 9, 11, 18, 21, 49–50, 55, 59
World Down Syndrome Day, 78
Down syndrome (people with). *See* Bérubé, Jaime; Brandon, Steven; Coppinger, Kieran; De la Fuente, Paco; De Sanctis, David; Espinàs, Olga; García, Jaime; Gerrier, Marin; Goldenberg, Ariel; Gottsagen, Zak; Guzmán, Rita; Iannucci, Kevin; Jirau, Sofía; Kelly, Charlene; Manzo, Alejandra; Martínez, Andrés; Merigo, Giulia de Souza; Mujica, Bryan Russell; Muñoz, José Manuel; Piantino, Lucio; Pineda, Pablo; Pokk, Rita; Ramírez, Tonet; Ramos, Gloria; Rodríguez, Ana; Sage, Paula; Scott, Judith; Sneider, Evan; Springmühl, Isabella; Tevlin, Madison; Trias Trueta, Andy; Urzúa, Ricardo; Viola, Breno; Von Der Ahe, Matthew.

drawing, 16, 47, 111–12
Dublin, 3, 54

Eltit, Diamela, 67
England, 77
Espinàs, Josep M., 2, 7, 12, 33, 35, 41–51, 53, 55–56, 91, 94
Espinàs, Olga, 2, 33–34, 43–50, 53, 55–56
Estreich, George, 20–22, 26, 87–88, 91–92, 143–44

fashion, 1, 14, 139–40
Fanon, Frantz, 22
fiber art, 3
film, 38, 142–43
    as amplification, 141
    the close-up, 69–73
    Brazilian industry, 59
    casting of actors with disabilities, 62, 77, 85
    Chilean documentary tradition, 58, 66–68
    deep focus, 125–26
    disability film festivals, 61, 78
    expository documentary, 106
    interactive documentary, 107
    the gaze, 70
    genre-mixing, 78–81
    incidental treatment of disability, 115, 129, 131
    lone-figure trope, 80–81, 86, 114–15, 117–19
    new disability documentary, 12, 61–63, 68
    observational documentary, 88, 102
    performative documentary 107
    poetic documentary, 107
    reflexive documentary, 106–10, 113
film (directors)
    Alberdi, Maite, 8, 10, 13, 58–77, 79, 86, 88, 94, 128, 142
    Barrera, Lola, 3, 61
    Cabeza, Mateo, 10, 13, 88–90, 96–113, 120

    Carnevale, Marcos, 11, 14, 61, 114–30, 164n19
    Chaskel, Pedro, 67
    Collin, Len, 77–78, 81, 85
    Davenport, Reid, 106–7
    Dowling, Chris, 77
    Galvão, Marcelo, 8, 10, 62, 77–86, 93–94, 158n95
    Gull, Jane, 77
    Jackson, Mick, 116
    Lerner, Justin, 77
    Magaña Vázquez, Jesús, 11, 13, 61, 114–20, 130–38
    Mocarzel, Evaldo, 60
    Naharro, Antonio, 1, 77
    Pastor, Álvaro, 1, 77
    Peebles, Alison, 77
    Peñafiel, Iñaki, 3, 61
    Ríos, Héctor, 67
    Rivero, Breogán, 140
    Sette, Renata, 60, 155n12
    Silveira, Gilca Maria Motta de, 60
    Vallée, Jean Marc, 77
    van Dormael, Jaco, 70
    Vertov, Dziga, 66
    Wiseman, Frederick, 67
film (fiction)
    After-Life, 77
    alien y yo, El, 2, 11, 114–20, 130–38
    Anita, 2, 10–11, 114–130
    Café de Flore, 77
    Campeones, 1
    Champions, 1
    Colegas, 2, 8, 62, 77–86, 93
    Girlfriend, 77
    My Feral Heart, 77
    Peanut Butter Falcon, 1, 61
    Sanctuary, 78, 85
    síndrome Cacareco, A, 1, 140
    Where Hope Grows, 77
    Yo, también, 1, 6, 20, 61, 77, 97, 147n22
film (documentary)
    agente topo, El, 63
    batalla de Chile, La, 58

I Didn't See You There, 106–7
Kiss, The, 70
niños, Los/The Grown-Ups, 2, 62–77
Once, La, 63–64
Praying with Lior, 61
Que nadie duerma, 2, 10, 88–90, 96–113
¿Qué tienes debajo del sombrero?, 3, 61
Testimonio, 67
Titicut Follies, 67
Vital Signs, 9
Foucault, Michel, 9

Galdon, Anna, 43
Gallardo, María, 46–47
Gallardo, Miguel, 46–47
García, Jaime, 2, 13, 88–90, 96–113, 139, 161n59
Garland-Thomson, Rosemarie, 16, 18, 69–70, 162n62
Germany, 98, 142
Gerrier, Marin, 77
Goffman, Erving, 128
Goldenberg, Ariel, 2, 13, 80, 82, 139
Gottsagen, Zak, 1
Gramsci, Antonio, 91
Guatemala, 1, 139–40
Guattari, Félix, 41
Guzmán, Patricio, 58
Guzmán, Rita, 2, 13, 62–65, 69–74, 76, 94, 139

Hartwig, Susanne, 13, 91, 98, 101–2, 105, 109, 123, 128, 142, 159n1, 161n50, 163n4
Hayles, N. Katherine, 25
Huffer, Lynn, 23
humanism, 25–30, 141

Iannucci, Kevin, 1
IDD, 20, 25, 33–38, 48–49, 95, 129, 141, 144. *See also* autism; Down syndrome.
Ireland, 77

Jewishness, 122, 164n12
 AMIA, 14, 119–21, 125–26, 129–30, 164n19
 identity/community, 61, 116–21
 Yiddish, 121
Jirau, Sofía, 1
Jörgensen, Beth, 6–8, 40, 69–70, 146n16
Juárez-Almendros, Encarnación, 6

Kafer, Alison, 10, 18, 27, 35, 85
Kelly, Charlene, 77
Kittay, Eva Feder, 19, 36, 150n12, 156n24
Klein, Jay, 54

Lane, Harlan, 95
Latin America
 dictatorships in, 58–59, 67
 See also individual countries; disability rights (and Latin America); disability studies (in Latin America)
law/legal system, 6–7, 9, 59, 67, 75–76. *See also*, Spain (LISMI).
Lazzara, Michael J., 58–59, 67
Lefebvre, Henri, 93, 95
Leuzinger, Mirjam, 59–60, 79, 84
life writing, 2, 12, 33–56
 autobiography, 40–41, 44–45, 51, 55
 biography, 44, 46
 (co)biography, 44, 46–47, 55
 and dangers of, 46, 53
 embodiment vs. identity, 41
 El teu nom és Olga, 2, 33, 42–47
 Fables and Futures, 20–21
 Ignorant la SD, 2, 34, 51–56
 new disability memoir, 41
Lindstrom, Naomi, 120–21
Linton, Simi, 9
literature, 6, 13, 38–40, 55, 67, 161n53
Lyon, 54

Maldonado Ramírez, Jhonatthan, 8–9, 82, 91, 142, 146n20
Manzo, Alejandra, 2, 14, 116–30, 139

Markotić, Nichole, 11, 115–16
Martínez, Andrés, 2, 13, 62–65, 69–74, 76–77, 94, 139
Marx, Karl, 28, 31, 95–96, 150n12
McRuer, Robert, 9, 18, 25–29, 31, 36
Merigo, Giulia de Souza, 82, 85
Mexico, 2, 6–8, 61, 116, 142
Mitchell, David T., 5, 9, 18–19, 22–26, 35–37, 46, 61–62, 119–20
Mollow, Anna, 26
Morris, Jenny, 19
Moscoso, Melania, 8–9
Mouesca, Jacqueline, 58
Mujica, Bryan Russell, 1, 140
Mulvey, Laura, 70
Muñoz, José Manuel, 2, 13, 88–90, 96–113, 139
Murray, Stuart, 25–28, 30, 141
museums
   Ixchel Museum of Indigenous Textiles and Clothing, 139
   MoMA, 3
   San Francisco Museum of Modern Art, 3
music, 11, 14, 34, 42, 55, 72, 77, 108–10, 116–17, 124, 128. *See also* film (fiction: *alien y yo, El*)

Nicaragua, 8
Nichols, Bill, 107, 113, 157n45
Norden, Martin, 11, 14, 61–62, 114–15, 125

queer studies, 3, 9, 23, 27–28

paintings, 3, 16
Parrilla, Arturo, 13, 88, 99–104, 108–11
Peru, 1, 73, 140
performance. *See* theater.
photography, 16, 67, 87, 129
Piantino, Lucio, 60
Pineda, Pablo, 1, 6, 20, 77
Pokk, Rita, 2, 13, 80–82, 139
posthumanism, 15, 22–30, 141

publishing industry, 33
Puerto Rico, 1

radio (BBC), 43
Ramírez, Tonet, 1, 140
Ramos, Gloria, 1
Resina, Joan Ramon, 40
Rodríguez, Ana, 2, 13, 62–65, 69–74, 76–77, 94, 139
Ruiz, Sergio, 43
Rush, Chris, 16

Sage, Paula, 77
Scotland, 77
Scott, Judith, 3–4, 61, 95
sculpture, 3, 100
Sedgwick, Eve Kosofsky, 3
Siebers, Tobin, 3–5, 10–12, 15, 24, 30–32, 38–39, 115–16
Smith, Kieron, 13, 18, 90–96, 121, 136–37, 139, 142, 144
Smith, Sharon, 13, 18, 90–96, 121, 136–37, 139, 142, 144
Smith, Sidonie, 41, 46
Sneider, Evan, 77
Snyder, Sharon L., 5, 9, 18–19, 22–26, 35–37, 61–62, 119–20
Spain, 77, 98
   Barcelona, 2, 33, 46, 51
   Civil War, 42
   Concèntric record company, 42
   Convergencia i Unió, 51
   Down syndrome population, 43
   Francisco Franco, 7, 42
   Galicia, 54
   Girona, 43
   LISMI, 7, 41–42
   Lleida, 1, 140
   ratification of UN Convention, 6
   Sevilla, 2, 97
Springmühl, Isabella, 1, 139–40
Stavans, Ilan, 120
Stiker, Henri-Jacques, 94–95

Straus, Joseph, 15, 27, 33–34, 36–37, 39, 55, 141, 151n22

television, 6, 51, 67, 74, 78, 91, 140
  Born This Way, 62
  Temple Grandin, 116
Tevlin, Madison, 1
theater, 10.
  En vano, 88, 97–101
  See also Cañadas, Manuel; Danza Mobile; Parrilla, Arturo.
Thomas, Carol, 19–20, 29
transhumanism, 26, 29
Trias Fargas, Ramon, 42, 46, 51
Trias Trueta, Andy, 2, 12, 25, 34, 42–46, 50–56, 91, 139, 141, 144
Trias Trueta, Katy, 53–55
trisomy 21. See *Down syndrome*
Trueta i Llacuna, Montserrat, 53, 55

United States, 7, 54, 60, 77, 128–29, 142
  Bethel, 106
  Oakland, 106
  Orlando, 54
  Philadelphia, 61
Urzúa, Ricardo, 2, 13, 62–65, 69–72, 74–75, 94, 139

Valderrama Vega, Esmeralda, 97–98, 100–101
Venezuela, 7
Velázquez, Carlos, 13
Viola, Breno, 2, 13, 78, 80, 82, 139
Vohnsen, Mirna, 120, 128, 164n19
Von Der Ahe, Matthew, 1

Wendell, Susan, 19
Wolfe, Cary, 30